THOUGHTS ON THE ROAD
WRENCHING, RIDING, & REFLECTING

Road Dog Publications was formed in 2010 as an imprint of Lost Classics Book Company and is dedicated to publishing the best in books on motorcycling, motorsports, and adventure travel. Visit us at www.roaddogpub.com.

ISBN 978-1-890623-45-6
Library of Congress Control Number: 2015932922

An Imprint of Lost Classics Book Company

This book also available in e-book format at online booksellers. ISBN 978-1-890623-46-3

On the cover: The author's Triumph Bonneville T100 parked on the side of the road before crossing the Mississippi River to Helena, Arkansas.

THOUGHTS ON THE ROAD
WRENCHING, RIDING, & REFLECTING

by

Michael Fitterling

Publisher
Lake Wales, Florida

To my family, for their patience while I attempt to be a husband, father, rider, and writer and to the Vintage Japanese Motorcycle Club for their faith in me

About the Author

Mike Fitterling was born in 1957 in northern Indiana and grew up just across the state line in Niles, Michigan, graduating from Brandywine High School in 1975. Mike did a two year stint at Anderson College, in Indiana, before dropping out in 1978. In 1989, he returned to school at the University of South Florida, where he graduated in 1992 with a Bachelor in Fine Arts.

Throughout Mike's youth, family trips hinted at the world awaiting him if he just got on the road. Starting at an early age his family made camping trips to over twenty states.

After his first stab at college, Mike tagged along with his brother on a biology and archeology excursion Anderson College had organized to Central America. Those five weeks of camping in the remotest areas of Mexico and Guatemala added the twist of adventure to his love of travelling.

As time went on, Mike was drawn to the sea, bought a small sailboat, and took off along the southeast US coast and through the Bahamas and Caribbean. He captained an excursion sailboat in the Cayman Islands for three summers and earned his US captain's license in 1993.

Returning to the States from the Caribbean, Mike settled in central Florida, where he worked as a graphic designer. He married his wife, Andrea, in 1997 and started a family in 2000. He became interested in woodworking during this time and worked semi-professionally at that craft.

Motorcycles had been a distant dream for Mike since his childhood, but bike ownership escaped him until he was in his fifties, when he discovered a 1968 Honda tucked away in a dusty corner of a relative's shop. He extracted the motorcycle and applied himself to learning about fixing and riding them, starting a new episode in his life, which provided him a new means of adventuring. By this writing, that first bike has carried him over 30,000 miles. A modern Triumph was added to his garage in 2012, which has now accumulated similar mileage.

When he married, Mike was working as cover designer and illustrator for Lost Classics Book Company, and later became Managing Editor. He acquired the company in 2010. Finding himself owner of a publishing company, his natural inclination was to turn to publishing books on motorcycling and so, in 2011, the Road Dog Publications imprint was started.

In 2013, Mike became Editor of *Vintage Japanese Motorcycle Magazine*, the official publication of the Vintage Japanese Motorcycle Club, where he also currently serves on the board of directors.

TABLE OF CONTENTS

Preface

Looking back now, my attitude toward motorcycling is predictable, although when I first started dabbling seriously in bikes I didn't consider what kind of biker I might be—I just rode, or fixed, motorcycles.

When I was in high school I rode a bike, the kind with pedals, and I rode it a lot. My friend, Joe Frucci, and I rode Italian "racing bikes," also then known as "ten-speeds." We rode together often. We even entered a road race one year through the farm-festooned countryside around Niles, Michigan. As I recall, Joe did well, while I finished in the back of the pack, after an bloody encounter with the road surface in a curve on wet pavement. We both favored performance bikes, but Joe did more so than me. He had a seriously light bike with Campagnolo gears, no less, while I rode a mid-weight Olmo, sporting the utility version of Italian gearing, the poor distant cousin to Joe's mint green Bianchi. If Joe rode a motorcycle today, I have no doubt it would be a Ducati Panigale or the likes. I , however, favor a middle of the road "standard."

As much as we rode together, Joe and I also rode alone, and, with the exception of that race, we never road in big groups. I rode alone to school and to work after high school, both about ten mile round trips, every day except when the snow was flying and the temps dropped to freezing. Years later, when I took up sailing, the same pattern emerged, sailing *Aries* by myself at least as often as with others. I didn't participate in the many regattas and clubs in Tampa Bay. Getting together with others was for after the sailing, at the anchorage or marina, not out on the salty waters. When I did sail with someone else on my boat, it was usually with one other person or, on rare occasions, two. I rigged *Aries* for single-handing, and on her practically everything that needed to be done on a small boat could be done by one person, without leaving the cockpit. It's not surprising that, after all these years, when I mount my motorcycle it is almost always one-up. Once on the road, I am usually in the company of just my motorcycle or, on rare occasions, one other rider on their own bike.

When I took up riding and did ride with someone else, it was often with my brother, Tim, who took over Joe's role as road companion, before he moved to South Carolina. Riding together with someone I know well and with whom I can intuitively predict their riding intentions is a nice change from long hours of riding alone, and Tim and I rode together on both short and long rides, always in harmony.

Of course, riding with others when you ride motorcycles as old as my CB350 and as battle scarred as my basket-case Savage, is reassuring because, in case something goes wrong, support will be close at hand. I've ridden in large groups for short rides when joining in on vintage motorcycle rides, but, while interesting and not unpleasant, I found it difficult to enjoy the road and scenery, having to watch the bike behind and in front constantly and adjust to each new rider's style. On long rides where I have joined up with a small group of riders for part of a trip, it was always a bit of a relief once I was on my own again, and I always found that part to be more serene and pleasurable.

Group support notwithstanding, I get the biggest thrill

from going it alone. There's a sense of self-reflection and independence when alone on the road. This is an internally quiet time for me when the motorcycle's motor thrumming pleasantly beneath me often becomes my om, and riding becomes a kind of meditation, where single-mindedness of riding makes me part of the machine and free of life's distractions. Alternatively, riding alone can be a time for clear-headed thinking, where troubles that seemed complex or insurmountable at home may become simpler and paths to resolution clearer. Riding alone, without the necessity to interpret other riders' intentions or accommodate their needs, becomes a journey into new lands, each with its own smells and sounds, landscapes and lighting, and its own feel when the wind rushes past. Riding alone is the only time I have laughed out loud in my helmet and grinned and said simply, "Yeah!"

Solo riding, like solo sailing, builds confidence. What seemed impractical is proven practical, and what you think you can do increases with each mile. It seemed like after that first two hundred miles you could no longer sit on that cursed saddle and then, three hundred miles on, you are still seated and will be for hundreds more. You learn what-you've-got, so to speak. My guess is this comes from my childhood, from what obscure impetus I do not know, but I remember always pushing things farther, always trying to do a little more. There is something in me that makes me stick to tasks, even sometimes past the point of practicality, just to finish what I set out to do. I do not mind at all losing to someone else, but I hate losing to myself. With age, hopefully, came some wisdom, and, picking up motorcycling at the age of fifty or so, my push to succeed will be tempered by a modicum of restraint.

As a youth, if I could ride twenty miles to school and back and around Niles, then I could ride to camp at Yellow Creek, near Akron, Indiana, a seventy mile trip each way, so I did. If I could do that, then Joe and I could ride at least a hundred miles in one day, and we did, one hundred and forty, to be exact. I got more interested in going farther and farther. Riding ten-speeds around Niles was fine, but beyond was adventure. When I bought a boat, sailing around Tampa Bay was fun, but heading out to the Keys was adventure. Eventually, I was slipping out of Tampa Bay for the Bahamas and beyond. It didn't matter much where I was going, as long as it was far, and, ideally, it was new. Now that I am on a motorcycle, the rides that interest me the most are those that take me far from home. If the trip involves multiple days, all the better. With a young family and the attendant responsibilities at home, those opportunities are few, but when they do arise and it is possible without overly burdening my wife and family, I am off.

Tied to this push-yourself mentality, perhaps partly fueled by seemingly endless lack of funds, is a desire to succeed with as little as possible. Willpower is my key to successfully riding long distances. I now recognize this when thinking of my younger days.

Further reinforcing this abandonment of superfluous accoutrements was a trip my brother, Bob, and I made, after my short stint at college. Both of us were free from academic chains, but knowing the leaders, we managed to join a trip organized by Anderson College to Central America as non-students. The journey started in Anderson, Indiana, with twenty-some students crammed in two vans, who were headed south for a crash experiential course in tropical biology and pre-Columbian archaeology. Bob and I were along for the ride, not matriculated into either class. We were allowed to bring: one sleeping bag; a mosquito net; a minimum of clothing; a bowl, knife, and a spoon; and some American money, which Bob and I were short on. Taking turns at the wheel, we drove those vans from Indiana, crossed into Mexico, and wound our way through mountains to the rainforests of Guatemala and back, rarely visiting populated areas—something close to 15,000 miles, as I recall.

Some of the troupe broke the rules and brought tents and, on occasion, would even sneak out of our usually isolated camps for the comforts of modern hotels they were lucky to find close by. But Bob and I took a simpler, if more painful ,path. We rolled sleeping bags out on the ground—sometimes in the tropical rain, sometimes in the frigid mountains where frost coated us in the mornings. We propped up military mosquito nets just big enough to cover the bags; put the clothes bag under our heads; and more than once stuck the knife in the ground close by, in case it was needed in the night; and said good night. Bathrooms were anywhere you could find out of sight, where a hole was dug, filled, and covered up again. Our miserly supply of money taught you could keep on going even when hungry. We shared the meagre fare doled out at camp in the community meals, and while those better endowed could buy what they wanted in the village markets, we made do on a seemingly endless consumption of pineapples. In spite of hunger and sore backs, we managed to bring back memories that will last us a lifetime.

Later, the diminutive size of my sailboat, twenty-five foot and small by anyone's standard, didn't seem a hindrance to crossing seas. All it meant is more preparedness and ingenuity, and I took it as a challenge to get by with what I had rather than put off my dreams of sailing away. I worked hard, prepping the little boat for rough service. More sweat was spent than money outfitting the vessel for single-handing and rough seas. I spent time with my head under the forecastle bunk, fiberglassing stringers in the too flexible bow. A small, but efficient galley was put together of plywood and laminates and attached over half the starboard settee. *Aries* was much smaller than most would ever consider taking offshore, let alone into the Caribbean, yet years later and after many sea miles she rode the trades successfully along the north coast of Jamaica and on to the Caymans.

Setting the stage for my predisposition for small boats and seat-of-your-pants self reliance were books I had devoured like

Voyage of the Dove, in which a sixteen-year-old circumnavigated the globe on a twenty-six foot sloop; and *Sailing Alone around the World,* by Joshua Slocum, an old sea captain who was the first to accomplish this feat. Slocum put the circumnavigation under his belt after already sailing his family home from Brazil in a sailing canoe, which he described in a earlier book, *Voyage of the Liberdade*, and all this before the turn of the twentieth century. I had also read the book *Fatu Hiva*, by Thor Heyerdahl of *Kon Tiki* fame, who had attempted to live a simple and natural life in the Marquesa Islands of the South Pacific, and similar books like *Typee*, by Melville, that not only showed me one could do much with little but also pointed to exotic destinations. With these books as my inspiration, I would substitute simple for complex, and cheap for expensive.

Part of that mindset led me to admire smaller things, especially things that moved. I've mentioned my small sailboat, or "pocket cruiser" as they came to be called, that also served as my small home until 1990. My first car was a diminutive Datsun Roadster with a 1600cc motor, smaller than the motors on many modern motorcycles these days. Next up was a MG Midget, with an even smaller 1500cc engine. I later had my share of "big" cars, but none I ever really liked, with the exception of my Montero four wheel drive, which served as tractor, swamp buggy, and trailer hauler.

When I was catching the bug for motorcycles, a big bike was 750cc. Unheard of were bikes with 1700cc and 2000ccs. Now, in the 2010s, people's measure of a motorcycle seems to be its size; bigger equals better. But for me, those sub-1000cc bikes are the sweet spot. The ability to haul a loaded trailer or pull a wheelie in fourth gear will never be requirements of any bike I buy. I am unlikely to ride two-up more than a few miles each year, so comfort for two is wasted. I prefer a bike that is efficient, good on fuel, flickable without being tiring, and capable of carrying the minimal amount of gear I need to camp, without getting too much in my way when I ride. If the bike will do highway speeds, and for me that is sustained speeds of 60 mph, with enough power in reserve for passing and emergencies, and have a saddle that is comfortable for a few hundred miles at a stint, then I will be happy. I will also be glad that my pocketbook will drain that much slower due to better fuel mileage, equating to the possibility of more miles on my usually limited amount of funds.

Since my old love of bikes was reignited by the find of my CB350, "Old Faithful," I have logged enough miles to wrap over twice around the world on the back of one bike or another, and, hopefully, I have learned something about bikes, about riding, and about myself and life in the process.

What follows is a collection of stories and thoughts on this motorcycle journey I have been on. Some of the stories have been gathered and edited from my blog entries, others are from magazine articles I've written, and a few are new material. Because these stories come from different sources, they may not be in sequence, and I may repeat myself here and there; for that I apologize. Most were written as stand alone stories with the anticipation that the readers would not have read the other stories and been familiar with some of the common characters and events that the stories share.

My opinions, are just that, *opinions*. Riding is a very personal experience and what one thinks is good or bad, right or wrong, wise or foolish varies in exact proportion to as many riders that there are. I don't pretend to think that my opinions about riding are going to be shared by every reader. My goal is simply to tell how riding has affected me. Maybe some will relate to my experiences and some will be entertained. If so, I will be happy.

A book isn't the author's work alone. Before I get started, I would like to thank those that read the manuscript, corrected it, and helped me refine it. A special thanks goes to Randy Lyons, who does the proofing at *Vintage Japanese Motorcycle Magazine,* who gave me invaluable advice as I worked to finish this book.

WRENCHING

WINDFALL—CB350

I first got interested in motorcycles many years ago. We had a small mini-bike as we grew up in southern Michigan. We lived in the country and had five acres, but combined with our accessible neighbors' land, we had plenty of room to try our skill at riding. Our mini-bike was a garden variety, lawnmower-motor type, with centrifugal clutch and chunky tires on tiny rims. I don't remember where my dad got the bike, but it was used, for sure—well-used—my dad never being inclined to buy anything new or expensive.

Looking back now it seems we were working on that mini-bike more than riding it. But ride it we did, all over the rolling hills, under the black locust trees that clicked with cicadas in the warm summer nights. We rode it, without permission, across "Old Man Well's" property, to our friendlier neighbors, who had kids our ages and toys of one sort or another themselves. We tore dirt paths over the rolling glacial unused farmland, when we weren't doing the same on horseback, and accompanied our neighbor two houses over on his "new" Honda Trail 70. This neighbor kid had all the luck, having a real motorcycle and snowmobiles for the winter. Once in a while, we even got to ride the Honda, but most times, between repairs, our mini-bike served as mount for my two brothers and I.

Riding and fixing that old mini-bike and blazing around on Danny's Trail 70 set the stage for my interest in getting a motorcycle of my own. I must have been in junior high. Counting up from the year of my birth, 1957, that puts it around 1970, jiving with the timing of one of my favorite television shows, *Then Came Bronson*, which added further fuel to the fire. To this day, when I hear the word *motorcycle*, an image of that red Sportster, with the eye enclosed in a pyramid on the tank, is what comes to mind. Wandering about the country all by yourself on a bike seemed like heaven and the most logical thing to do with one's life.

With a naive confidence in somehow making it work, I started planning to build my own "real" bike. I would get pipes and weld a frame, after I learned to weld, or buy a beat up rolling frame, and then buy a second-hand motor to put in it. Then all I would need is gas in the tank and I would be rolling thunder, although still in the fields, not on the road, with my sixteenth birthday still way in the future. I vaguely recall seeing makes like Bridgestone, Hodaka, Triumph, and Honda as I searched classified ads for used motors or made calls to shops in the area.

But somehow the idea faded, perhaps with the realization that without a job or money, or a dad willing to lay down some cash for my hair-brain scheme, which was more than far-fetched, I would not be able to pull off this mechanical feat.

Years passed. My cousin, Denny, got a motorcycle sometime later when I was in high school and let me ride it across our pasture. His was a real motorcycle, and while I don't remember all the particulars, it was a universal Japanese bike with a huge engine, probably 600cc, and had a real transmission with clutch and all. I managed that short ride, dodging road apples and sliding in the sand, miraculously without dropping the bike. The ride reignited that fire, the embers of which smoldered for many years in the background of my mind as high school passed, and college loomed ahead.

That sleeping coal of interest might have extinguished itself if it wasn't for a couple of friends over the years succumbing to the magic of motorcycling themselves and buying bikes and puffing a little life back into the coals. After a couple indecisive years at Anderson College, I moved to Pratt, Kansas, the home of my dorm mate, Dean, where I worked for his dad, installing sprinkler systems and doing concrete work in the almost unbearable Kansas summer heat. Dean's brother, Darryl, picked up a Kawasaki KZ650, a very fast bike at the time, which he rode across the plains to exotic lands— like Nebraska. Darryl let me give the KZ a go, keeping the ember alive for my future affair with motorcycles.

In the meantime, I also was keeping my interest in motorized things alive by driving and tinkering with my first automobile, a white 1968 Datsun SPL311 Roadster. I had bought that non-running convertible for six hundred dollars back in Anderson, and with my meagre mechanical expertise I got it running in time for summer break and the run out to Kansas. I even got a little track time in once by sneaking onto the Lake Afton Grand Prix track the night before the races and doing a lap. The little car really could run, and I must have had a smile on my face all the way back to Pratt after that drive.

After that summer in Kansas, my life took many turns—a move to Florida with my brother, Bob; a short, miserable, and failed marriage when I was twenty-five, for which I had sold my beloved Datsun to provide funds for the engagement ring; years more of near poverty in spite of my working full-time at dull and discouraging jobs.

Eventually, I found some kind of equilibrium in my life and also a new love—for boats and sailing. I worked to save money and bought myself a little sailboat. She was an Irwin twenty-five footer, one of those typical '70s boats made of 5,000 pounds of white fiberglass with an interior similar to the inside of a bleach bottle.

I was in Lake Wales, Florida, then, a small town in the geographic center of the peninsula. I kept the boat in Tampa Bay and drove over, often with my dad, who loved to nap aboard while the boat bobbed in the chop of the bay. I practiced sailing every chance I could, while I studied every book I could find on the subject. Back in Lake Wales, I was saving every dime and paying off all my debt in anticipation of taking off for the warm waters and exotic places I had been dreaming of for years. I acquired some woodworking and fiberglassing skills and slowly turned the little cruiser into a strong and comfortable boat that could stand up to most anything short of a hurricane the Atlantic, Gulf of Mexico, or the Caribbean could throw at it. Leaving my job in Lake Wales, I sailed for a couple years before returning to Florida and college, once again.

I kept my boat until my third year at the University of South Florida in 1992, when I finally finished that degree I had started back in Anderson in 1976. Motorcycles had slipped my mind. School, then work, a move back to Lake Wales, then marriage to Andrea, and then kids all almost drowned out that last ember.

But then I saw it. My father-in-law had a modular home business which included a large shop, where he and I would do woodworking from time to time. The last of the four bays held tools and junk gathered over years of Andrea's family gophering away this or that. In the farthest corner, under a blanket and piles of family debris, I saw a motorcycle. It was hard to see what it was exactly until it was pulled out from under the piles of boxes and behind the unused exercise equipment—a 1968, I later found out, Honda CB350.

It had been a long while since I had fooled with bikes, but I asked Andrea's dad what the story was behind the CB and whether he would mind if I "messed with it" and "see if I could get it running."

Andrea's dad, Ronnie, said that he had picked up that bike a long while ago, which was evident from the 1986 license plate it still bore. Someone in his neighborhood had gotten the bike as a family toy and, apparently, had not had it long before one of the kids took a spill on it. From then on, the owner was afraid for anyone to ride it, and it sat until Ronnie bought it for one hundred dollars. Ronnie rode it the entire mile from his house to his shop on the other side of US Highway 27, until my mother-in-law decided it was too dangerous and that he should stop riding it. So to storage in the shop it went, until I spied it in 2004.

With the bike stored in my garage, I worked on the CB. The bike was in almost perfect condition cosmetically, with only a small dent in the left fork cover—a result, I surmised, of the original owner's spill. There were little specks of rust on the chrome, but nothing that would not buff out with an application of steel wool. The bike was teal and white, with that typical 1968 tank paint scheme of teal on the top half and white below, and no stripe between. The knee pads were still on and looked like new.

I pulled the then-unfamiliar CV carbs apart and did my best to clean them. Somehow, I managed not to damage them, and, with a new battery in, the bike fired. It ran, let's say, reluctantly. Popping and buzzing and firing on one side only, Ronnie decided to give it a try. He popped and wheezed from our driveway across the street to the next corner and back. I also talked to Hank, a motorcycle restorer-collector friend of my dad and was told how to clean and reline the tank, which I did, resulting in a nice clean and silver-interiored tank. The bike had no power, but it ran, and that encouraged me—then hurricane season set in.

In the fall of 2004, our little town, which is usually the refuge town for friends on the coast during these times, being so far inland, instead hosted three hurricanes within one month. All three eyes passed over our home, but it was the first one—Charlie—that changed our priorities for several years. Our old Cracker house, built in 1914, had a veranda across the front and down half the side, which I had just rebuilt as part of our ongoing restoration process. We had expected Charlie to hit Tampa, but it changed course at the last hour and charged down upon us, ripping the roof and columns off the veranda and depositing them fifty yards behind the house. With the front of the house opened up above the veranda, the rain poured in, ruining most of the old heart-pine, tongue-and-groove ceiling, which now looked like a washboard suspended above our heads. The pine floors got a similar treatment, and the walls had been shaken with such ferocity that the horse-hair plaster unkeyed from the wooden lathe, leaving the interior walls covered in cracks and failed plaster.

It took over three years to repair the damage, and all work halted on the CB, which still sat in the now precariously leaning, detached, one car garage. The bike's home was torn down. I erected a new one on the old foundation, while roofers clumped about on the house roof installing new metal shingles and the sounds of hammers and power drills came from inside the house.

After three years and over a hundred thousand dollars later the house was back in shape. By then our growing family impressed upon us the need for another bedroom and bath, and for me a dedicated home office, instead of the forever mobile hallway/sunporch/back porch office I had been working in. Another year and a half passed as more construction took our time as the addition went up. Finally, by the spring of 2009, I was ready to once again dig that old Honda out and pick up where I left off, now years ago.

How Not to Line a Tank

In 2009, early in the year, I once again got the old CB350 out and tried the starter—just for kicks. No click, whir—nothing. With a run down to the local auto parts store, a new battery was acquired and set in place. It would now turn over, but nothing more.

Once again, off came the carbs. We were about to become thoroughly acquainted, again and again. Getting this little bike back into road readiness required all the typical stuff—cleaning carbs, new battery, cleaning carbs, new engine oil, cleaning carbs, new fork oil, cleaning carbs, new spark plugs, cleaning carbs, new tires, cleaning carbs. During this time, I peered into the tank and an obvious problem was revealed to me—rust. "No problem," I thought, "I have done this before."

Getting the gunk out was quite a challenge, but nothing me and five gallons of muriatic acid, not to mention the acid etch from the Kreem kit, couldn't overcome. And I was right; two days later I had nice gray metal showing inside the tank. The previous rust coating and sketchy old liner was gone. A swish around of the liner prep, and I was ready. Now it was time for relining, and that is where things started going terribly wrong.

The instructions of the vanilla milkshake bottle of Kreem liner said you needed to pour in the liquid with all the tank holes plugged, then roll the tank around to get even coverage. Then let it sit with the lid off for eight to ten minutes, recap it and roll again. Let sit uncapped in a different position for eight to ten minutes, recap, and repeat.

I was smart before all this started and made a nice tight fitting plug by tapering a wooden dowel to insert in the petcock neck. I also had the foresight to run some wire up into the crossover barbs to keep those from filling up with the liner liquid and becoming useless. But the big hole for filling the tank was a challenge.

I had an old rubber printing blanket from back when I worked in that industry, and so I made a round wooden cap with the blanket as a gasket to make sure nothing leaked out when I was sloshing the stuff around. A bolt through the middle of this wood and rubber disk connected to a maple bar about one inch wide and slightly wider than the mouth completed my cap. I could loosen the bolt, slide the cap on sideways, tighten the bar up on the underside of the filler, and have a leak-proof seal.

I was so excited; one more, uncomplicated step and I would be in tank nirvana, completely removing the tank as a possible suspect in my carb problem.

In went the Kreem, on went the cap, and slosh, slosh, slosh, around went the white liquid. "Hey! This is not so bad." OK, sloshed enough, it was then time to uncap, and let it sit that first eight or ten minutes. When I made this cap, I used a thumbscrew, so no tools would be needed for capping and uncapping. But one thing I did not think through very well was how little of that screw was still in that bottom nut when loosened enough to get the cap off. A little too much unloosening and...off came the maple clamp bar, nut still embedded in its clever little recess I had so carefully chiseled out so the nut would not rotate as I screwed or unscrewed the cap.

I could not see the clamp bar and was starting to panic. This Kreem, let's just say it is thick—think of Elmer's Glue—thick and sticky. Anything sticking to it has a tendency to stay stuck, and the stuff dries quickly, increasingly adding to the tenacity of the hold. The nice smooth back side of the clamp bar was stuck like a suction cup to the inside of the tank.

By then, I figured the least of my worries was the paint on the tank or preserving my supply of Kreem, which was all inside the tank. I turned the tank upside down and started shaking. At least this was performing the function of distributing the liner around the tank's inner surfaces. Once in a while I heard the bar pop loose and settle somewhere else, again as tight as a barnacle on the bottom of a ship. If I could only get it near the filler hole; I could pull it out with a pair of needle nose pliers, I thought.

So I shook, and I shook, and meanwhile the white glue-like stuff was flying out of the open fill hole. It was now on my legs, my shoes, the deck by the shop, and all over the top and sides of the tank. I frantically, but lightly, tapped the upside-down tank on the wooden floorboards of the shop deck where I was working. Surely, the fairly soft wood wouldn't cause any damage to the tough metal tank.

Now I was getting desperate; the Kreem was drying and I'd yet to get the bar to break loose and come anywhere near the fill hole. I figured my best hope was to at least get it up toward the front of the tank so it would not obstruct the crossovers or petcock attachment. Thump! I heard it smack against the front top of the tank and figured that was as good as it was going to get.

I turned my attention to the spilled Kreem all over the nice original factory teal paint of the fuel tank, formerly with hardly a scratch on it. Not too bad; the stuff was still a little soft. I just got my lacquer thinner and my disposable shop towels and wiped and wiped, and I was making progress. Some of the Kreem was being stubborn, so I rubbed a little harder. "What's that?—gray metal? Oh, rats!" Damage done,

I continued to remove the white gunk along with teal paint here and there.

With the white remnants of the liner gone from the outside of the tank, I could clearly see how the harmless pine deck boards have created divots in the top of the tank, a result of my tapping the tank to expel the clamp bar.

What was once a pristine tank with original paint was now a sloppily lined, scratched, and dented tank with a piece of maple and a nut coated white and glued onto the underside of the top. At least it was now coated with liner.

The tank fiasco behind me, I then turned to professional help with the motor. I could get it to run; sometimes quite well. I could actually ride it. I had not gotten my license yet, so back roads only, in the groves near my brother's house, was where I justified a little road testing. Sometimes it would run like new. Unfortunately, that was not a typical ride, with most ending in a loss of power from one side of the motor and usually a slow crawl back to the house. On occasion, the flatbed trailer I had for hauling lumber for my woodworking projects would come in handy to get the bike home.

I eventually got a lot of experience loading my bike on that trailer. In spite of all the practice loading and unloading the CB, still things could go wrong, and one night it all went wrong in a spectacular way.

How Not to Load a Bike on a Trailer

I thought I had finally gotten the CB350 running correctly. This time we thought it might have been the float level. The float might have been cutting off the gas too early and causing the cylinders to starve after the initial load of fuel in the bowls ran out. My brother, Tim, and I messed with it on a Saturday morning, bending the little tab on the float so the bowl would fill higher. We were getting together at his place that evening for some barbecue, and it was about five miles away—the perfect distance to ride and check out our "fix."

I sped along with the little motor running well and got past the double curves just past Mountain Lake, which I had never been able to pass before without the bike cutting out. Alas, I was awoken from my dream when I got about as far as "Fuzzy's," the local biker bar, about midway between Tim's place and our house, when the bike started to sputter. Oh well, I had gotten farther than I had ever before, so that was a sign we might be on the right track.

A little break at Fuzzy's and off I went again, now with a carburetor full of fuel. I got all the way to Tim's with no more incidents and parked in the perpetually open garage, beside his big Kawasaki Vulcan Nomad 1500—a bike which actually ran and kept on running, something that was amazing to me at the time.

Because of the longer distance I had ridden, I was hopeful, and I, once again, for about the hundredth time, closed off the petcock, pulled off the fuel line, poured gas all over myself, got out a Phillips screwdriver, and proceeded to remove the left carburetor, disassemble it, and take out the float bowl. The left one seemed to be the only one infected with this fuel supply problem.

This time that tang got bent, and then bent some more. I refitted the bowl, turned on the fuel, only to have it pour out the overflow. I then repeated the whole process with the same results. Finally, I got the tang bent just to the point where it would turn the valve off at the last possible second, just before overflowing the bowl—no leak. On went the carb, the air cleaner, and covers. I fired her up and moved out onto the road, with Tim following me on the Nomad. I took it for a fairly long ride, and when we returned we reversed it, and I rode the Nomad and Tim rode the Honda, again for a decent run, maybe five or six miles. That day, on a long straight stretch I watched the speedometer reach close to eighty miles per hour.

Aha! The bike refused to die or sputter. We had found the sweet spot, or so we thought, and I sat back in my chair in the garage and downed a cold one in celebration, while waiting for the Boston butt to finish smoking. Cheers! All around!

I was there a bit early, but soon my wife, Andrea, along with our daughter, Tess, arrived and the butt was carved and more beer opened. After a nice long evening of barbecue, and, after having taken long enough of a break from the beer drinking to be safe for riding, I got ready to head home; now on a trouble-free bike. Andrea loaded up our five-year old and started the car. I woke up the CB350, donned my helmet and gear, and put 'er in gear. Andrea followed me down the now dark back road toward home.

Things were going swimmingly, with the forty-one year old bike now humming along under me and the road passing quickly under my headlight. I passed Fuzzy's, then onto the first of the double curves, then the second, and then whizzing past the Mountain Lake entrance, with only a couple miles to go. Then it happened; the left cylinder, again, decided to not cooperate. "So, I guess it is still not right." I was not too worried; the bike had usually gotten me home running like that before, and I only had a couple miles to go. Then the right side went, with only the sound of compression and dwindling revolutions coming from below me. Other than Andrea, there was no traffic behind me, so I pull it over off the road. Andrea stopped behind me.

Here the shoulder was very narrow and sloped; it was hard for me to get the bike to balance on its side stand, but I managed. We were in ankle height to knee-deep grass. The shoulder went about three feet from the pavement, where it sloped suddenly into a ditch, filled with deeper grasses and weeds. Directly below us, was a drainage pipe coming out of the side of the hill and emptying into the ditch.

Andrea and I discussed what to do; with me thinking it was best for her to head home while I stay with the bike, and for her to retrieve my trailer and come back. Andrea, however, was sure she would not be able to hitch up the trailer properly and decided she would stay with the bike while Tess and I went to get the trailer. It would not be long, and she would stay well off the road while waiting, she promised. With no other options, I agreed, and Tess and I drove off in the car watching the orange glow from Andrea's cigarette fade in the rear view mirror as we headed for home. I made it there as quickly as I could and when we returned, Andrea was still there, alive and unharmed. I made a U-turn and pulled off as far as I could, directly in front of the bike.

The worst was over I thought, and I was more concerned with what to do with the motor next, rather than the work of loading the trailer. After all, I had done this plenty of times when this or that experiment had failed with the bike, sometimes with help and even by myself. I had one of those four foot by seven foot little flatbed tilt trailers that Lowe's used to sell for four hundred dollars. I had hauled countless loads of hardwoods on it to the wood shop I had in our back yard, and countless cabinets or pieces of furniture were hauled back out on it. I had even gotten clever, when the trailer had been designated my official motorcycle carrier, and had built a stop at the forward end of the deck to keep from pushing the bike on and then over the front. I had even made a small "chock" in which the front wheel could rest while I strapped the bike down with four ratchet straps that I always kept handy.

The procedure was simple. Release the pin at the front of the deck which held the deck to the tongue, put some weight on the rear of the deck, and the back would tilt to the ground, making a ramp out of the entire deck. You simply rolled the bike up to the ramp, getting the tire on far enough to hold the rear down, gather up all your strength, and push and pull the bike up the slope until the weight was over the wheels, then push just a bit farther and the deck would level out, and you could push the bike forward into its chock. Then in the proper position, someone would hold the bike upright, while the other pinned the deck to the tongue again and then attached the straps. That's it, pretty simple, and then off you go, bike in tow. That's how it was *supposed* to go.

Unfortunately, I had not taken into account a couple things. First, that it was night and pitch dark, and I had forgotten the importance of picking up a flashlight when I went to get the trailer. Second, it now being well into the night, the wooden deck had been covered by a nice slick covering of evening dew. On top of that, my state of mind of being frustrated once again with my efforts to restore this bike were not aiding in my clear thinking and neither was having a young child in the car screaming at the top of her lungs. "I'm cold!" "Turn off the air conditioning!" "I'm cold!" "Turn off the air..." Well, you get the idea.

Still, it should've be a snap, but I failed to take into account that the bike was possessed, proven earlier in my botched tank lining incident.

I managed in the dark to get the pin out of the trailer while working in an invisible cloud of exhaust from the car's pipe blowing directly into my face. The tail end of the deck went down. I walked back to the bike, and cursing under my breath, moved it forward and managed to get the wheel onto the back of the tilted trailer. I was on the left, the road side, and Andrea was on the right, the ditch side, and we each took hold and heaved the Honda up the ramp, and, just as planned, the deck tilted down and we rolled it to the front wheel chock. Andrea held the bike while I re-pinned the deck to the tongue. Nothing to it. I felt a bit better knowing we would all be home in a few minutes, and tomorrow I could take my time and see what could be done about the motor.

I reached into the back of the car for the straps, the volume of Tess's entreaties increasing with the opening of the tailgate and decreasing again when I slammed it shut. I started the job of strapping the bike down at the front left side, while Andrea stood at the right front side, on the wet deck holding the bike upright. I hadn't gotten the strap up to the fork when I heard Andrea squeal, and I felt the bike leaning toward her. The deck had become a slippery, algae-covered platform, and Andrea was going down. I recall telling her to jump, not wanting the bike to fall on her, but from then on everything went in slow motion, like a bad movie effect, even the sound: Oooooooooohhhhhhhhhh,   nnnnnooooooooooooooo! "IIIIIIIIII""""""mmmmmmmm   ccccccooooooooollllllll dddddddd!!!!"   Sssssshhhhhhhhhhhhhhiiiiiiiiiiiiiiiittttttttt! Ttttthhhhhhuuuuummmmmppp!   "IIIIIII'mmmmmm cccccoooooolllllldddd!!!!   Ddddaaaaaaaddddyyy!" Cccrrrraaasssshhhh!

In time-suspended horror I watched the bike go over. That would have been bad enough, but that little trailer was not wide enough for the bike to simply plop down on its side and land on the deck—no! The center of gravity of the bike was far enough out, and the top of the bike on its side was far enough over the side of the deck, that the bike did a sickly elegant side somersault off the right side of the trailer. It was like something alive, and when the handlebars and all their attachments and the saddle hit the ground three feet below, it bounced effortlessly over again to do yet another flip. The bike stopped exhausted in the grass-filled ditch on its side.

When it had fallen, the Honda had caught Andrea at the shin, and a huge bruise was forming. I had gotten cut on the shin by something clear through my jeans, which were miraculously unscathed, in spite of the blood, as evidence of the scrape, coming out of my pants leg. At least we were lucky enough to still be standing, Andrea doubly so in her more dangerous location.

I quickly unpinned the trailer bed again, and with invective-spewing lips I walked down into the ditch. I tilted the bike back upright and muttered, "That's it! This is the end of my motorcycling days!" I took a quick look at the stuff dangling off the handlebars, and then with adrenaline strength I yanked the bike back out of the ditch. Meanwhile, Andrea was standing beside me, where, unknown to her, she was in the middle of a nest of fire ants. These ants are insidious in Florida, and you usually don't know you are in them until your legs are covered, and they seemingly all decide to bite at once. I, too, could feel them crawling and biting under my pants legs. Andrea fled for her life, and I kept hauling the bike until it was behind the trailer once more.

I was at the point of tears with discouragement by then. I got this bike for free, and I had hoped with some perseverance and hard work I would be able to ride. I definitely was not in a financial position then to simply buy a bike. If I could not get this bike going, I was not going to be a motorcyclist for the foreseeable future. And then, having gotten to the point with the engine that it actually ran, I had, it seemed, innumerable new things to repair before I would even get back to where I was, which was still not a place that allowed me to ride, other than on an occasional, futile, road test.

In spite of my frustration, I couldn't leave the bike there. So, we both got beside the bike again and pushed it up the hill of the deck. The bed tilted down, and this time being careful to keep her feet off the slippery deck Andrea held the bike, while I pinned the deck to the tongue once more. I stooped down into the exhaust again, still hearing Tess complaining about her fate inside the car, and fumbled in the pitch black under the front of the trailer deck to try to pin it level. I called out to Andrea, "I got it!" and at that instant, the back of the deck tipped backwards and threw the bike once more over the side. At least this time it landed beside the trailer and not ten feet away in the ant-infested ditch. Andrea was unscathed this time, except for the assault on her ears by the expletives exploding out of my mouth, not aimed at her, because I knew damn well I had been the cause of yet another catastrophe.

Once more, I hauled the bike back around, and this time we got it on the trailer and tied it down without incident. I got back in the driver's seat, seething with self contempt and discouragement, and drove slowly away toward our house.

At home, Andrea and Tess left me to my misery while I unhitched the trailer from the car and then re-parked in the driveway. Things were quiet in the house when I got in and stayed that way until sleep overtook us.

The next day, I went out sheepishly by myself to survey the damage in the daylight. Mirrors and clutch and brake levers were dangling from the handlebars like garish Christmas ornaments. I was surprised, however, that no major damage was done. There was a new small dent in the right fork cover to match the original one on the left, but it was cosmetic. Both the wheels and the fork were undamaged. The handlebar was unbent, and all the turn signals were intact and working, except that the headlight and front turn signals were now aiming in a new direction. The mounting ears were not kinked or creased, though, and a simple pull back to alignment is all that would be required to fix them. In the end, all that was needed was new handlebar switches, the levers still were unharmed because the attachment tabs for the levers sheared off, instead of the levers themselves. Still discouraged, it took me a couple days to decide it was still worth the effort and to pick up the phone and start calling salvage yards.

Within a week I had procured the switches, and the work began anew, with me swearing that I would never load that bike onto a trailer again.

CB350 Motor Restoration

After repairing the damage the trailer incident caused, I turned my attention back to the motor. I sought the advice of the two shops in town, with no resolution. We put the bike on a dyno, but with no conclusive result. The petcock, the design of which I have never trusted, was replaced and the same thing happened. These petcocks are simple gravity feed valves, but they split into two chambers where there is a barb attached for a separate fuel hose for each carburetor.

Of course, more carb cleaning ensued. By now, I was thoroughly familiar with the CV carb and think I could have taken one apart and rebuilt it in my sleep in five minutes or less. A carb cleaner dunk tank and a compressor were the biggest help getting the carbs thoroughly clean. When the bike ran, it ran well—for a while, then one side would go.

Of course, frustration was mounting. Every time I had a new, bright idea and ordered one thing or another to try, there was at least a week of waiting for the part to arrive, moving the date for me to get out on the road and ride further and further away. I took the Basic Rider Course and got my motorcycle endorsement and still had no bike to ride.

Talking to Vince, the owner of B.A.B.'s motorcycle shop in Lake Wales, convinced me the only thing left was a bad coil. I ordered a pair of aftermarket, generic coils, and built a special mount to attach them to the aluminum mounting bracket the original coils sat in. I was confident I had found the problem. I hooked up the new coils, hit the starter, and pulled out—but not before the smell of burning electrical components and smoke came billowing out from under the tank. I shut it down fast and, discouraged, rolled it back into the garage, thankful the whole bike didn't go up in smoke. The end of one new coil was ruptured and burnt. So much for that idea. I started scouring the salvage yards for anyone having a set of original coils for this bike and eventually found them. Installing the new old coils, I fired the bike up and took it for a test ride. Both sides stayed firing, although the bike still ran rough, and hand-free idling eluded me. At least one major issue was solved, now on to the next.

I acquired the CB350 *Honda Shop Manual* from Bill Silver, along with his restoration guide, and now had a more authoritative source for information than the old Clymer manual I'd purchased before. Bill included all the shop bulletins for my bike, and I found out that this bike over the years, and even within the same year, had different carbs with different jets.

My CB was a very early one, the first model, in fact, before any changes were made. My bike had a different "hot rod" cam, which produced a bumpy idle that was not received well by Honda's customers in 1968, so the cam was changed just after my model, along with the carbs. I looked closely at my carb and very indistinctly stamped on the right front "fin" under the diaphragm housing were the numbers. My bike was supposed to have 350A carbs, which looked like the others but internally had a rectangular float and different jetting, which was listed in the carb bulletin I had gotten from Bill. I looked at my left carb and indeed it was a 350A, but looking at the right carb I saw the number 3D stamped on the fin. All the times cleaning these carbs, I had noticed the float being round on the right and rectangular on the left, but thought nothing of it. My bike had mismatched carbs, jetted completely differently, and no matter how many times I cleaned them it was never going to run smoothly.

Armed with this new knowledge, I went in search of a right side 350A carb. I searched everywhere and finally found one, "new old stock," at Western Hills Honda, in Ohio, priced well over four hundred dollars. Well, it was nice to know they had it, but my income had never been extraordinary, and I could not justify that money when there were bills to be paid. I started to see how my dad had gotten to be—frugal because he had to be, and now I was, too. The next best thing, I thought, would be to find two matching carbs, even if they were a different number, then I could re-jet them similarly to how the 350As were jetted. Making some calls, I found a pair of 3Ds in a St. Petersburg salvage yard, so off I went to pick them up. While there, I picked a few other choice pieces for future possible use off the old 350 sitting on its center stand in the rambling, raucous pile of rusted bikes. The carb's jets could be had from Sudco, so I ordered the primary main and secondary main jets in a couple different sizes. I could not change the air jets on the carbs, so I knew I was going to have to be creative and flexible getting these to work.

My goal was to balance the air/fuel ratio between the jets. The original 350As called for number 60 primary main fuel jets and number 50 primary air jets, while the 3Ds came with number 70 primary fuel jets and number 150 primary air jets. The jet numbers increase in diameter as their number increases, so a number 60 fuel jet lets through less fuel than a number 70. So while the fuel jets were close, the air jets were not. Because the air jets were 50 percent bigger on the 3D than the 350A while the fuel jets varied by only about fifteen percent, this essentially made the fuel mixture leaner (more air, less fuel) on the new carbs than the carbs originally installed on this bike.

I ordered number 62 and number 65 fuel jets from Sudco and installed the number 65s, hoping to mimic the air-to-fuel mixture of the 350As. I could see how this would work by riding the bike for a while and then checking the plugs to see if they were rich, lean, or just right. If this proved the bike was running too rich, I could swap out the number 65s for the 62s and then try the test again. If the bike proved to be running too lean with the 65s, I would have to order another set of jets and try again. Luckily, the 65s turned out to be the right combination, with the plugs showing evidence of a close to perfect balance of air to fuel.

A little more work was needed synchronizing the carbs. This was accomplished by watching the throttle levers closely and making sure that when the throttle was rolled both levers moved at the exact same instant. Finally, the little CB would run smoothly and with more power and, for the first time, I could take my hand off the throttle at idle and be assured the bike would keep running without me fiddling with it.

After months of messing with this or that, I finally had a bike I could ride confidently on the road. I spent a lot of time staring at maps—detailed local maps with small roads that were ignored on others. I also scanned other state maps, with hopes of long trips. I spent hours staring at aerial images of winding roads in the mountains on the Internet. I started locally and slowly pressed farther on those little side roads. My brother would often ride with me on his big burly Kawasaki Nomad 1500, a bike weighing close to two and a half times my CB. We spent time riding close to Lake Wales, eventually expanding our circle, making it all the way to Tampa Bay and the marina in Ruskin, where I used to live on my little sailboat. Life was good and riding was better.

SAVAGE

Not long after I returned to Florida from a trip to Michigan on the CB350, I had a chance to go fishing off Panama City, Florida. My father-in-law's nephew, Lloyd, lived in Dothan, Alabama, but kept a couple boats down at the coast at Panama City. Most years, when the kingfish migrate north as the waters in the Gulf of Mexico warm, we got together with Lloyd to try our hand at catching them, usually quite successfully. Lloyd was a friendly guy and generous to a fault and offered his boat and experience to my father-in-law, brothers-in-law, brother, nephew, and whoever else wanted to tag along. Lloyd never asked for anything in return.

This time, Lloyd and I were on the flying bridge enjoying cold beers while others manned the downriggers. Wandering around the Gulf waiting for a hit and a call to action, we got to talking about motorcycles, somehow. I was telling him about Tim and my trip to the upper Midwest when he mentioned he had bike that I could have, if I wanted it. He had no time to fool with it, with all the other projects he had going.

Lloyd told me the bike was a 650cc Suzuki that he had bought at an auction a while back. He had ridden it on the street for a while, then handed the keys over to his son when he bought another, bigger bike. Lloyd's son, Andrew, was in school and used the bike to ride around the thirty-five acres they had in Dothan. One day he came back to the house saying it would not start. There it sat, until then. All I had to do was drive up to Dothan to pick it up.

After all the experience I had gained working on the CB350, I figured there was not much I could not fix on a bike, and, if the motorcycle was free, what did I have to lose? There was no report from Lloyd that the motor was seized or had a hole in the crankcase, or even had any bad signs like knocking. I figured a carburetor cleaning, perhaps a look at the wiring, and I would have the motorcycle up and running

Making the entire prospect more appealing, too, was that the CB needed some babying after the long trip. The CB had a head gasket leak. I had tested the compression and everything was in spec, almost like new, so the leak was from the oil passage to the outside of the jug only. Still, the leak made a mess and required checking and adding oil more frequently than was convenient, and I owed it to the little bike that had served me so well to take care of the problem. The electric start had quit on me before the Michigan trip, too. Although the starter would spin, the motor would not, indicating a problem with the starter clutch.

Pulling the motor would be required for the head gasket repair, and, while I was at it, the starter clutch rebuild would be much easier, and I could also do a careful job adjusting the valves. The problem with doing this work was I would have no motorcycle to ride while I benched the CB motor.

Since I got the Honda, my plans to replace my Montero had changed. I had hardly started that truck for months. I decided to put new tires on it and fix the air conditioning sometime in the near future and just keep it for occasional hunting trips, pulling stumps, and hauling lumber to my woodshop or the dump-trailer to the landfill. But none of those repairs had seemed pressing as little as I used the Montero now, so it was not a practical alternative for everyday transportation if the CB was disabled. The motorcycle Lloyd offered seemed to fit the bill nicely; it could be my daily transportation while I took my time caring for the CB. None of the repairs on the 350 were pressing, so I thought I could pick up Lloyd's bike, get to work doing whatever minor things were needed to get it road worthy again, then turn my attention to the Honda. It was a perfect plan.

My brother, Tim, and I, armed with ratchet straps, hitched the trailer to my wife's Element and headed north to Dothan.

We arrived at Lloyd's mid-afternoon. No one was home yet, so we took a look around the place. In a corner of the yard was a large Quonset in front of which was a large, flat concrete pad. There sat a bike, tankless, on the uncovered pad. The front fender was spray-painted black and overspray was on the forks, while the rear fender was teal. One side cover was missing, as was the tool box compartment that was supposed to be on the side of the battery compartment on the right side.

It proved to be a Suzuki Savage, also known as an LS650, and later I found out from Lloyd it was a 1986—the first year for this bike which was still being made and was called the S40. The 1986 model was four speed, while the later ones were five.

When they got home, Lloyd and Andrew helped us look around the Quonset for parts of the bike. There was a rear footpeg, and in another spot was a second front fender and a second rear fender, this one in black. Two tanks were found, one teal and one black, and both were filled with rust and dented here and there. Extra handlebar mounts were discovered and another, left-side cover in teal. The bike was missing the front left rider peg, but this was not to be found anywhere, although we did find the missing passenger peg. Back at the house, Lloyd's wife, Kay, dug out the paperwork on the bike, but the folder, in spite of being filled with Alabama registrations, was missing the title. Knowing the bike had been registered for several years and up to a couple years previously, I figured a duplicate title would be possible to procure.

Lloyd and his family offered us their home for the night and cooked us a full breakfast in the morning before we headed out. Tim and I started loading the bike on my flatbed, while everyone headed off to work. We gathered up all the various loose parts and loaded them into the back of the Element and started for home with the Savage's headlight bobbing in my mirror fifteen feet behind us.

Arriving home, with the disapproving grin of my wife as a greeting, I wondered what I had gotten myself into. Well, I thought, I have not spent more than my time and the cost of fuel to Dothan and back, so I might as well give it a go and see what I could do. After all, there was no hurry, and I could tackle each problem as I found them until the bike was rideable once again.

Now, one thing I should mention is that the designer of the Savage had one of those little red devils on his shoulder while he figured out how to put this bike together—no angel in sight on the opposite shoulder. Tolerances are tight. What was quick and easy work on the CB350 was a nightmare of knuckle-busting procedures on the Savage.

For doing almost any work on this bike, the inevitable first steps are to remove the saddle and tank. The saddle is easy enough, but the tank sits over the top rail so that the attached petcock tucks under the left rail with the vent line nipple pointing inward and under the rail. This means that to remove the tank, you first remove the two bolts holding it to the bike frame at the back; the front is held in position, just like my CB, with half moon flanges on the tank resting around rubber pegs on the frame. Removing the two bolts is easy enough, but there are two steel and rubber bushings which sit under the rear tank flange and which protrude through two holes in the flange and through which the bolts pass. These bushings sit on a cross rail that sits below the top of the side rails and which has a turned lip along both its long sides. Once the bolts are removed, one cannot simply lift the back of the tank up and slide it backward off the front mounts. First, you are limited to how high you can lift the rear of the tank because of the petcock being stuck under the side rail. You also cannot slide the tank backwards because the bushings will not clear the raised lip on the cross rail's rear edge. You can almost do it, but not quite. The tank and its appurtenances are all tucked in place so tight that the only way I have yet to find to get it off the frame is to twist and slide and wrack it until somehow, I know not how, the bushings can be cajoled out from under the flange. This will give you a tiny bit more space to further twist and pull and wrack the entire tank rolling it to the left and lifting the rear while holding your tongue just so, hoping you don't tear the petcock from the tank, and eventually, once you have just about given up, the whole thing comes off almost magically. I have yet to figure out what happens to let it go, but it does...finally.

So, now, after a half hour or so of all these manipulations, you can start to actually work on whatever the problem was that you needed to fix.

And, God help you if you have to get to the rotor or stator under that damnable left-hand engine cover. This is something that should be easy—just take off the cover screws and pull it off. No, no, that would have been too easy for the bedeviled designer. "Can't have any ugly clearance space; that just looks too tacky. Lets tuck that kickstand and footpeg assembly closer." This results in you having to loosen a bolt that runs entirely though the engine and out the other side to the opposite footpeg to loosen up the assembly enough to slip the cover past it. This works much more easily, also, if you have the bike sitting perpendicular to the ground so that the bike's weight is not pressing on the kickstand. Of course, there is no centerstand. My solution, not having a motorcycle stand, was to run ratchet straps across the garage to strong points on either side attached to the bike, then adjust them to balance the bike between the two. Thus suspended you stoop under the straps back and forth every time you need a different tool from the workbench. You also must use a wire tie, or something, to hold back the spring-loaded kickstand switch plunger that is directly in front of the engine case. Next, loosen up all the screws on the perimeter of the case, except for that last one—the one directly behind the kickstand bracket and shift lever linkage. The linkage will have to be taken apart, with the loose end flopping around in the tight space behind the bracket. Now, the fun begins. You hold the flapping linkage out of the way and thread the small wrench back in behind the bracket to that last screw head. You turn the screw one degree, then withdraw the wrench, flip it around, reinsert it so you can get the box end on at the right angle to turn the screw one more degree, then withdraw the wrench, then do it all over again, and again, for the next ten minutes, one degree at a time. Then, once you do whatever you have to do inside there, you get to do it all again, while putting it back together.

First, I pulled the carb and did a thorough cleaning, pulling all jets, clearing their tiny holes with fishing line, put in a new float valve O-ring, and reinstalled the carb. While I was ordering a couple new O-rings for the carb (one spare; always buy one spare), I also ordered rubber tank mount bushings, which were missing from this bike. My Suzuki dealer didn't have anything in stock, in spite of this bike still being sold new with almost no changes since 1986. Every time I needed something, it was a week's wait for the part. I was pretty confident that the carb would now function properly after all the experience I had with other CV carbs on my CB350.

There was no air filter on the bike when I picked it up, so I ordered and installed a new one, then changed the oil and installed a new oil filter. I also installed a new plug, properly gapped. Before putting in the plug, I put a teaspoon or so of oil in the hole to soak down past the rings, because the bike had sat since 2008 and there was zero oil in the top end.

I chose the least dented and rusted tank and cleaned it with muriatic acid, flushed it out with water, and immediately followed that by denatured alcohol to prevent flash rusting. It was then all clean with bare gray metal inside. Relining would wait. First, the bike would have to prove to me that it could run.

I also discovered the fork legs were reversed, with the rotor on the wrong side, so I put them right.

The first big challenge was the petcock. Of course, Suzuki did not sell any parts for this; they sell an entire petcock for about seventy dollars. It did not look bad inside, but I found an aftermarket rebuild kit which fit this one perfectly, so I renewed the inside of the petcock. Next was to mount it. I remounted the petcock on the cleaned tank but had bad fuel leaks. I tried anaerobic sealant, which failed. I next tried Hylomar, a highly touted racing sealant, but the leak was still dripping. I flattened the mating surface with a file, followed by fine sandpaper, where the petcock flange's lozenge-shaped "O-ring" seated; but it still leaked. I once again removed the petcock, and this time I saw tiny pin-holes in the bottom-to-side flange, right next to the petcock base, which is what fooled me into thinking the petcock was the culprit. A bit of JB Weld cured that leak, and a fine film of Hylomar on the petcock base, the mating surface of the tank, and on the bolt threads finally did the job of stopping the leak.

Next up was mounting the tank with all the attendant struggles outlined above. Tank on, I plugged in the instrument lights, put on the speedo cable, and remounted the tank. Then I hooked up the vacuum and fuel line from the petcock. Next, a new battery went in. Switch on, and the headlight worked, at least. The front turn signals came on but didn't blink. I even had a working neutral light.

I hit the start button and whirrrr!—the starter turned over. I left the bike for the rest of the day, planning to try a real engine start after work, with fresh fuel in the tank. Unfortunately, the whirr was only the starter. The engine was not turning over. I pulled the starter, one of the rare, easy tasks of working on this bike, and could turn the gear it meshed with inside the engine easily in either direction through the hole with my finger. I drained the oil and started the arduous task of pulling off the left side engine cover.

The starter clutch is a gear which engages the gears driven by the starter. The starter clutch is made so if turned one way it will turn the motor over and start the bike; if turned the opposite direction it will spin freely so once the motor is running the gear doesn't keep spinning and turning the starter. Being able to spin the starter clutch gear freely in either direction was a sure sign it was shot. The starter clutch is hidden underneath the rotor, which requires a special Suzuki tool—of course. I took out the allen head screws holding the rotor to the clutch. Then I tried just loosening the middle nut that holds the rotor to the shaft, but to no avail. I was afraid I was going to damage something doing that. Grrrrrrr! I cursed the scoundrels who think they have to put every nut and bolt on a motor as tight as they possibly can! I used a three-quarter inch pipe on my ratchet in an attempt to break that rotor bolt loose but only succeeded in breaking the extension in two. I sprayed it with PB Blaster and thought I'd give it another go the next day.

Day dawned, and I tried my hand at the bolt again. This time I had my half-inch breaker bar and a 17mm half-inch drive socket, instead of a wimpy three-eighths-inch drive. No luck again. I went to my local bike shop and talked to the owner, hoping he might be willing to get it off with his impact tools if I loaded the bike on the trailer and brought it to him on the weekend. Instead, he was kind enough to offer to lend me his air powered impact wrench along with a 17mm impact socket. I brought it home, wheeled the bike out to my woodshop, where my big compressor lives, made sure it was on 125 psi, and used the impact wrench on the bolt—it didn't budge.

I loaded the Savage onto the trailer. I couldn't hold that hex shaft of the rotor securely with my big adjustable wrench while I tried to turn the rotor bolt, so it was going nowhere. The manual called for an offset 36mm wrench to hold the shaft which, of course, I did not have, and the cheapest one I found was over fifty dollars. Even once that bolt was out I would need to pull the rotor, which calls for another special Suzuki tool costing more than seventy dollars. I chatted with my bike mechanic cousin, Johnnie, and he gave me an idea for making a special puller, but finding what I needed to do that and then welding it up was not going to be very cheap or easy either. Finding a really big metric nut that would fit the shaft, welding a tube to it, and then welding a center nut in which to thread the puller bolt would not be a piece of cake. I admired the ingenuity, but it would be a lot of work for one-time use. I called the local dealer, and, for between $20 and $40, they would pull my rotor for me. So off the bike went to the shop. For $42.27 and after an hour wait I got the bike back with the rotor pulled. That was less than the cost of the 36mm offset wrench, alone, that was required to do the job.

With the clutch off, now I could address the problem of fixing or replacing it. Unfortunately, Suzuki, in their great wisdom, did not offer a clutch by itself or parts to repair one; they only sold the entire assembly, which included the clutch and large driven gear. So, I started the search for a used one. I thought with this bike being made virtually unchanged since 1986 to that day I could find parts easily, and actually I could, with the one exception of the starter clutch. After many days checking eBay, I had no alternative but to spend the $155 on an assembly from Suzuki, which entailed another wait of a week. Upon arrival of the clutch, I installed it and closed up the motor again, and refilled the bike with oil.

I hit the starter—nothing. The starter would spin and whir, but the engine just sat there motionless. Then I had a terrible thought—when I received the new clutch it came together as an assembly, with the driven gear already inside the clutch. I installed it as it came to me, but, halfway on, the drive gear parted from the clutch. I had to take the parts off and put them together again before putting them on the shaft. I wondered if the clutch was reversible. If so, when the starter turned everything, it would turn the clutch the direction that turns free in relation to the driven gear. Taking this thing apart was a bear, and now I had the realization that I would have to do it all over again, including paying to have the rotor removed, which was now affixed to the crankshaft with the bolt and red, permanent, threadlocker.

I paid the dealer to once again pull the rotor. I then reinstalled it the correct way. Finally, I hit the starter button, and lo and behold, the engine turned over. It took a while, some battery recharging, and some little blips on the throttle with the choke all the way out, but, eventually, the beast roared to life! And, man, was it loud!

Looking closer, I saw the muffler was ruined; someone had haphazardly mangled the baffle and the whole unit would have to be replaced. All that was holding it to the head pipe was a wimpy hose clamp. I took the old muffler down with me to see my local bike guy, Vince, and see what he thought. He took me out back and showed me a pile of shiny mufflers that people had left with him when they had him put aftermarket stuff on. We pulled a few out and found one off a Harley Softtail that looked like it would work. Price—nothing!

I took it home and cut the front pipe shorter, behind the crossover connector, and it slipped on like a glove. I also had received the rear pipe shield from eBay the day before, that was missing from the bike, and it would hide any ugliness at the connection. I thought about getting a foot or so of heat wrap or maybe fiberglass cloth to use as a gasket at the connection, but after talking to a couple knowledgeable people about using the exhaust wrap, the consensus was that it was unnecessary. I installed it without the wrap, although I used some high temp silicone sealant (red) to help air-tight the joint, and this time I used a proper exhaust clamp. There is a tapped, reinforced plate on the muffler made for mounting it to the FXS1450, and, luckily, it lined up with the mount on the Savage. It wasn't a perfect fit, but it was not visible, and it worked. I could not help but fire the Savage up to hear what it sounded like. It produced a nice, low rumble—loud but not obnoxious—and very little backfiring. I had listened to online recordings of several custom muffler installations that people had mounted to their Savages, and I thought this one was the best sounding I had heard.

After getting the muffler installed, I noticed that the rear fender I had just put on to replace the teal one that was on it before was bent—no dramatic dents in it or anything like that, it just did not line up with the rear tire, and you could see a line around the left side of the tire where the fender had cut into it. I guessed that whatever bike that rear fender had been on had crashed and fell on its left side, shoving the fender over when the turn signal hit the ground. I got out the handy ratchet straps and hooked one of them around the fender about mid-way and secured the other end to a strong point on the wall. I rigged the other strap similarly, but farther up on the frame, where it could act as a fulcrum. The rear ratchet strap was tightened, pulling the fender into somewhat better alignment with the back wheel. It was not perfect, but the wheel would no longer rub.

Vince, my muffler supplier, told me he had some parts for me I had ordered. I had forgotten all about them. They included a tiny contact for the front brake switch and a clamp/mirror perch for the right side controls. I then ordered some other missing parts: an aftermarket rear left turn signal; a front right signal; the front left peg which, like the starter clutch, do not seem to exist in used-parts-world for some reason; and a new clutch cable.

Now that I knew the bike could run, I had to tackle the electrical mess. A lot of, um, "customizing" had gone on there. Safety interlocks had been by-passed, even though the safety switches actually worked, and the decompression lever did not work. It also needed a new rear turn signal, but I took solace in the sound of that motor roaring to life.

I started troubleshooting the wiring. Most was OK. I considered leaving the safety switches by-passed, but finally decided to reconnect them. I checked the decompression solenoid, and it was working, so I moved on to the timer/

controller unit. I made up a bunch of jumpers and, carefully following the shop manual, checked both timers. Timer one was bad on this unit. I found one on eBay, so soon I would be able to wire this properly with a working decompression lever. I also checked the neutral switch, the wiring from which was dangling under the bike. It tested OK, so I spliced it into the wiring. I still had no winking turn signals, although they lit up now that I had put in new bulbs. I looked at the relay and it was very corroded, but a good cleaning did not fix it. Luckily, I found a generic flasher unit at the local auto parts store for $2.99, compared to the $38.52 for the same part from Suzuki. It plugged right in with the same connector and restored my turn signals to working condition.

About this time, my title arrived. If I could get this thing working I could put it on the road, but getting it road-worthy still eluded me.

There was a myriad of other little issues with the electrical system. The solenoid had no mount or insulators covering the terminals and was flopping around under the seat. The clutch switch was dirty and had to be cleaned to get working consistently. A unmountable fuse holder was replaced and mounted. The front brake switch was not lighting the brake light. But soon I was ready to start up the bike again. This time, I had hoped it would be the final time. Fingers crossed, I turned on the choke, gripped the clutch, turned the ignition key, and hit the start switch—nothing.

First things first. I checked the resistance of the coil. Both resistance measurements were spot on. Next, I hooked my spark tester up to the spark plug lead, snapped it onto a head fin, and hit the starter. I got a weak spark for just an instant and then nothing. I checked continuity for the leads between the ignitor and the coil, and both were good. Just for good measure, I sprayed the contacts down with contact cleaner and cleaned up the coil terminals and then reattached everything, hooked up the spark tester again, and got the same results—a spark, then nothing. I concluded I had a bad ignitor. The manual gave me no way to test the ignitor, but all indications pointed to it as the culprit.

I started thinking about the possibility of the problem also being in the "pickup coil," "signal generator," or "pulse generator" (all names for the same thing in my manual—confusing, huh?). That seemed to be the only other possibility. Someone in a Savage forum also mentioned it, and that they had a similar problem. Replacing the signal generator had fixed it for them. I checked the manual, and it had a testing procedure for it. The resistance tested right in the middle of the correct range, so that eliminated the signal generator as the cause. I also tested the continuity of the leads from there to the connection to the ignitor and they checked out OK.

Eventually, a member of a Savage forum posted the resistance figures for testing the igniter. I got out my meter and started testing. I got nothing even close to what I should have. The readings I had were not even consistent each time I tested. I found an igniter on eBay and ordered it.

When the new igniter arrived, I plugged it in, and the Savage started right up—after I remembered I had to hold the clutch in to start the bike, now that I had reconnected all the safety interlocks. I wish I had remembered that before I took the saddle and tank off again to check out things! The Savage ran pretty well, and, with a little adjustment to the idle set screw, it idled without throttle input from me. It backfired quite a bit, but other than that, it ran smoothly.

I noticed a lot of smoke coming from the header where it attaches to the exhaust port, as I had before on the couple occasions I did get it to run. There was a lot of oil around the pipe there, and, as I suspected, I would to have to remove the head cover and replace a plug that sits right up above the exhaust pipe—a typical Savage issue. The plug fills an access hole to get to an head bolt right next to the exhaust port. At least the motor does not have to come out to get to this.

It also looked like the exhaust to cylinder connection might need some attention, perhaps a new gasket. I would not be surprised to see, once I opened that up, that there was no gasket at all.

All the lights and electrical systems were working as designed, so despite the exhaust and oil leak issues, I was about to take it for its first test ride.

The next morning, I mounted up for a bike ride on the Savage. It started out rough, with lots of popping and backfiring. I almost brought it home after once around the ball field complex, across the street from the garage, but as I rode, it smoothed out. I passed the house and kept on riding up around back streets. The backfiring diminished. It was hesitating and coughing when you tried to open the throttle at first, but that got better, too. I came back by the house and decided to run down Lakeshore Boulevard to Kiwanis Park, about a mile away, so I could get in all four gears. All the gears worked fine, and, by the time I got home, it was running much better and was quite rideable.

I still had that oil leak above the exhaust, so when I stopped billows of smoke came from there where the oil had dripped onto the exhaust. It looked like a simple enough fix, just removing the cover on the head, replacing a plug, and sealing it all up.

The bike felt really good and had lots of torque. The brakes both worked fine, and all the electrics, lights and all, worked perfectly. Even the speedometer worked. At least now I didn't feel like I'd been wasting my time with this thing. Another afternoon of work and the leak should be fixed, and I could take it for a real ride. I applied some high temp silicone sealant with a long q-tip on the outside of the leaking plug, which, indeed, proved to stem the oil flow.

My wife heard the news and mentioned it was like new—a "virgin" bike. I corrected her and said it was more like a resurrection—being old and worn out but now running like new, a "Virgin Whore"—the name stuck.

My joy did not last long. I got insurance on the bike the next day and went to take the Virgin Whore out to Fuzzy's, our local biker dive, about three miles away from home. The Savage started right up but was still backfiring. I thought it would settle down once it was warmed up, like before, so I took it for a short ride around the neighborhood. Unfortunately, this time the backfiring never stopped, and the bike would not rev up smoothly. It would surge up, then cough and slow. I had to stay in the middle of the friction zone the entire time and never got past second gear. It quit completely on me a mile or so from the house, but, eventually, I got it to start again and I rode it "pop, pop, popping" all the way home. I parked the Savage in the garage and took my CB up to Fuzzy's, instead.

I thought about the problem and came up with, and dismissed, a bunch of possible causes. I guess the cam chain could have jumped and messed up the timing. The backfiring was in the exhaust, not back through the carb. I thought fuel was being drawn into the combustion chamber and not getting burned and then going out the exhaust only to be ignited in the pipe. It was backfiring pretty much all the time. I checked the coil again while it was still warm, and it still checked out perfectly.

My cousin gave me an idea. He said to check the decompression lever. If it was not working properly, it could certainly have caused my symptoms. I unplugged the wires on the decomp solenoid and started the bike without it and it ran much better.

Looking at the decompression system, the lever, once released, did not have a positive snap-back, so I thought that might be the crux of the problem—possibly the decomp kept "decomping" at times. So, I pulled the tank to take a closer look and to pull the cable to see if it ran free. Now that I was more familiar with this bike, I saw that parts of the decompression system were not even there. First, the decomp solenoid was being held on by only one of the two bolts. Also, there was supposed to be a bracket that held the cable at the solenoid end, which was completely missing from my bike. Also, the cable itself, although seemingly free, was frayed pretty badly and had a kink in its casing. So, I ordered another decomp solenoid, complete with cable and bracket from eBay and bolted it on when it arrived.

Another good thing resulting as a result of removing the tank was getting a good look at the top engine mount. There were supposed to be two bolts at the frame and one at the engine, but mine only had one frame bolt, leaving the motor "unmounted" at the top and the brackets dangling. Thankfully, I could pick up new bolts for that locally. I knew there was an issue with the mount before, but I had thought the mounting bolts were broken off in the holes; luckily that was not the case and I wouldn't have to easy-out anything (which is anything but "easy"), just plug in new bolts.

I went out to start it, and the Savage fired on the first try. While running on choke it popped a little, but very little, and nothing like before. I never got it to warm up completely. The choke on this carb would not stay put and popped back in before the bike was ready, and the bike stalled out. I tried to start it again, but I only turned it over a couple times before the battery would not turn it over again. I figured, even though it was a new battery I had bought when I first got the bike and had kept on a battery tender, that sometime during all those first attempts at starting the bike I wore it down beyond charging, maybe using a charger while starting. Now the thing was good for one or two starts and then had to be recharged.

A load test showed the battery bad, so I had Vince's shop replace it under warranty. The mechanic installed the replacement battery. The bike turned over fine but had no spark. The mechanic and I looked the bike over and found a loose lug on a wire going to the coil. He re-attached it, plugged it in, and we got spark! The bike immediately fired up and ran nice and smooth. He kept it on idle, slowly letting in the choke until it was running without it. While I was settling the bill, I saw him ride past the window and around the drive of the shop. I guess he couldn't resist a test ride.

Once warmed up and he was riding, the bike did not backfire. It had a softer pop when he decelerated, but that was pretty typical of this bike, and nothing at all like the continuous shotgun blasts I was getting before.

So, my conclusion was that the decomp lever was not returning properly and leaving the exhaust valves open, causing the bad backfiring. Replacing the solenoid cable bracket and cable solved that.

It had been a long road, but I was glad to be getting to the end. I was able to ride the Savage once in a while. I didn't go far, because my confidence had not been won over completely yet, plus it still wore the old tires that needed replacing. By then, I knew better than to assume all was well.

I had ridden out to my brother's to help with some work on his house that he was going to put on the market soon. Leaving for home, the Savage wouldn't start. My brothers gave me a push and it fired right up, so I was not too worried. My other brother, Bob, who had come to help, had his new wife with him and he wanted to introduce her to Fuzzy's. I said I would meet them there, knowing we could pop-start the bike again, if need be, but, really, I thought it would not be necessary. It should start much more easily when warm. Leaving Fuzzy's, the bike, once again, refused to fire. Bob pushed me down the road—nothing. We pushed the bike to the top of a hill and tried again—nothing. Dead as a doornail. Bob gave me a ride back to my place where we attached the trailer to my Montero and returned to pick up the recalcitrant motorcycle in Fuzzy's parking lot.

Later, in the garage, I checked the voltage while trying to start the bike after recharging the battery fully, and the bike fired up, but the voltage did not increase as the revs did. I pulled off the saddle and checked the stator wires— no continuity on one of the leads—definitely bad. I found a used eBay stator that had been tested, and I tested it on arrival, too, and had continuity from all leads as I should have had.

It was time to get tires and bearings, so, with the help of one of my brothers, we hung the bike from the rafters with ratchet straps. (The Savage only weighs about 350 pounds.) I pulled the wheels and brought them in to my local shop for tires. While the bike was hanging there I pulled the left side cover—again—and installed the stator.

Another thing about this bike is that the handlebars were swept way too far back, making it terribly uncomfortable to hold onto, having to hold your wrists at almost right angles to your arms. I pulled the bar and, of course, broke the wire from the controls to the recently repaired brake switch. After some struggle getting all the controls off, I took a closer look at the bar. It looked like the bar had been in a wreck sometime in its past life, probably causing the severe back-sweep. I found a crevice between my porch rim joist and brick columns and yanked on the bar ends until I had something more reasonable.

When the shop pulled the tires off the rims they were found to be very rusty inside. I picked them up and with a brass wheel and Strong Arm I got them back in shape. They were not pretty inside, but would not poke any holes through the new tubes. The outside looked almost new.

I had suspected the front bearings were on the way out, so had the shop preorder new ones, but, upon removing the back wheel, we found the rear to also be going, so those were ordered, as well. I picked up the front wheel with new tire and bearings and reinstalled it. The bars went back on, and the engine was buttoned back up and filled with new oil. My back-ordered from three months ago right front turn signal finally arrived, so that was installed, too. After the rear bearings and tire were installed, I hoped to be back on the road again.

Finally, I pulled the bike out of the garage and started it. I checked the voltage as the motor revved up and down, and it never increased above the regular battery voltage. There was no doubt the stator had been bad, but now I suspected that the regulator/rectifier was also shot. Looking closely at the output three-prong connector, I saw that the red connector was suspiciously burned.

I determined that my regulator was toast, putting out no charge at all. I bought a brand new aftermarket one. When it came, it had only two wires coming out of it and into the triple connector going to the harness. I called the manufacturer, who assured me it was supposed to be that way and not to worry about there being no third wire to match up with the third wire coming from my harness. Looking at the wiring diagram it did seem superfluous. I plugged it in and fired the bike up. The new regulator seemed to be doing its job just fine.

I took the bike out for a test ride, but did not get more than two miles before it started sputtering. Discouraged, I took a look first at the carb and saw that, once again, the crappy fuel line I had bought from the auto parts store had softened, and the clamp had chewed a hole through it. There was fuel leaking around the connection to the carb. At least I was relieved to know it was a fairly simple problem and not a continuance of the electrical nightmare.

I got the bike home, cut off the end of the fuel line at the carb, reclamped it, and took another test ride. It worked until about the same distance, when I had the same issue, this time at the tank end. I was using this same line on my CB350 and, on the way to Birmingham, it also had developed a leak, which required a roadside stop, cutting off the end of the line and discarding the mushy tip, and reclamping the line to the bike. Lesson learned: buy good fuel line, not just any generic kind. Vince's shop supplied me with an appropriate length of good fuel hose. The clamps I had been using (plain old screw type hose clamps) were exacerbating the problem, too, by digging into the softened cheap fuel line, so I bought some new spring type clamps for this reinstall.

I rode the bike and, finally, everything went smoothly, no popping, stalling, fuel leak, or anything bad. While the wheel work had been proceeding, I had also repaired the saddle covering's loose edges, restapling them to the underside of the saddle. I had read that the seat is found by many riders to tilt forward too much, making the rider slide forward when braking and making for a more uncomfortable ride, so I made a "riser" for the front saddle mount, making it much more comfortable to ride.

There were still some things that needed attention. At Vince's shop, we found was that the clutch was slipping. In fourth (top) gear, if you throttled up quickly, the motor would spin up quicker than the bike would accelerate. I adjusted the clutch, but that did not solve the problem. Riding normally, this was not a big problem, but I would have to order new clutch plates and springs. It was a simple job to replace them which I had previous experience doing before on the CB.

The free bike was not so free anymore, and the simple task of getting it running was not so simple. But, with some experience, help from others, a little ingenuity, and relatively few dollars; I had a bike I could ride while the Honda got its much deserved repairs—maybe.

Two Bikes Down

Whenever I get back from one of my road trips, a funk settles in as the contrast of the excitement of the open road and new places is replaced by the day-to-day monotony of everyday life. As I slowly adjust back to sedentary life, I usually do local rides on one of my bikes as relief to help in the transition. I got one ride in on the CB since my return from the Blue Ridge Mountains and was looking forward to more riding.

Before leaving for the Motorcycle Kickstart Classic ride and the Barber Vintage Festival, the Virgin Whore, my ratted out 1986 Savage, had been reluctant to start, requiring way too much throttle and too many spins of the starter. I had dutifully cleaned the carb and replaced a slide and diaphragm unit that had developed a hole and figured that would solve the problem.

I was asked by my son's fifth grade teacher to come in to class and help the kids carve a pumpkin for a class competition the school was holding. The school is less than a half mile from home, so I thought I would hop on the Savage and see how she did, and perhaps take a spirited ride after my school duties. The old girl fired right up, and I thought the problem had been solved as I parked her and walked into school.

Two students at a time, I cut and carved with sharp tools, being the responsible adult, while the kids glued a wild assortment of things onto their entry—antlers, an alligator head, palmetto leaf "ears," goofy buckeye eyes—the pumpkin was...um...eccentric, but imaginative.

I stayed a bit past lunch so all the children would have a chance to participate and then walked outside to the waiting Savage. I pulled the choke, flicked the key to "start," made sure the bike was in gear and the clutch was pulled in, and hit the starter button. The Virgin Whore roared to life...for about thirty seconds. Try as I might, the bike would not start again, and, eventually, I gave up, put up the kickstand, and coasted down the hill in front of the school and around the corner at the bottom, hoping to get as much distance as I could toward home. I made it almost a block after the corner, then, after a couple more attempts at starting her, I dismounted and started the push back to the garage.

The Savage had played this trick on me before, and the culprit had been a loose connection on the coil. Once back in the garage, I pulled the wires to the secondaries and made sure to reattach them firmly. I rolled the bike outside and hit the start button. She flew to life. "As always," I thought, "it is something simple," and I rode off. Thinking my ride was saved, I headed up FL 17.

My hopes were soon dashed as I was rounding the large sweepers just south of Fuzzy's when the bike died, restarted, popped, and snorted. I rolled into the parking area at Fuzzy's disheartened, but knowing that if I could not get the Savage running, I could leave her here safely until I could retrieve her with my trailer. "Might as well have a cold one," I thought, as I went in to get in the cool air conditioning and think about alternative solutions, hoping the bike would start when I left. Coming up empty of brilliant ideas for repairing the Virgin Whore, I went outside to fire her up and coax her the three miles home. The Savage fired up instantly, but I hadn't gotten two hundred yards before it started cutting out, popping and groaning, and then rolled to a quiet stop. I tried starting it again, but this time I got nothing, just the whir of the starting motor. I rolled the bike back to Fuzzy's and went inside to leave my jacket, helmet, and gloves before walking home in the now hot Florida afternoon. Luckily, a friend offered me a ride and took me home, where I would have to wait for Andrea to come home from work so I could haul the trailer up to get the bike. I called my brother, securing some help for the loading, and by evening the Savage was back in her spot just above the oil stain on the garage floor.

With the Savage down for the time being, I figured I could always count on Old Faithful, my 1968 Honda CB350, for my second attempt at a therapeutic ride. I had taken her on one ride since I had been back, over to Plant City to meet up with some folks I knew from *Born to Ride* magazine and had no trouble on that ride. However, now upon kicking her awake, my ears were greeted by a strange and unhealthy grating and rattling sound I swear had not been there during the 1,700 mile ride from which I had just returned. Other than the sound, the bike ran as well as ever—no hesitation and no loss of power. I had only gone a couple blocks and returned immediately to the house and started my investigations.

As I listened to the idling motor, I swore the sound was coming from the left side exhaust, and sure enough, the joint between header and muffler was loose, and, if I tapped on the muffler, I could distinctly hear rattling inside. (Every CB350 parts diagram I had ever seen showed a solid pipe here from header to tip of the muffler, just like the one on the right side, but mine was in two parts, and obviously not a homemade concoction. I am still wondering why that is. The muffler is stamped clearly CB250/350. [I've since learned that the two part exhaust was the original for my year. Honda switched later to a one piece, to prevent riders pulling off the muffler and running plain pipes and making a racket, or so I've been told.]) I also noticed that my chain guard, which had recently been repaired, was once again broken at the rear mounting ear. That could have been contributing to the rattle, too. Happy to have found the problem, I dismantled the exhaust. I tapped the muffler end on the ground, but the expected rust didn't come out, and, holding it out and shaking it, now free of the bike, I could hear no rattle. I removed the chain guard and reassembled the exhaust, this time ensuring the joint was tight by cutting some additional shim out of a soda can. The exhaust back on, I kick started the CB and could not hear the scraping sound I had heard before, although listening over the clackity clack sewing machine sounds of the valves and points was difficult to do. Always an optimist (OK, not always), I thought I was set.

I had my heart set for a long while on picking up, if not a new, at least a newish Triumph Bonneville. As much as I like vintage bikes, they take a lot of care. It would be nice, I thought, to have a bike to just jump on and ride, while I took all the time I needed to do a proper frame up restoration on Old Faithful. I had made a few trips to Hap's in Sarasota, a local dealership, to sit on Bonnies, dream, and plan. My hopes were high for finally being able to make this happen toward the end of the year, or early 2012. When I learned from a fellow VJMC member that Hap's was having an open house, I figured that would be a great opportunity to get out and ride, make a final check of my intended next bike, and perhaps pick up some new riding gloves, as mine were becoming threadbare from use.

A friend of mine from Fuzzy's, a new rider with a new-to-her H-D Sportster 883 Anniversary Edition, had been wanting to do a ride together so she could gain a little more experience. I thought the ride to Hap's would give her some useful saddle time. The rural route I had planned was a step above the straight-line, flat roads usually found in Florida, and I thought she would enjoy the ride off major highways.

Saturday morning came, and I was looking forward to the ride to Hap's, although my friend had canceled at the last minute because she had to work. I hopped on the CB and started out alone in a soft drizzle, but I knew that the rain would soon be gone and the rest of the day would be nice. The route was via back roads starting out running through the groves between Lake Wales and Ft. Meade. This stretch had a couple wide sweepers and a few nice hard turns that kept it interesting. As I neared Fort Meade, though, the grating sound returned and grew worse, although the bike, like before, still ran flawlessly. By the time I had descended the hill in the groves and got to the last corner at the road that would take me into Fort Meade, I thought it wise to turn around and abandon the ride. Back through the empty groves I rode, worrying all the time at the increasing scraping noise of the engine. I made it home, the engine still running smoothly, in spite of the sound. I rolled her back into the garage, next to her wounded companion.

Next on the list of things to check will be the starter chain and starter clutch. I'd had starter trouble on the CB for a long time then, and had been kick-starting it for two years. I had rebuilt the starter clutch, but upon reassembly, it behaved the same as before, spinning but only occasionally catching. The starter itself looked good when I had taken it apart to clean it, with still substantial copper on the brushes. The starter system had mystified me, and now I wondered if the starter clutch was totally messed up and perhaps turning the starter chain all the time and causing the new sound. Checking that would entail draining the oil (1,500 miles early), pulling the crankcase cover, and removing the rotor. The CB would be down for a while. If it proved not to be the chain/starter clutch, then the motor would have to come out and be disassembled. Either way, it was off the road for a considerable time.

Meanwhile, the Savage, after more investigation, may have had a coil and/or igniter problem. A spark tester I used showed inconsistent firing of the plug. The seat and tank came off and the next step would be to find another coil and then testing once again. If that didn't do the trick, I would try the much more expensive igniter.

After pulling the CB motor and some investigation I found that the 350's cam chain tensioner had failed. Well *failed* is probably the wrong word; *exploded* was more like it. Bits and pieces of the guides were scattered around the innards of the engine. New parts were ordered and were going to have to be installed, and while I was at it and had the cylinders off, new rings would go in, too, just for good measure. That was going to take some time.

So, for the time being, I was stuck. No riding therapy for me. I would just have to do my best to dispel the after-ride blues on my own. But you never know, my truck was for sale, and, if it sold soon, I might have the down payment for a Bonnie. At least I could dream.

Old Faithful, Back on the Road

After the second Motorcycle Kickstart Classic Ride deposited me in Denton, North Carolina, with a broken frame, I found a local welder to weld the bike back together enough for me to limp home to central Florida. Once home, the motor would have to come out so the frame could be fixed properly. Once that was done, it seemed like the logical time to strip down the bike, clean it up, and restore it properly.

I disassembled the bike down to all its component pieces with the hope of powder coating the frame parts before reassembly and restoring all the shiny bits. As usual, my meagre budget got in the way when I priced out powder coating and rechroming. So, instead, a good cleaning, followed by a rattle can paint job, would have to suffice for the frame The chrome and body part painting would have to wait. I did, however, take the opportunity to replace all the loose bearings and races in the steering head with modern tapered bearings.

With the frame repaired and repainted, the motor went back in. It had been running fine, so it required no attention other than bolting it in.

Now that the bike was reassembled, it was time to test fire her and see where I stood. I had the Vintage Japanese Motorcycle Club National Rally coming up in about a week, and the bike had to be ready and able to be ridden 1,200 miles or so to Helen, Georgia, in the Blue Ridge Mountains, and back to Florida.

The bike had never had the proper 350A carbs on her, so while it had been in pieces, I went on the search for a matched pair of 350As. I found them, thoroughly cleaned them, and finally put them back on the motor as soon as everything else was restored to its proper place.

A little non-ethanol fuel was picked up via jerry can, then deposited in the CB's tank, the key was turned, and the starter thumbed. Old Faithful came back to life. (You can't say "roared back to life" when referring to a CB350 motor, which sounds more like a muffled lawnmower engine combined with the whirs, clicks, and rattles of a sewing machine.)

But something was not right. Fuel was pouring out of the overflow weep-hole on the bottom of the left carburetor. I had done this many times before—pull the carb, clean the float valve seat and needle, reinstall, and try again. This done, I reinstalled the carb and tried again. Nope, nothin' doin.' Still leaking.

After a few (meaning a couple dozen) more cycles of disassembly and reassembly, I had the foresight to fill the bowl with fuel off the carb. It still leaked. This could only mean the fuel overflow tube had a leak around where the brass tube attaches to the aluminum bowl, just above the weep-hole. I had an extra bowl for a 350A and it was playing the same trick. "Sounds like a job for JB Weld," I told myself, and off I went to Autozone to pick up some.

Back with the magic epoxy mixture, I went to work on the drain tube, making sure I got a good bead of JB all around the circumference of the tube where it attached to the floor of the float bowl. While I waited the required twenty-four hours before reattaching the bowl to the carb and filling it with fuel, I dreamed of instant gratification upon hitting the starter the next day.

The following day, I put the carb back together, attached it to the motor, and turned the petcock to Reserve. Not a drop! Aha! Now, we will listen to the sweet sound of the Honda twin once more. And it did start, but the bike would only run on the right cylinder. The fuel line going to the left was devoid of gas.

"OK," I said to myself, "I need to pull the carb and adjust the float; no biggie! Standard operating procedure." Once again, I fired her up. The motor sputtered to life, but still something was wrong. Now, although she seemed to be running fine, fuel was pouring out of the left carb. "Can't have that," I thought. Off came the carb again, along with all the related lines, cables, air filter, and side cover. Back on and now the carb was dry. I repeated the entire cycle, next time resulting in an overflowing carburetor, then repeated the entire cycle. Now I had a dry carburetor, then...repeat this cycle, oh, I dunno, perhaps two dozen times. No matter how I adjusted the float valve tang, if the fuel flowed at all, it overflowed; and if it didn't overflow, the carb was dry. Between all the offs and ons, the carb was dismantled and cleaned once again. An order was placed for a brand new OEM float needle and seat. (This would surely solve the problem!). The vents and the jets were all blown with compressed air, but, even with the new valves in place, the carb would still not cooperate.

Finally, with my deadline for departure for Helen approaching and wanting to have ample time to test ride and make sure everything was OK with the bike, I abandoned, at least temporarily, the attempt to make the bike all original with the 350As as it was designed. Luckily for me, just before the frame break caused a year-long pause in riding the bike; the motor had been running perfectly on the old pair of 3Ds, which I jetted to simulate the 350As' settings. I dug out the dirty old 3Ds, wiped them down the best I could, and replaced the 350As with them.

In the meantime, I ran down a few remaining electrical gremlins. Now, when the key was turned, the neutral light worked, along with the gauge lights and headlight. All I needed was a running motor.

I hit the starter and Old Faithful came alive, on both cylinders, with no leaks! I hit the streets and did a short test ride. All was fine now and the motor purred just like it did on that last ride to North Carolina, where the frame had given out.

The gauges are the only things that I had not tried to fix, and the tach was bouncing all over the dial, while the speedo was stuck at 30 mph, until I gave it a good whack with my fist. The tach was disconnected. Who needs a tach anyway!? I mean I can feel what rpm I am at on this old bike. Just in case the speedo continues to ignore the wheel revolutions and posts its own less-than-accurate opinion of our speed, I Velcroed to the bars, once more, that old handheld GPS that had served me before as a speedometer on my way to Michigan.

With four days to spare, I got the bike back to road-worthiness, and come Thursday, I was to, once again, have the experience of enduring...er...I mean enjoying, a ride of over five hundred miles on the back of that old 350. For a year I had been attending VJMC rides on my modern Triumph, and while that allowed me to participate, there was just something not right about riding a modern Brit bike among all those vintage Japanese motorcycles. Now, I was back in the saddle, and Old Faithful would have the chance to ride once again with her two-wheeled brethren.

RIDING

.

To Biketoberfest

With my bike repair nightmare behind me, Tim and I started planning a long ride to Daytona's famous Biketoberfest. While the festivities in Daytona were fun, the ride there and back was really the most exciting part. The weather was crispy cool. I took my little CB350 and rode it alone, while my brother took his wife on his Nomad. My wife, Andrea, drove up to Deland where we had booked a room and then rode the rest of the way into Daytona and back to Deland on the back of the CB with me.

Checking mileage on the Internet gave me 218 miles from Lake Wales to Daytona Beach and back, but by the time we returned my odometer would read 439.

The weather was chilly in the morning, but warmed up enough by afternoon for me to be comfortable in my mesh jacket, with the liner installed for the first time that year. Still, the first couple hours were on the frigid side, and I wished I had gloves that covered more of my wrists between my hand and jacket sleeve and that weren't riddled with holes like my perforated gloves that are needed for the usual hot weather riding in Florida.

On the way up we went north on US 27, making a quick breakfast stop at Waffle House, then off to Howie-in-the-Hills and SR 19 up to Tavares, where we caught SR 44 to Deland. That's some very pretty country, and the roads were filled with bikes on that weekend, outnumbering cars two to one. At one time we found ourselves trailing a solid line of perhaps fifty bikes, also heading up to Biketoberfest. We hit the Cabbage Patch before meeting up with Andrea at the hotel, where we watched some uninhibited women wrestling in the cabbage and oil, while numerous others wandered around in different levels of undress.

We headed back to Deland and got to the room well ahead of Andrea, who had gotten held up with babysitter misunderstandings. We checked in and emptied the contents of our saddlebags and tail bags plopping them into the room's dresser drawers. Andrea finally arrived, and we all hopped on the bikes and headed back eastward on International Speedway Drive to Daytona Beach.

Downtown at the beach bikes were everywhere, and the parade down the main street was quite a spectacle, not to mention the dancing girls at Froggie's and other hot spots. After enough beer was consumed, dancing girls were tipped, and after a healthy period of temperance to ensure a safe ride back on the bikes, we headed to the hotel in the now very chilly night air. A seafood dinner at Deland's Fish House next to where we were staying was devoured and it was back to the room and a good night's rest before our trip home in the morning.

Before leaving Deland, we had a slow, hearty breakfast, giving the sun time to warm things up, and after a good-bye to Andrea, off we went again, this time deciding on a untried route home.

On the way back we went through parts of Florida I had never been in, and I had lived down here more than half my life. South and east of Orlando there is low, swampy ground running north and south on the east side of the

Lake Kissimmee area with no crossovers, until you get far enough south to hit State Road 60, which runs west into Lake Wales. We shot south from Deland and skirted swamps and farmland, making numerous turns and doubling back often.

For anyone interested in riding this quiet and untrafficked part of the state themselves sometime, the route is a maze of turning instructions: south out of Deland on US 17/92, east on Graves Avenue which becomes Howland Boulevard, south at SR 415, also known as Cabbage Patch Road to Biketoberfesters; east then southeast on SR 40 to Geneva and Snow Hill Road (Don't miss this turn!); south on Snowhill; left on Brumley; then south and then west on Second Street in the metropolis of Chuluota; south on Chuluota Road to Lockwood; then east on SR 50; followed by a southeast veer onto SR 520; pass under the Beeline (SR 528 toll road); left on CR 532 (Snow Road); don't miss the next left after the curve onto CR 419 (Deer Park Road); left on US 192; south on US 441 to Yeehaw Junction; right at Yeehaw onto SR 60 and finally west through flat land on to Lake Wales.

Throw in a couple of unplanned, um, "detours" and backtracks (see: "Don't miss this turn!" above), about fifty miles worth, and you can see why our mileage was so much more; but we were in no hurry. In Pirsig's words: "...we were interested in making good time, emphasis on good." Still, if the isolated crossroads had road names on them, names that matched the ones on our maps, we might have saved ourselves an hour or two of confusion.

The wind was surprisingly strong that day and knocked my little bike to and fro; sometimes I had to lean like I was in a curve just to keep going straight. The wind wreaked havoc with my fuel consumption, giving me a low of 41 mpg and a high of 55 mpg. Revving up around 6,500 for 65 mph doesn't deliver the best mileage on my CB350, but otherwise it gave me no trouble all the way, other than having to re-lube a noisy tachometer.

Finally, at Yeehaw Junction, we turned onto the final stretch, the arrow-straight SR 60, passing one of our usual hunting spots at Three Lakes Wildlife Management Area, crossing the Kissimmee River, and forcing ourselves west through the oncoming wind to Lake Wales.

This was the first really long jaunt on the CB350 since I got it back into running condition, and it showed me it had the gumption to take on the road and gave me the confidence I needed to put it, and myself, to the test on longer rides.

FLORIDA TO MICHIGAN ON A CB350

PART ONE

My brother, Tim, had been planning a visit to Niles, Michigan, to see his old high school friends for some time. Unfortunately, he lost his job before he was to fly up. Chatting in his garage one afternoon he proposed a motorcycle trip, instead, now that he had time, and, once re-employed somewhere new, it would probably be a long time before he would have another opportunity to do a long ride. I agreed, looking forward to a long ride myself and thinking that the trip might be just the ticket for Tim to clear his head and get a game plan going for his future.

I thought Tim would want to go in a few weeks, the departure time when he had planned his flight, but Tim said, "How about next Wednesday?" which was only five days away. Not much time to plan, but I had already said, "Yes." I guessed I *had* to go.

I rode my old Honda CB350, and my brother rode his 2001 Kawasaki Vulcan Nomad 1500. My speedometer jumped all over the place from 35 to 100 mph and was totally useless, so I Velcroed a small, handheld GPS from a boat I used to have onto the middle of my bars to be my speed gauge in its stead and got ready to go.

We left Lake Wales, in the center of the Florida peninsula, Wednesday morning on the seventh of April before full light. I barely got out of my driveway, headed to my brother's place, when I realized I had left the atlas in the garage. I went back the few blocks to get it and proceeded to stuff it in the already overfull luggage. When I shoved it in, I moved the bike, the kick-stand folded, and the bike rolled forward, falling onto its side and into the fender of our parked car. The windscreen shattered into a myriad of small pieces, which I angrily threw into the garage. Disappointed with myself, I once again left for my brother's, where I quickly readjusted the handlebar and mirrors, which were misaligned, but unbroken. So, off we went, me windscreen-less, on our way north, with over a thousand miles ahead of us to go.

We took US 27 north to US 129 at Branford, in North Florida, and followed US 129 to US 41 into Valdosta, where I have a high school friend who teaches at the university there. We met Julie for lunch at an great little Cajun restaurant downtown named Antoine's, the Flavor of New Orleans. After a meal of andouille sausage and rice, we continued north, stopping just before getting out of town at a bike shop we were told might have a windscreen replacement.

Having no luck there, we were off again, taking GA 125 out of Valdosta to GA 37, then east to US 221, where we once again headed north. At Douglas, the road hooked up with US

441, which we took all the way to Athens, where we stopped for the night.

All through Georgia the air was filled with the smell of flowers in bloom—a fragrance reminiscent of incense. Most of the trees were still bare, but the pecan trees were just starting to bud. The sun was warm, but the breeze was refreshingly cool.

We had planned to camp on the way, but I learned you need much better guides than a simple atlas if you are going to do that. You are probably not going to get as far as you thought, and it's impossible to plan to be at that little state park tent icon on the map, which is the only campground they point out, before dark every time. Or you are going to ride much farther, maybe into the night because of the need to beat the weather, which is what happened that first day.

There was a strong front with tornado activity heading east, and we decided to get as far north as we could that day, so the front could pass through in the night while we slept somewhere dry. It was a good plan, but by morning the front was still lingering. We left the hotel late, giving the weather a little more time to clear, then headed north on US 441 toward Franklin, North Carolina, which we hoped would be dry by the time we arrived. The weather, however, did not cooperate, and at Franklin we headed northwest on NC 28—a thrill ride, for those who want to try it—and then west to the Cherohala Scenic Skyway. The Tail of the Dragon was closed due to rockslides, but we thought in this weather the Cherohala was a better choice, anyway. At least by going west we would eventually get behind the front and in clear skies.

On the Cherohala the rain was coming down. We saw our lives flash before our eyes more than once as we wound around the twisties in the rain, and into the foggy cloud tops. My little mount did me proud and handled like a dream, and I often left my brother and his dragging floorboards behind, or when he had the lead, I had to slow down a bit to stay a safe distance behind him.

At Tellico Plains we left the Cherohala and headed up TN 68, slowly leaving the high mountains. We continued to US 27 and got just north of I-40 when we decided to stop— wet, cold, and tired. We decided to ask for directions to *any* campground. Our first stop ended up being a dead end, being at a "campground" that catered only to motorhomes. We stumbled across Roane County Park, backtracking just south of the Interstate and east, where we chatted with a Tennessee State Police officer, who was doing paperwork in her car. She was not sure where we could camp. She made a call to her brother, who happened to manage the park. A surprise to her, she found that the park did have primitive camping, and she led us, via the directions her brother gave her, holding up a locked wire "gate" so we could ride under and into the campground. What a beautiful place, with fire ring already made, split and stacked firewood, and a short drop down to an inlet of the Tennessee River. We had the entire campground to ourselves. We pitched the tent and hit the sack while temperatures dropped. By early morning, I was freezing, but by putting on more clothes in the dark I got through it. After drying our wet things around the fire in the morning, we took off again, only slightly less wet.

We headed on US 27 toward Danville, Kentucky. From Danville, we took US 127 to Frankfort, where we hopped on US 421, which provided a surprisingly twisty ride to the Ohio River.

Crossing at Madison, Indiana, we now followed US 421 to Greensburg, then IN 3 to US 52. From 52 we took IN 9 north. The smell of flowers was gone and now replaced with a surprisingly pleasant, earthy smell of cow manure and rich, turned soil. We gave thought to continuing on to Niles in the night, but by Anderson we were tired and knew that a short ride to Niles in the morning would get us there easily by noon. There was no point in arriving exhausted in the middle of the night, so we stopped and checked into a hotel.

The following morning, we continued on IN 9, and then IN 15 from Marion. On 15 we rode on empty highway through cornfields all the way into Michigan. Once inside Michigan, we turned west on US 12 and on into Niles, with a detour to ride past our childhood home on Redfield Road, a block south of US 12 and a stone's throw from the Indiana border.

The GPS said 1,335 miles when we arrived at my brother's classmate's house in downtown Niles. The little CB made it all the way there with no mechanical problems. I had a slight oil leak from the head gasket, but no loss in compression, so all it took was an occasional oil check to keep her healthy. I never did find a windscreen on the way up, and the toll on my arms from hanging on to those bars was obvious by the time we got to Niles. I determined I would make sure to have a new windscreen back on the bike before I left for Florida.

Florida to Michigan on a CB350

Part Two

After our arrival in Michigan, Tim and I did some well-deserved partying. We both went to high school there and were only a couple years apart, so high school pals were called, and, along with a pile of old friends, we closed more than a couple bars. We also have a lot of aunts, uncles, cousins, second-cousins, and friends of our parents in the area, so we made appearances at most. It was a little early for morel mushrooms, which Tim was really hoping to find and bring back, but we gave it a good try and found only thirty-five one morning. Those ended up being cooked in three different ways at a cookout we were invited to. Unfortunately, we never found any more to pack for the ride home.

A friend of my dad, Hank, is a motorcycle collector, along with collecting many other things, and, of course, we made a couple stops to see him and his bikes. He had three completely restored bikes in the basement—a couple BSAs; an Ariel Square Four, no less; and another 1965 Harley in pieces in the process of restoration. I counted three Whizzers down there, too, with one being an odd, off-road looking version I had never seen before. Out in the barn there was a line of bikes, each under cover from the front to the back, side by side. I noticed more BSAs, a couple World War Two Harleys, Honda Trail 70s, and more Harleys of different years and models while squeezing by each bike as Hank lifted the covers. Most were ready to kick-start and ride away.

While at Hank's, we took my front wheel off to investigate an odd scraping sound coming from my front wheel. We found a very dry speedometer gear, which received a good dose of grease, While we had the wheel off, we cleaned the inside of the drum brake, too. The shoes had plenty of life still on them so, with the gear lubed, we remounted the wheel. A few days later, between parties, we ran back out to Hank's to replace Tim's worn out rear brake pads.

During the week, I had made time to go past Behind Bars, a Niles motorcycle shop, and ordered a new National Cycle Deflector Screen DX, which arrived Thursday. We installed it in the parking lot of the bike shop—pretty quick work because I had left the old mounts on the bars. I also received a new front sprocket that had I ordered before I left, and which my wife had mailed up. The sprocket had one more tooth than the stock one (seventeen opposed to sixteen on the stock) and was intended to reduce my revs for the ride back, when we expected to take Interstates on occasion to save some time. The sprocket exchange was easy, and the chain had just enough clearance to fit the new sprocket without interference with any other parts. We ended up riding only a few miles on Interstates, but the sprocket worked as expected, giving me a bit more than five more mph at the same rpm than the old sprocket gave. Doing 65 mph had the CB revving at about 6,300 compared to close to 7,000 before, and my fuel consumption dropped considerably, topping out at over 61 mpg and hovering just under 60 on average, where my previous very best was 59, but averaging mid to upper 40s.

After a rambunctiously wild last Friday and Saturday nights with old friends, we took it easy on Sunday to rest up for the long ride home. We packed and finished mounting all the gear in the cold and dark before sunrise on Monday, the 19th of May. I went out to throw on my seat pad, tent, and sleeping bag and thought I should first wipe the dew off my saddle. One wipe and I realized the saddle was not wet; it was covered in ice.

We left in about 35 degree temps and headed back east on US 12, then retracing our steps all the way to Madison, IN. There we crossed the Ohio River, and continued to Danville, KY, where we took US 127 instead of US 27, trying to stay more west on the way back, with a plan to miss most of the mountains in order to save some time.

A bit after nightfall we were in Jamestown, Kentucky, where we thought we would hit a motel for the night after the long ride we had and to avoid trying to find a campground still open after dark. While stopped on the side of the road to discuss our plans, we rolled out again to find a motel, when I realized after shifting into third that I had no other gears. I could not shift down or up. Nothing happened. There were no sounds from the transmission, even though the clutch was working properly—it was just lift and nothing, press and nothing. Tim went on himself to find the nearest motel and came back to tell me one was just a mile or so ahead, and they were waiting up for us. We pop-started my bike, and I rode to the motel, tired and, now, discouraged. The response to a call home, telling my wife I may be delayed, did not lift my spirits. A quick check around gave us the final slap in the face when we found that we were in a dry county and would not even get our well-earned evening after-ride beers.

The next morning brought rain and more self-doubt about fixing the bike. I had wrenched just about everything on that bike when getting it back in shape after twenty-three years of it sitting idle, but I had never gotten into the transmission. I also only had the original tools in the small plastic pouch that stored under the air box cover. Intimidated, I made up my mind I needed a bike mechanic. The night before, a local police officer made a couple calls for me and got the name of "the only bike mechanic in the county," so I decided to call him, but he was not open until nine o'clock. In the early morning we wandered about the little town, eventually finding a café that was open for breakfast, where we killed some time chatting with the young waitress on her first day on the job. When I did get hold of the mechanic, I found out he had a strict rule about not working on "anything over fifteen years old." I asked him a fruitless couple questions about the possible problem, thanked him, and hung up.

Now I learned how lucky we were to have chosen this particular motel—The Jamestown Court Motel. I went to the office to see if they had a phone book so I could see what other options mechanic-wise were available. The young owner was very friendly and helpful, and let me use the phone book while we chatted about the trip and bikes. I got the number of some other shops in towns not too distant and went to call a Honda dealer about forty-five miles away. I asked them about the availability of parts for my transmission in general. They were pleasant, but not encouraging.

My brother talked me into taking the bike apart and at least taking a look to see if we could do anything ourselves. I again went to the office to ask the owner if he would mind if we put the bike up on its centerstand on the covered walk in front of our room while we did some mechanical investigation. He was happy to oblige and soon the bike was out of the rain, and the footpegs and kickstand were off, followed by the right side exhaust. I drained the oil and removed the side cover. I knew I would need some rags, more oil, and a ratchet set to get the job done, so Tim rode off to pick up those items.

I could not see anything obvious, and it looked like the working end of the shift lever was intact. I took off the clutch disks and outer basket, thinking I needed to get deeper in to see what might be the problem, perhaps taking it back to the inner case by pulling the gears off behind the basket. Before I got that far, I took another look at the shift lever just behind and in back of the clutch basket, this time noticing that there was a small "ear" on part of the lever with a hole in it; an ear that looked suspiciously like it should have a something attached.

I returned to the office with my manual, which I had brought along on a little USB thumb drive "just in case." The owner gave me access to his computer and let me load the PDF manual. Sure enough, a spring belonged there on that ear and stretched to another ear on another lever pivoting on the shift arm. Voila! We had found the problem, and, luckily, it was not deep inside the motor.

As luck would have it, I found the broken spring in the outer engine case, along with the broken hook from its end, so I did not have to worry about that part being somewhere in the oil system, waiting to wreak havoc on the motor. I called the Honda dealer and found that the part was still available and cost a whole two dollars. Unfortunately, it would be four to five days for them to get it.

Asking around, we found out that a nearby hardware store had a large selection of springs, located, where else, but in Russel *Springs*. Tim rode off in search of a suitable spring, while I put the drain plug back in. Tim came back with three possibilities, each probably costing less than one dollar. Comparing them to the broken one, I picked the most likely candidate and hooked it onto each attachment point. I re-attached the clutch disks and outer basket, put on the engine cover, reattached the exhaust and pegs, finally put in new oil, and then crossed my fingers.

I pulled in the clutch and clicked the shifter—it worked! We cleaned up our mess and prepared to head south, trying to get a couple hundred miles in during what remained of the day. By then, it was about three o'clock. We thanked our motel host and rode south. What a relief it was when I completed the final shift into fifth and then all the way back down to first with no issues.

In about a half hour we were in Tennessee once more and were free from the rain. We followed US 127 as far as Pikeville, where we turned southeast on TN 30 in an attempt to avoid the traffic in Chattanooga. We rode into Dayton, where we found a motel about dusk. Being in Tennessee, we once again could enjoy our evening beers while sitting in our room watching the weather channel and planning the next day's ride.

The next morning dawned foggy, and we delayed leaving by having a good breakfast. After breakfast, the fog was still hanging low, but we decided to take off anyway, hoping the fog would lift soon, which it did. Out of Dayton we took TN 60 to Cleveland and there caught TN 40, which soon became US 64/74 east of town. This morning we were trying to get east of the I-75 corridor and down to US 129 for the trip south through Georgia. US 19/129, crossing perpendicular to 64/74, looked tame enough on our map, an almost straight line to the southeast and into Georgia. We hoped we were far enough south of the Smokies to avoid the time consuming mountain twisties, and 19/129 looked like just the ticket.

Once on 19/129 our illusion of a straight route down into Georgia disintegrated as curves, twists, and switchbacks kept rolling under our wheels. Later we realized that this was the road that eventually became the so-called "Tail of the Dragon" farther north where it crossed from North Carolina into Tennessee. Here the route was mainly a downhill grade and much more challenging than the Cherohala, but at least the pavement was dry. We wound our way down, rarely getting above third gear in an attempt to keep our speed down.

Making a hard right then left, on the outside of a curve we saw two riders in full leathers, standing and gazing over the side of the roadside cliff. We stopped on the narrow shoulder just below them and walked back up to the riders. Over the edge, about ten feet below and upside down, was a red Ducati, held from another non-stop tumble of a couple hundred feet by a sapling perhaps three inches in diameter. The rider, luckily, was unscathed, in spite of riding the bike over the edge and also being saved by the little tree. His outfit was unscratched and he stared at his totaled bike just below. His friend had stopped down the road and had walked back up to help and was staring over with his friend and not believing the luck of his fellow rider. There was not much Tim and I could do to help. The bike would need a steel cable and a winch to find the pavement again. A State Police officer had stopped not long after us, in addition to several other riders, so they were in good hands, so we walked back to our bikes and headed south again, this time much more cautiously.

Gradually, the mountains receded in our mirrors, then flat Georgia land passed by us on each side, the trees becoming fuller with new leaves the further south we rode.

US 129 connected to US 441 at Athens, Georgia, and when they diverged again just south of Eatonton, we took US 441 south.

By the time we were in South Georgia, the pecan trees, bare on the way up, were in full foliage and bright green.

I kept peeling off layers of clothes as the day warmed to the mid 80s. The day before I had shed my wind-shredded rain pants and top, which kept the wind from getting through, and now I got rid of the sweat pants, then sweat shirt, next off was the long sleeve shirt, followed by unzipping the thermal liner in my jacket. Eventually, I got rid of the thermal undershirt and replaced it with a light T-shirt.

We decided to visit my friend again in Valdosta. At Lakeland, we took GA 37 west to Ray City and US 129 again south to GA 122 and then the Interstate. We got on I-75 and headed south two exits and went west on GA 133 just a few miles to Julie's house, arriving just as the last bit of light disappeared in the west. Beer, burgers, and beds were waiting. While talking over the trip and old times with my friend and Tim, I nodded off to sleep in an easy chair, eventually reawoke, and hit the mattress for the rest of the night.

Stopping at Valdosta was a great idea, giving us an short final day—under three hundred miles. We rose late, and, after a few cups of coffee, Julie made us a hearty breakfast. After the meal, we loaded the bikes for the last time and got on the road again, taking US 41 across the Florida line and connecting to US 27 at High Springs. US 27 would be the last highway until we made our final turns into our own neighborhoods in Lake Wales. The ride through Ocala was painfully slow, with countless red lights and bumper-to-bumper traffic. I thought to myself that this was probably the most dangerous part of the entire ride, and if there was going to be an accident, it would likely happen here, but we got through the mess all right, and things cleared up a bit as we neared Leesburg. This happened to be the Thursday before the very popular Leesburg Bikefest, and there were bikes buzzing north and south, behind, beside, and in front of us. A big cruising bike passed us, and the leathered-up biker chick on the back was snickering as she passed, probably thinking how un-cool I was on my little toy bike. But I smiled in my helmet, knowing my bike had proven itself.

South of Leesburg, we both needed a break, so we stopped for a beer and a rest at an Irish Pub at the crossroads of I-4 and US 27. Sufficiently rested and restored, we headed home, arriving about six o'clock. My GPS had us logged at about 2,875 miles, 2,670 of which was the way up and the way down, leaving 205 or so ridden in the South Bend and Niles area.

I guess the trip had answered a question I had posed to myself and motorcycle forum friends on whether I needed a big cruising bike for traveling, or could I ride and be comfortable on something smaller. Truthfully, I never was very uncomfortable on my bike during the whole trip that was attributable to the bike itself, except for the forty-two year old, worn-out saddle. The ride itself was smooth enough and any discomfort was attributable to the weather and not the bike. Sure, the little CB buzzed like crazy and needed occasional chain re-tensioning, but all in all it was a fine road bike and even better than many on the twisties. The main limitation was the size of the motor for super-highway riding and it was not suited for riding 70 mph on the interstate all day long, but on smaller highways and back roads, running around 60, the little bike really shined.

Ride through the Green Swamp

With the CB down until Wednesday, when it's new seal would arrive (Twelve dollars, by the way; Honda still stocks them, for a 1968 bike!), I decided to take the Savage for a ride yesterday. On the first Sunday of each month there is a motorcycle and old car swapmeet up in a little town called Webster. There are usually tons of old bike parts, heavy on the Harleys, but plenty of metric stuff, too.

My left mirror had vibrated apart a few weeks ago while riding the Virgin Whore, and, although I was able to retrieve it intact from the road, my attempts to take it apart to get at the now loose parts rolling around inside failed and resulted in a broken mirror-glass. I thought someone at Webster was sure to have a cheap set of mirrors, and it was going to be this weekend, so off I went on a much needed ride.

The only problem with riding to Webster from Lake Wales, however, is it is located northwest of the Green Swamp and Lake Wales is southeast of the swamp. It is normally a decent enough ride, taking back roads to Auburndale, then

Berkley Road to Polk City, and then SR 33, a straight, almost curveless run through the heart of the swamp, to Groveland on the north side. Turn west for a few miles, passing through the little village of Mascotte, then north on FL 471, and you are at Webster. It is a pleasant run of about seventy miles with very little traffic from Auburndale north, with forest on both sides most of the way, but who doesn't like a twisty or two thrown in? Besides, I had run that route numerous times and I was looking for a change.

I called up the great and powerful Google Maps and started looking for roads that an arrow could not follow. I found a route that would also let me hop up to the swamp without going through the whole suburban Winter Haven/Auburndale area. Instead, I took State Road 17/US 27A north, to the little town of Haines City. From Haines City I caught Old Polk City Road (Main Street inside the town) across US 27 and into the swamp.

Once past the houses on the outskirts of Haines City, Old Polk City Road trends northwest past a couple lakes then meanders west to CR 557 (Old Grade Road). This road has many large sweepers. While not challenging twists, they do bring welcome relief to the usual straight line riding that prevails here in Florida. Traffic, too, is very sparse on this route through the wilds of the Green Swamp.

At Old Grade Road, I turned north and headed to Deen Still Road then west to 33, finishing the ride as usual. But what I should have done, as I discovered on my way back, was to turn off Old Grade Road, north of crossing I-4, and taken Fussell Road over to FL 33. Fussell Road is a winding, fun road that takes you to FL 33 just south of Deen Still Road. There are many curves on this road, and most of them are serious curves, not sweepers. Extra caution is required on this route as some driveways enter the roadway on these curves, so you must watch for vehicles entering the road before blasting through them. Most of the suggested speed signs on these curves are 10 to 15 mph below what they can reasonably be taken at. I saw no sand on these curves, either, but that can change from time to time, so it's important to stay alert. You're not going to feel like you are "ridin' The Dragon," but you ought to have some fun and smiles on this little country road.

Normally, Webster is a fun destination with much to offer for those looking for vintage motorcycle or car parts, and usually there is an antique car and motorcycle show on the grounds, too. On my ride, as I was passing west of Groveland on FL 50, I passed through a small rainstorm. This was fortunate for me as it provided some welcome relief from the mid-90s temperatures, but, unfortunately, this same small storm had passed over the swapmeet and by the time I arrived about noon at the swapmeet location, now in sunshine, almost all of the vendors were packing up, with only a smattering of parts here and there, and almost all of them for H-Ds. Attendance is smaller in the summer, so I guess any disturbance like this rain makes continuing on for the rest of the day unprofitable for the vendors. I ended up with a beer and a pair of sunglasses. They fit under the helmet nicely and allowed me to keep the visor open for the ride home; making the heat a bit more bearable, but I came home with no new mirrors.

When riding these roads another thing to look out for is "road gators" and by this I don't mean shed truck tires laying in the road, I really mean alligators on the road. I passed a small three footer on the side of the road on my way up, just off the road in the right side bike lane. I don't know if it was alive, but it wasn't there on the ride back, so chances are it was. I don't think hitting even a little one like that would be kind to your bike or your hide.

Going up, once on 33 and approaching Groveland, an alternate route is to go left on Lake Erie Road to Bay Lake Road/CR 565 north to FL 50. An interesting route, judging from Google Maps, too, for dual sport aficionados is to turn left, instead, at CR 565 and go until you pass Van Fleet State Trail, where the road changes to dirt and is called simply

"Logging Road," becoming "Center Grade Road" further on. This route will take you to FL 471, which you can take north directly into Webster. I might have done it on Old Faithful, but I had not ridden dirt on the Savage yet, and didn't want to try it for my first time on an unfamiliar road.

Florida to North Carolina on Old Faithful

Back in May, the sixth to be exact, I had originally planned to ride north, meet up with my brother, Tim, just east of Greenville, South Carolina, and together hit some mountain roads, for once in nice weather. The last time I had passed through them we rode the Cherohala Skyway in off-and-on blinding rain and through cloud tops, with a cold wind whipping across the ridges and threatening to topple me off my light bike. I was looking forward to the projected nice mid-80s weather and sunshine this time while I packed the bike. "Old Faithful," my 1968 Honda CB350, was ready to go and waiting in the garage.

I had almost gotten used to the feast-or-famine lifestyle of being a small independent publisher, so I was not too surprised when a series of business setbacks made me suddenly, but reluctantly, reconsider the wisdom of leaving, just hours before departure. A month passed and business improved, and the ride was back on. It would still have to be on the cheap, but it was do-able.

I worked most of the afternoon on June second trying to load too much stuff onto my little CB350, and if it hadn't been for the miniscule second-hand saddlebags, I might have gotten away with it. I was going to blog each day during this trip, so my netbook was essential along with a camera, and it became obvious other things had to go. Out came the Kindle, out came an extra pair of jeans, out came underwear and T-shirts, out came my sweatshirt—my jacket and liner would have to do if it got cold in the hills—and off came a handlebar bag that was obviously going to get in the way of steering. Finally, I was able to zip, snap, and buckle the tail, tank, saddle, and fork bags. I backed the bike back into the garage, and climbed into bed about nine, anxious to leave early in the morning.

I rose before four and was on the bike and out the drive by ten after. My plan was to do the least enjoyable part of the ride, up US 27 and through construction zones, in the pre-dawn darkness. With any luck, I would be in the Ocala National Forest at dawn and far out of the way of the rush hour traffic around Orlando.

In spite of it being June in Florida, it was chilly as I started north, so my liner was zipped into my jacket. I made good time through the cool darkness, and, after a quick breakfast and fuel up in Umatilla, I was in the forest and on empty roads. The fog was patchy, but thick. Now too late in the season, the smell of orange blossoms that usually fill the Florida air was replaced by an earthy smell like wet hay and yellow pine, and smoke added to the foggy haze. The smoke became almost unbearable for a while but eventually dissipated enough for me to breathe easily again, although it never completely left until well into Georgia.

Once north of the forest, my Google Map printouts, slipped under the clear vinyl top of my tank bag, told me to turn west on FL 310, then north on FL 215. At the place where 215 should have intersected I saw a sign for FL 315 instead. I must have written the number down wrong. Still not completely sure of my bearings, I turned north on 315 hoping to intersect FL 21. With a sigh of relief, I soon came upon 21 and turned right, following it to Middleburg and FL 218, that shot northwest joining US 301 at I-10. 301 took me north to Callahan in the little "bump" of the Florida border, northwest of Jacksonville. Here the highway joined US 1, which crossed into Georgia at Folkston, east of the Okefenokee National Wildlife Refuge, and continued on to GA 121. Continuing to Baxley, 121 joined US 1 again, and I rolled on past Vidalia, where the distinct smell of sweet onions replaced the smell of smoke in the air. Leaving Vidalia, the onion odor faded and the familiar smell of pine wafted in the hot east Georgia air again.

By then, I had much earlier removed the liner from my mesh jacket, and I replaced it with an evaporative vest as the temperature soared in the east Georgia emptiness. By Wrens it was already dry, and I removed it before it added to, rather than reduced, the temperature inside my jacket.

US 1 went almost due north until Wrens. Here I was supposed to pick up US 221, which by a careful scrutiny of the map shows it obviously going north and east. I flew by an exit that said "221 West", which "Couldn't be right," I thought. A mile past it, without seeing any other exit to 221 East or 221 North, I stopped and asked directions. "Yep. You're going to Greenville? You need 221 *West*." Could it be? I took their word for it. I never did figure out why they considered it *west*, but soon the route was confirmed when I entered South Carolina, crossing the J. Strom Thurmond Dam.

As I made progress into South Carolina, the climate moderated, and I was fairly comfortable in my mesh jacket. US 221 carried me north and east past Greenville and to SC 290 which crosses I-85, at exit 63, where Tim lived then.

That day was a hard 580 miles, and my butt had suffered, in spite of the new upholstering in my saddle and the ATV cover on top. I like countryside, and that route had plenty of it, and I never passed through any large cities the entire way up. Fourteen hours and ten minutes, just ten minutes over my estimate, was the total time—not bad for a forty-three year old bike and a rider with ten more years on him than the bike. I settled in at Tim's for the night, thankful for the air conditioning.

Tim was in Duncan and a stone's throw from the Blue Ridge, so we took our time getting started in the morning, knowing we would not have a very long day heading up to Maggie Valley, North Carolina. We mounted our bikes and headed north to US 176 under sunny skies and in warm temperatures. We decided to hop over to I-26 at Hendersonville for a quick commute up to the Blue Ridge Parkway.

We headed out on the Parkway in cooler temps, enjoying the curves and spectacular scenery to the right and left. The hills were a bright summer green and the haze and cloud cover so common here was gone, revealing the detail of the ridges in all their beauty.

Upon entering the first tunnel, I discovered that my headlight was not working; not the best place to find that out. I followed the taillights of the car in front of me, until I remembered I still had my low beam and switched to it. I always leave my high beam on because the headlights on 1968 model bikes were not exactly powerful, so the low beam filament was almost unused. The tunnels continued to be hair-raising as I passed through them, illuminated by the dull yellow glow of my low beam the rest of the way to the valley. Even with a high beam, the tunnel passages were other-worldly because the quick change from bright sunlight to the darkness of the tunnels made it difficult for vision to adapt before coming out on the far end. Nothing was visible except the reflection from the road markers and side markers. The road and walls were invisible and it was like riding a motorcycle in space. When I got to Maggie Valley I replaced the bulb, reducing the effect, at least a little, on the return ride.

We occasionally stopped at overlooks and enjoyed the views. At one of these stops, Tim decided to bungee his camera onto his handlebars and try some video following me.

After passing the southern dip of the Parkway and heading northwest, and climbing to the highest point on the Parkway, the temperature dropped dramatically. I was tempted to replace the liner in my jacket, but I knew the cool would be short-lived. It proved to be, as we descended east off the Parkway and into the valley on US 19.

In Maggie Valley, Legends Sports Grill provided rest and refreshment, while Tim downloaded pictures and surprisingly clear video to his laptop. Just down the road was the Wheels Through Time Museum, one of the places I had wanted to see since I was told about it last October at Barber Vintage Festival, and it certainly lived up to its reputation. The museum was filled with life-sized "dioramas" into which were placed appropriate motorcycles—a military depot and military bikes, a 1940s bike shop and 1940s bikes. Who'd have thought that Harley-Davidson had dabbled in electric motorcycles ages ago, along with all manner of experiments and prototypes? Indian was also well-represented, with other products they had produced, such as chainsaws and outboard motors.

At the museum was a Harley-Davidson I had only read about before—a copy of a captured World War Two German military motorcycle made by BMW—a Harley with horizontally opposed cylinders and heavy off road tires. Out front were the museum's two bikes that had competed in the Motorcycle Cannonball Run from Kitty Hawk, North Carolina, to the Santa Monica Pier, in California. One even sported a CB350 front wheel, which Dale Walksler, the owner of the museum, told me was chosen because of the great brakes those bikes had, especially compared to the originals. We were treated to a show as Dale fired one of the bikes up and rode it around the museum grounds.

Tired and looking for refuge for the night, Tim and I headed up Jonathan Creek Road (US 276) and then Cove Creek Road toward Cataloochee Campground, inside the southeastern end of the Great Smoky Mountains National

Park. Our waitress at Legends had told us about this spot, "… up Cove Creek Road and across a stretch of gravel road…," and we were looking forward to a nice rustic mountain site to pitch our tent. Starting up Cove Creek Road we stopped at a sign saying, "Reservations Required," with a phone number to call. Finding out it was full, we turned around and made our way back to Jonathan Creek Road where we had seen "Camping" signs. It was getting late now, and a commercial campground would have to do. We turned into Winngray Family Campground. It appeared to be more of a RV park than a campground, but we were told there were tent sites, so we followed the manager around back to a quiet, nicely shaded grassy strip along a creek reserved for tents. We were the only tent campers, and, looking creek-ward, we could imagine it was a bit more rustic than it actually was. We pitched the tent and tore into the subs we had bought before heading out to camp. The night fell, and the temperature along with it, as the trees and patches of night sky that found their way through the branches filled with fireflies.

Well-rested in the morning, we reloaded the bikes Before setting out, Tim thought he would check his rear tire. He had left knowing it was not in the best shape, but he thought it would be all right for such a short trip. Upon inspection, Tim found he was wrong. The ply was showing through in a patch about two inches long. A bit worried, with all the mountain riding we planned on doing, we headed back to Maggie Valley, thinking if any place was open on a Sunday that could change the tire, it would be in that biking mecca.

We stopped at one shop, but the owner was leaving and would not be back before one. He thought he might have a tire that would fit, but wasn't sure. We headed back to Wheels Through Time hoping to get some info and some other options to call. Calls were made to no avail, however, so I called Craig, a buddy of mine in Asheville who rides in the area frequently, to see if he had any suggestions. A dozen back and forth calls and he had procured a used tire that would fit, but both of his friends with tire changing machines were out and unavailable. Without a tire changing machine we were not equipped to change out a rear tire on a heavy 1500 Nomad. Tim and I discussed the situation, and Tim made the call to ride it home, trying to baby it as much as possible.

We had planned on taking US 441 across the Smokies to Gatlinburg and back, but we scrapped that, not wanting to add any more miles than necessary to the tire, and headed back. With good local knowledge now from Craig, we returned to the Blue Ridge Parkway, back to the southern dip where NC 215 crossed it. We headed south down 215, which Craig had told us had just been repaved, and enjoyed the downhill run to US 64 on the new black pavement. In spite of worrying about seeing a blue puff of smoke from Tim's rear tire in front of me, I relished the curvy ride, inwardly wishing I could carve the curves at a bit more lively pace than we were going.

At US 64 we headed east. Luckily, we could camp at a great spot without going more than a couple miles out of the way, so we could still enjoy the full three day weekend. We turned left on US 276 trying to find a campground that Craig had recommended, only to find out it was for groups only. We were given another option, almost across the road from the Ranger Station where we had stopped, and went back down the road and turned in at Davidson River Campground, in the Pisgah Game Reserve.

After setting up camp, we walked the trail along the river and watched the tubers floating by. We walked to the swimming hole, about a mile up the river. There it makes a bend and forms a deep pool on the outside bank, above which rock-faces hang over the water from which kids jumped into the cold water, while on the inside of the bend others were wading in the shallow water.

Back at camp, friendly neighbors offered us firewood, and we soon had a campfire going and were reheating the roast chicken over it that we had picked up earlier in Brevard. We had forgotten to eat all day, other than some jerky, so the hot chicken tasted especially good and was soon all but gone. Tim set up his cellphone connection to the Internet and we both did our Facebook and blogging tasks while, ironically, sitting in the forest. We were at a lower altitude than the night before and it was warmer, but it cooled slowly, and we crawled into the tent for the night and for warmth and were soon asleep.

We headed out leisurely the next day, knowing Duncan was a short ride home, with only a short stretch of real mountain riding left. We went back towards Brevard and then turned south back onto US 276 and headed into South Carolina.

We stopped at Caesars Head to check the tire again. The bare patch had now grown to six inches. We remounted our motorcycles and started the ride down the mountain.

This road, so far, was a nice ride, but nothing challenging, but we knew from a previous car trip up to Caesars Head that the ride down to the south would be wild, and it was. Going down-grade is always more challenging: you don't want to ride your brakes on the straightaways and you can't on the curves; you want to accelerate out of the curves, but you don't want to increase your speed too much or there won't be time to slow before the next downward curve. Going uphill, of course, gravity acts in your favor giving you more control, but on these downward spiraling rides it becomes a matter of finesse and restraint. Add to that the worry about a blow out and you can imagine the thrill of that ride down the mountain. Nevertheless, we made it down safely and turned onto SC 11, also known as Cherokee Foothills Scenic Highway, and headed east on the relatively straight road. 11 took us to US 25, which we took south just a couple miles, turning southeast on SC 290, which took us all the way back to Tim's.

By the time we arrived, the tire's bare patch had grown to an unhealthy twelve inches. Tim and I both breathed a sigh of relief, picked up a pizza, and hit the rack early after our Internet tasks were complete. We had ridden 320 beautiful miles in the Blue Ridge since Saturday in near perfect weather.

Monday was a work day for Tim and the start of my return home, which I would split into two days this time.

Tim and I said good-bye outside his apartment at six-thirty on Tuesday morning, and then headed our separate ways. I threaded my way back the way we had come the day before. I had decided I could spare an extra twenty or so miles taking the scenic Cherokee Foothills Scenic Highway back. SC 11 rolled west and joined I-85 at the Georgia border, with picture book views of the mountains, now on my right. I passed Caesars Head, by which time I was getting hungry for breakfast. I was disappointed when I pulled into Aunt Sue's, a place I had enjoyed for lunch a couple times in the past, only to find they were not open for breakfast. Continuing west past Table Rock Mountain and the turn-off to Devils Fork, I stopped at a convenience store and was told my wish for a diner would come true just a few miles down SC 11. "Jes' look for the cars," I was told. Sure enough, at Tamassee, in tiny white letters in the window was written "Abby's Grill." I pulled in. Breakfast on the road at small out-of-the-way places is one of my favorite parts of traveling, and Abby's did not disappoint. I ordered scrambled eggs, sausage, grits, a biscuit, and coffee. It was all delicious and the grits were some of the best I've ever had and tasted like freshly-plucked corn. All this for three and a half dollars! I gratefully left a fifty-five percent tip.

At Tamassee, 11 shifts southwest on its way toward Interstate 85, and I merged west-southwest into Georgia on 85 and rode to Exit 149 and US 441 South. This took me to Athens and its "loop" then back out the south side, continuing on 441 all the way to Florida. The air was filled with that Georgia pine smell, the smoke now gone, as I buzzed my way south through central Georgia.

I entered Florida soon after crossing the Suwannee River, where the highway veered southwest to Lake City. Here I made a twelve mile detour north on US 41 to White Springs, where I planned to stay the night. This town was known in the late 1800s for its therapeutic spring. An unusual building, looking a bit like a reconstructed Globe Theatre, can still be seen, built around the "White Sulphur Spring," right beside the road.

I checked into the Stephen Foster Memorial Folk Center State Park then went back into the village to have dinner at Fat Belly's, a barbecue place I remembered from a previous trip to the Florida Folk Festival that is held each year at the State Park. Just a half mile south from the park, Fat Belly's served up good food.

Back at camp, I turned off "Old Faithful" after 475 miles and pitched camp in the quiet, while the sound of the bike and the road dissipated in my head. I had decided earlier that I did not want to bother with the tent tonight, so I had bought a small cheap tarp, which I now fastened to the bike in a kind of lean-to in which I could sleep beside, almost under, the bike. With the "tent" set up and the mosquitoes starting to buzz, I crawled into the sleeping bag next to the still warm exhaust and waited for the darkness and sleep to overtake me.

Breaking camp was quick and easy thanks to the lean-to, but I wasn't in a hurry, as I had business at the park's gift shop and it would not be open until nine, when I would also be able to borrow their Wi-Fi to post the blog from yesterday, which I had not yet written. While I waited, I typed the details of the previous day, then cleaned up a bit, at least as much as a person who was still wearing their riding jeans (my only armored pair) from five days ago could. When the shop opened and I had taken care of my business, I quickly posted my blog from the porch of the shop and loaded up the netbook for the ride home.

I retraced my route back to Lake City, continuing south on US 441 to High Springs, where I took US 27/US 41. US 27 goes all the way home to Lake Wales, but the traffic and never ending traffic lights from Gainesville all the way to Leesburg convinced me to veer onto US 41 in Williston, heading south past Dunellon to Floral City. The roads between Lake City and Dunellon were practically empty, and I made good time flying through the smoke ,which once again wafted through the air for a short time.

At Floral City, I turned east on FL 48, then took FL 471 south to FL 50, which took me east to Groveland and FL 33. This road headed south through the Green Swamp to Polk City, and from there Berkley Road took me into Auburndale and well-known territory. Now it was via a variety of familiar back roads I wound my way back to Lake Wales, parking the CB in the garage about 4:30 PM after 235 miles, and arriving to the shouts of "What did you bring us?!" from our two children, who ran out to meet me.

I had managed to do the trip "on the cheap" as I had planned, spending about $150 on fuel and another $150 on food, accommodations, and miscellany. Keeping the cost down on fuel is easy on the CB350; it managed about 54 miles per gallon on average, with a high of 60 and a low of 40. I had a great time on the ride and a much needed break from my often sedentary day-to-day life in my office in front of my computer screen, and I was reminded of the importance of careful pre-ride checks in a very real way. The straight run north to Greenville was kind of a personal challenge and I am happy I could tough it out enough to do it. I had ridden 1,610 trouble-free miles on the "Old Faithful," once again proving herself worthy of her nickname.

The Blue Ridge Mountains are spectacular, both for their views and their exciting riding, and the camaraderie of fellow riders in that bikers' heaven was great. I have many trips planned for other places in the future, but you can be sure I will find my way back to the Blue Ridge on two wheels again.

KICKSTART CLASSIC TO BARBER VINTAGE FESTIVAL

Every year, Barber Motorsports Park in Leeds, Alabama, hosts the Barber Vintage Festival. In 2010, I was again invited to ride up to the festival with a group from Pinetta, Florida, a little community just south of the Florida-Georgia state line below Valdosta, Georgia. The group ride was sponsored and organized by Luis and Deb who have a motorcycle shop there and are the H-E-L distributors for the US.

This year when the time for the Barber Vintage Festival rolled around, I was determined to join my north Florida friends once again for the ride. Just about the time I was planning the ride to Pinetta, I found out about a ride being sponsored by Wheels Through Time Museum and by *Road Bike* [later called *Motorcycle Rides & Culture*] and *American Iron* magazines. Called the Motorcycle Kickstart Classic, it was slated to roll out of Maggie Valley, North Carolina, and end at the festival in Leeds. To join the ride, all you needed was to pay a small fee and have a kickstart bike, and Old Faithful fit the bill. With my fledgling motorcycle book imprint just getting underway, I thought it would be wise to join the ride and get to know some others in the motorcycling industry, especially those in the publishing field. I also offered to provide copies of our first book as a kind of door prize to all the ride participants, thinking that having the book in all those hands would make it more likely that the imprint would be noticed when the second and third and fourth book were released.

I let my ride buddies in Pinetta know I would not be going up with them, but would join them at Leeds for the festival and the ride back. They were very understanding of the need for me to join the Kickstart and offered me a tent site at their swapmeet spot when I got there and welcomed me to ride back with them.

I had been prepping the CB350 all along for the ride to Barber, so all was in good shape for the long ride to Maggie Valley, in the neighborhood of some seven hundred miles away. In central Florida we had just had our first cool spell, and the forecast for the mountains was cool in the day and cold at night, typical for early October, but October can be fickle, so I would have to pack for both cold and warm weather. I packed carefully on a Monday night, then piled the mountain of gear on the bike so it would be ready to go the next day. It wasn't exactly a streamlined pile, but it would do.

A ride of seven hundred miles would take me a while. The little bike's tank usually could only carry me for a hundred miles before hitting reserve and needing refilling. That's seven stops just for fuel, and then there would be much needed get-my-butt-off-the-bike rest stops, too. Add to that my terrible knack for underestimating the time required for travel, I thought I better give myself plenty of time cushion if I was going to make Maggie Valley in one day. I decided on a two am departure time, tucked myself in bed about nine, and tried to get some sleep.

The alarm went off at one-thirty, and, for once, I was prepared and hopped out of bed and pulled on the road gear, already laying in wait for my waking. Cold while riding is a different kind of adversarial companion than it is when just standing around outside. The frigid wind finds its way into every available crevice and gap. I decided I could not over dress. My bottom layer was a thermal undershirt, and on top of that a shirt, followed by a left-over from my sailing days—a fleece lined jacket with windproof nylon shell. Atop all this was my armored mesh jacket, into which I had zipped its thermal liner. My feet were wrapped in knee high "cold-weather" riding socks inside my thick leather boots. Below the waist was regular underwear, followed by long legged thermal underpants, topped by my heavy denim riding jeans that had armored knees and leather lining in the seat and around the knees.

In the dark I kissed my sleeping wife and clomped as quietly as possible out the door in my motorcycle boots. All was ready in the garage—oil checked, tire pressure checked and adjusted, gear secured. I rolled Old Faithful out into the chilly air. I kicked the CB over and while it warmed I put on my cold weather gloves and helmet. I clumsily climbed aboard the crowded bike and rolled out of the driveway at 1:40 AM.

I passed along the familiar roads heading north with the steady hum of the little two cylinder and the clackity clack sewing machine sounds of its points and valves in my ears. I passed Fuzzy's, the local biker watering hole, as they were closing and beeped a weak good-bye on the anemic horn of the little Honda.

I followed FL 17, also named US 27 Alt and Scenic Highway, toward Davenport, where I could jump over to US 27 proper, past the construction mess they had going just south of the juncture. I turned west at Davenport and within a couple miles was at US 27, where I once again turned my wheels to the north. On all but deserted tarmac, I rolled north past I-4, past Four Corners, past Clermont, and past Minneola to a little turn-off to Astatula, County Road 561— a quiet country road with a few fun twisties thrown in for good measure that would join up with US 19 for the jaunt north through the National Forest.

I had decided to take a route through the Ocala National Forest for a couple reasons. I often take a path through the Green Swamp further to the west, then jog on small roads over to US 41 where I turn north, but because I would be riding in darkness and in the wee hours of the morning, and because of the abundance of wild hogs in the swamp, I decided to take an eastern route rather than end my trip early by wrapping my bike around a wild boar or by flipping over a road-crossing alligator, which I had seen before in broad daylight in the Green Swamp. Ocala Forest has its own wildlife to be sure, and deer and bear were my main concerns, but the forest does not encroach the road as close or lie as low and it is not as wet, so I was hoping for better visibility instead of the almost inevitable fog of the swamp.

While riding through the darkness of the forest, the temperature kept falling. Every so often I could feel the little bike hesitate when we passed though a low spot of colder, denser air, as if the cold didn't want to let us pass. Then we would emerge into a warmer spot and the bike would surge forward and the engine would ease. Following the dim circle of light thrown ahead of us on the asphalt by the meager thirty-five watt headlight bulb we rolled north. During the recent cool spell, the atmosphere had dried and we were able to speed through the darkness, free of fog.

The wind started finding its way inside my jacket and helmet, and I started to shiver. As daylight approached and a faint lightening in the east appeared, I started to shake and my concentration waned, while feeling in my hands began to fade. I emerged from the forest and found the first diner I could. While the light grew brighter in the east, I sat in warmth and drank several cups of coffee, dawdling over breakfast while my body returned to normal. I spent at least a precious half hour in the diner. While eating and watching the sun rise, I heard a voice on a radio say it was fifty-one degrees, so my guess was that I had ridden through the mid-forties in the forest. I've been through much worse for much longer before, but something about the dampness of the woods, still humid even in a Florida dry spell, combined with the cool temperature worked together to make for one of the harshest colds I had ridden through.

Now, with feeling back in my hands, I returned to the bike, clambered aboard, and rode to the west on CR 310 until it "T"ed at CR 315. Turning right, I headed for FL 21, then in Middleburg took CR 218, which I followed to US 301. Now in light, I shot north-northeast, passed under I-10, my second Interstate, jogged around a forest fire via a detour, then returned to US 301, merging with US 1 and continuing again together until they split at Folkston, Georgia, just across the state line. 301 shot north and I shot northwest continuing on US 1 into the Georgia morning. US 1 would take me north all the way to Wrens, Georgia, through pleasant, empty farmland.

Pecan groves passed by in ordered rows, often next to stately antebellum mansions. I passed Lyons, Vidalia's eastern neighbor, and whizzed under I-16. Woolly rows of cotton soon replaced pecan groves as Georgia passed under the CB's wheels, which brought back childhood images of winter fields in Michigan when the snow covered all but the dead brown stalks of crops sticking up through the whiteness. Thankfully, in spite of the snow-white of the cotton fields, the temperature continued to rise and by midway through the eastern Georgia farm and pine lands I was able to, one after another, remove layers of clothing, although I could still feel a hint of northern chill in the air softly mocking the Southern sunshine, hinting of what was to come.

The incense I had so often found remarkable in Georgia, now returned. Georgia is the most wonderfully fragrant place through which I have ever ridden. In the spring, I rode through it while it smelled like sandalwood incense, and in the summer the smell of pine was everywhere. This almost autumnal time, it was the smell of balsam, earthy and clean smelling.

At Wrens I jogged north catching GA 17, eventually passing under I-20, my fourth Interstate, and continuing on to Royston. Another jog west and I was on GA 106 heading north to its junction with GA 17 and US 123 again, which ran west. I connected with 441, rolling north through the Georgia hill country and into North Carolina, while the hills slowly transformed into the early fall mountains of the Appalachians.

Earlier, before my northwest turn at Wrens, Georgia, I started to doubt the likelihood I would make Maggie Valley before nightfall. About the time I had decided to turn northeast and head to my brother's place in Duncan, South Carolina, for a bed and an early departure the next day to Maggie Valley, I remembered he had just moved into a friend's house and there would be no room for me. I had no choice but to continue on to Franklin, North Carolina. As I approached that mountain town, I had made the decision that I would need to seek out a hotel and finish the trip in the morning, not wanting to transit the mountains' roads I remembered up here in the cold and darkness. But as Franklin passed, I realized I would have four lane divided highways all the way to Waynesboro, and Waynesboro was not as far from where I was as I had thought, and only a hop from there would get me to Maggie Valley. I continued on, the sun setting lower, just above the western mountain ridges. I was able to keep my speed up, even though most of the throttle range was used to get up to the higher altitudes while keeping up a speed of 60 mph. The sun was still dawdling in the west when I arrived at Waynesboro, where I hopped north on US 276 to US 19 and Maggie Valley. I turned into the gravel drive and stopped at the closed, but unlocked gate at Wheels Through Time, opened the gate, rolled the bike onto the wooden bridge beyond, re-closed the gate, and rolled into the museum grounds, pitching my tent on the soft grass beside the stream in front of the museum as the sun settled behind the mountains.

I had left Lake Wales eighteen hours earlier, and now the odometer had 680 miles more on it than when I had left—the longest one day ride I had yet undertaken. Which brings me to this next tidbit. If you ride this far your butt is going to hurt—and I mean HURT with capital letters. On this ride I found a secret to being able to carry on: I cut a small piece of dense foam, about three by eight inches, out of one of those kneeling pads people use for gardening and house chores. I stuck this from time to time in various positions under my saddle pad; the secret being to position it each time so the pressure points are moved to another place. If successful, you will have a butt that is horribly sore everywhere but, with no particular spot aching more than the others. The change in location of suffering will allow you enough temporary respite to keep on riding farther.

After pitching the tent, I noticed that the crew from *Road Bike* magazine had arrived. I sauntered up the hill to the shop entrance of the museum, where the group had gathered, to say hi and chew the fat a little. I then made a quick run to Legends, a local sports bar, for a bite. Getting back to the museum, I climbed into my sleeping bag, fully clothed as the night came on chilly, and tapped out my blog entry for the day on my netbook, using the air card I had recently purchased to enable me to do business on the road without being chained to finding Wi-Fi hot spots as I traveled. As the cool mountain night air settled in, I fell asleep anticipating all the bikes that would be arriving at Wheels Through Time the next day.

In the morning, the sky was growing promisingly bright. The night had been very cold, but with all my road clothes on inside my bag it was bearable. The sun takes a while to peep over those mountains and show its face down in this little valley, but the sky was bright when I took a chilly walk out in search of coffee.

It took about a mile of walking to find Country Vittles restaurant, but their coffee was good and, most of all, it was hot. The breakfast menu looked inviting, with an all-you-can-eat special. I ordered a coffee to go and took a paper menu to go to show the crew from *RoadBike/American Iron*, whom I had seen earlier when I was walking, hanging out in front of their hotel around their bikes. I thought they might be looking for a place for breakfast and this place seemed to fit the bill. I was hardly out the door when I bumped into *Road Bike's* Buzz, Steve, Matt, and Tyler coming in. I turned around and joined them for a filling breakfast.

Back at the museum, riders started pouring in on bikes of every description. There were Harleys, BMWs, Honda CBs, a couple Royal Enfields, a few customs, and even an East German MZ. In addition to all those Kickstart Classic bikes were all the bikes of the regular museum visitors. By the end of the day there were fifty or so bikes entered on the Kickstart Classic check-in, with more expected tomorrow before we would leave.

I took off about noon and had lunch at a Mexican restaurant, then moseyed down to the Hardtail Saloon to cash in a chip for a free beer that Barry, a pal from Fuzzy's, had given me. The folks in the bar said it was old, and that they gave those away back when they had just opened. I guess Barry hadn't been up here in a long time. But they honored the chip, which was all that was important. I just happened to have a Fuzzy's chip in my pocket. A fellow patron said he was heading down to Lakeland, Florida, the next week, so I gave him the chip and we planned on meeting up at Fuzzy's when he came down.

I headed back to the museum to see what kind of new bikes had arrived and to visit with the riders. I made one more trip out to fuel up so I wouldn't have to mess with that in the morning.

As the sun was dipping behind the hills; hamburgers, brats, and other good stuff was offered by our hosts. While we ate, Buzz Kanter gave us a quick rundown of plans for tomorrow's ride. After dinner, the riders started trickling out to their hotels.

I planned to be up early to break camp and reload the bike. The departure time was ten AM. The route would take us to Tellico Plains via the Cherohala Scenic Skyway, then south into Georgia and to Rome. I climbed into the sleeping bag early and soon it was lights out as the air grew cold and night fell.

We left Maggie Valley the next morning at ten as planned. The route would take us through some of the best riding territory in the country. We followed US 19 west out of Maggie Valley, but just outside of town, before the day's ride had hardly begun, Old Faithful stopped running. It just shut down. I was riding in the middle of the pack, and I watched helplessly as bike after bike passed me on both sides and I rolled to a stop. Our support hack, a BMW with a modified sidecar rig that could load and carry any broken down bikes, stopped to make sure I was OK. Upon inspection, I saw that the headlight was not working, either, so I knew the problem was electrical. I feared the worst, but it turned out to be nothing but a blown fuse. I always carry a spare, so the hardest part of fixing the problem was simply unloading all the luggage to get at the fuse holder, then reloading it all back onto the bike. Soon I was once again on my way, and the hack and I caught up with the group by the first gas stop at Stecoah, North Carolina, sixty miles from Maggie Valley.

We followed US 28 west, the road that eventually leads to the Tail of the Dragon. Before the Dragon, we took 143 south and west which became the Cherohala Scenic Skyway flowing toward Tennessee in a series of beautiful sweepers and scenic passes. Many flock to these hills to try their hand at the Tail of the Dragon, a technically challenging but short ride; but for pure mountain scenic beauty and enjoyable curves, climbs, and descents the Cherohala is hard to beat. Yes, you can test your mettle on the Dragon, but you can relax and enjoy the ride and views on the Cherohala. The road number, NC 143, changed once out of North Carolina, the Skyway continuing to Tellico Plains as TN 165.

Our column of bikes stretched for at least a half mile as we wound our way along some of the best motorcycling roads in the eastern United States. The oldest bike was a 1933 Harley-

Davidson VL, while there were knuckleheads, panheads, flatheads, Indians, mid-1960s Japanese bikes, BMW airheads, sidecar rigs, custom bikes, choppers, bobbers, dressers, and a very light sprinkling of modern bikes making up the procession. Some intersections were commandeered so all the bikes could get through as one body. It must have been quite a sight for the local people as we rumbled and roared through their little towns in a seemingly endless line, and I am sure the gas station owners were thrilled to see seventy-five bikes pull up in front of their pumps.

From Tellico Plains we jogged north on TN 68, then west on TN 39 to TN 315, where we turned our bikes south toward Reliance, and onto one of the almost unknown, but no less enjoyable, motorcycling roads in the area, TN 30. After the twisty jaunt down 30, we turned on US 74/64 and rolled west. Picking up US 411 about nine and a half miles further on, we shot south into Georgia. Passing Eton, we jogged west on US 76, to GA 225 south into Calhoun, passing under busy I-75. From there, GA 53 led us to Rome and Panhead City.

We got into Panhead City well before sundown, where hot food and cold beer was waiting for us. Panhead City is a combination vintage bike shop and parts place in a quiet little bowl in the hills, surrounded by trees—shop up on the hill, with grassy spots and a combination bunkhouse and pavilion in the green bottom. Our bikes crowded the entire grounds. We parked in a long shiny, and in some cases rusty, line of vintage and classic motorcycles along the side of the shop and in clusters of old bikes scattered about in almost every open spot.

In addition to my minor electrical issue, other casualties that day included an old-timer Harley that lost the front cylinder and another Honda, a CL305, which quit two miles before Panhead City and required a lift from our hack. That, too, turned out to be a loose fuse holder and was easily fixed simply by tightening it. I thought, "Not too bad, considering how many of us there are and how old most of the bikes are."

A fellow rider and I pitched our tents on a soft grassy spot twenty feet down a grassy bluff below the shop and behind the pavilion/bunkhouse after a dinner of roast pork, spicy stew, bread, and the ubiquitous beer.

I located an electrical outlet on the outside of the bunkhouse, where a table and a few chairs were scattered about on a deck, and plugged my phone, computer, and air card in, settling in as it grew dark, typing out and posting my ride report on the Road Dog Publications website blog. My daily chores completed, and while my stuff continued to charge, I joined a gathering of fellow Kickstart riders and Panhead City staff around the corner for more beer than was probably necessary. Stumbling back, partly because of the beer but also because of the blackness of night that had descended, I disconnected the chargers and toted my equipment back to the tent, lying down in my bag on the soft grass that cushioned the floor of the tent. I was soon asleep and slept comfortably through the night, the night coolness never getting as cold as it had in Maggie Valley, now that our altitude was much lower.

We were to leave Panhead City the next morning at nine AM. As soon as I woke, I hauled my stuff to the bike and packed the tent and all the other luggage on top of it. At a few minutes before nine, I discovered my cell phone was missing. I looked everywhere I'd been, but to no avail. I asked a riding buddy to walk around with me while he called my phone. At the campsite we heard nothing. At the site of my charging station and of the last evening's beer drinking, we still heard nothing. Up at the bike, he tried to call it again. Standing near my bike, we heard a very faint and muffled ringing. It turned out the phone was in the tent when I packed it, and then, in its tent cocoon, it got loaded onto the bike. With about five minutes to go before I would be left in a cloud of dust and motorcycle exhaust, I unattached all the bungee cords securing the gear, unrolled the tent and withdrew the phone, re-rolled the tent and then repacked all the luggage, just in time for, "Two minutes to kickstart!" announced by Buzz

Kanter. Disaster averted, I got on my bike and we headed out to cross north Georgia into Alabama.

With a simultaneous kickstart of seventy-five motorcycles, we roared out of Panhead City and west out of Rome, following GA 20 into Alabama, where it changed names to AL 9. At Piedmont we switched to AL 21 southwest to Jacksonville. Here we started making course changes ever few miles—AL 204 west, US 431 south, and finally AL 144 west to Ragland and our last fuel and food stop before Barber. Some of us refueled the bikes, while everyone refueled their bodies at the barbecue place next to the gas station which probably had never had such a run of customers in the space of an hour. The roads had taken us across lovely country with rolling hills and forests, and the mountains once again grew large as we approached Leeds and the festival.

The bikes and our bellies full, we took another series of short jogs—144 west, then AL 53/US 231 south, to AL 174 just north of I-20 west, to US 411 that led us into Leeds. US 78 (Parkway Drive) paralleled I-20, now to the north, with the distance between the two highways closing. Just before intersecting with I-20, we turned left onto Rex Lake Road. Riding south for less than a mile, we turned right at the Barber Motorsports Parkway, continuing to the very doorstep of the Barber Museum.

Upon arrival, we were greeted by Mr. George Barber himself, who invited us to park our bikes as a group in front of the museum entrance.

So far, Old Faithful had hummed along for 1,050 miles with no more trouble than a blown fuse. We said our good-byes to our new Kickstart friends in front of the marvelous museum and then spread out to different parts of the park; me to the swapmeet area to meet up with Luis and Deb, my friends from Pinetta.

I found my friends and pitched the tent on the swapmeet site. It was getting late now and my friends were leaving for the day, leaving me alone for the night. After a while, I decided to make the short ride into Leeds and find something to eat for dinner and to pick up drinks for back at camp. I whizzed past a couple barbecue places on the way to town, but, after barbecue for the last couple of meals, I thought I would try to find something different. I remembered from last year an area up near a major highway north of Leeds where there were a clump of restaurants from which to choose. I turned north in town and soon was lost somewhere in a residential area of town. I backtracked my way to US 78 and, rather than spend a lot of time searching out the restaurant zone, I settled for another barbecue dinner close to Rex Lake Road before heading back to the park and my swapmeet camp. The next day I hoped to get in some race viewing and, hopefully, some riding in the rolling surrounding countryside.

In spite of my intent to hit some of the great roads in the area, the next day found me spending the entire day inside the park—there was just so much to do and see at the Barber Vintage Festival. I never got out except for a quick lunch and to pick up a can of chain lube, which Old Faithful was much in need of. I spent a lot of time wandering the swapmeet rows, looking for a NOS speedometer for the CB, but, while I saw literally piles of them, none had the exact same mounting arrangement as my original 1968 gauge. Apparently, Honda had used that particular configuration for only that first year. I next caught the Race of the Century for bikes one hundred years or older. My favorite, Dale Walksler from the Wheels Through Time Museum, took second, all the while looping the track with a cheap cigar clenched between his teeth in typical Dale fashion. Then I hoofed it over to the dirt course, miles away it seemed, to take some pictures of the dirt action for my son. I arrived there a few minutes late and missed the racing. That was a bit after one, and the next race, vintage cross-country, was at three. Retracing my steps, off I went in search of souvenirs for the kids. Once souvenir T-shirts were stowed in the tent, I returned to the cross-country area. This time I was smart and hopped on my bike for the ride over, idling past thousands of bikes, a mixture of new and old, glistening in the north Alabama sun. They lined both sides of the road in uninterrupted rows, forming a shoulder of metal and rubber. This time at the dirt track, I was not disappointed. The cross-country course allowed me to get right on top of the action at a few different dramatic turns, and I got some close up action shots before riding back to my camp at the swapmeet.

As the sun settled in the west and most shoppers were leaving the swapmeet area, Luis and Deb offered the bread, salami, and chips that remained in the cooler. My dinner provided, I stayed put rather than running out for restaurant food. The sun set and the partying in the adjacent sites began. I soon hit the sack, in spite of the raucous revelry, so I could be up early to pack for departure.

We left Barber about noon. Although I missed exploring the area outside of the park, we did take the "Mini Tail of the Dragon" on the way out of town. This is AL 25, or Dunnavant Road, and leads southeast to US 231. It is a nice mountain ride through lush forests with nice twisties, and a hairpin that can catch you if you are not prepared. I polished the tip of my kickstand making the hard left around that turn. I've dragged a peg from time to time, but this was the first time any hard parts hit the road. I surmised that all the weight of my luggage made the difference between my toe touching down or the kickstand. I escaped the hairpin unscathed, regardless, and we continued on our way to US 231, sweeping along the wooded, curving road.

It had grown cool and cloudy before we left Barber, and soon the rain set in. We had rain for most of the day, but it was off and on and mostly light, a mere drizzle at its worst. The wind, however, was whipping. Numerous times, I thought Old Faithful's motor was cutting out, and I had to lower my head and listen to the motor from below the windscreen. Each time the engine was purring like it always does. What I thought was a clogged fuel line or carb turned out to be no more than strong wind gusts, that hit in bursts and held me back, instantly lowering my speed by five or more miles per hour.

After US 231, we continued on US 280 out of the state of Alabama and into Georgia. 280 carried us to GA 520, which connected with US 82 running into Albany. There, we headed south on US 19 until we got to Thomasville and US 84. I got separated from the group there, making a turn I thought would take me to Valdosta, but I turned too early. I did a U-turn, and ended up catching up with my friends in Quitman. At a gas station there, we said our good-byes. They turned south towards Pinetta on GA 333, while I remained on 84 into Valdosta. A quick hop up I-75 just one exit, got me to Exit 18 where I left the Interstate and rode west for the last couple miles to my high school friend's home off GA 133, arriving about nine in the evening.

My Georgia friends and I had a pleasant rest of the evening catching up, while I devoured a perfectly cooked filet mignon that Julie had grilled for me. It grew late as we sat enjoying the Georgia evening, chatting on the porch. I was exhausted from fighting the wind all day. I had gone without a shower or even washing my hair for five days, but when I realized how late it was, I figured I could go one more, especially considering the forecast weather for tomorrow would make a mess of me, anyway. The wind had beaten me so bad on this day that I abandoned posting the blog for the night, too. I laid down on a mattress for the first time in almost a week and was instantly asleep.

I woke about eight in the morning after a comfortable night's sleep and spent about an hour chatting and drinking coffee with Julie and another friend, Lisa, before getting ready to head out for the last time. The forecast was grim, but I was determined to get back home that day. Andrea, by this time, had enough single parent child care for a while, so I repacked the gear on the bike, checked the oil, and waxed the chain, and waving my good-byes I drove out of the driveway, in full rain gear.

There was a huge tropical low swirling around north Florida that I had seen on radar that morning. Monday, I had the pleasure of riding through the heart of it. The wind was howling, and soon my boots were filled with water from the unrelenting torrential rain. Again, I ducked my head every so often when the little bike seemed to loose all power, checking the motor sound again, but this time I knew what I'd hear—a beautifully humming little gem of Japanese engineering. I headed south out of Valdosta on I-75 a short way into Florida until I could catch US 129 south. I took 129 to Branford, where I took a break from the wet and the wind and had a cup of hot coffee and a Cuban sandwich in Coffee Clutch, a little shop I found downtown.

A bit warmer and with renewed energy, I headed back out into the wild weather, following US 27 south. I made the poor choice of following 27 all the way to Haines City, just north of Lake Wales, forgetting how many traffic lights and how much traffic would be stacked up in Ocala and most of the way south to Leesburg. I lost a lot of time in that stretch, probably only averaging thirty miles per hour.

After Leesburg, speed improved, and the traffic opened up. I had a pleasant ride as the clouds started to disperse, and from time to time I could see the sun peaking through. The winds slowly abated. After crossing over I-4, I turned left off 27 and jogged over to FL 17, which rolls right into Lake Wales, twenty miles or so farther along. Arriving in our driveway about 5:30 PM, the kids ran out to see what I had brought them. I was worn out and glad to be home, but also a bit sad when I backed the little CB350 into its spot in the garage, closing the door on another adventure together.

By the time I arrived back in Lake Wales, I had added 1,717 miles to the odometer and had done my longest one day ride so far—680 miles, close to 18 hours in the saddle. I had used a capful of Startron engine treatment in each tank, which is suppose to cure many of the ethanol gas ills. That's not all it does, though—I got roughly 66 mpg on the ride, compared to my usual 54 average without it. I even hit a high of 70 mpg once. Startron proved itself to be a good investment. That good mileage resulted in a total fuel cost of only $87, or five cents a mile. The only trouble I had with that forty-three year-old bike over all those miles was one blown fuse. By being frugal, camping, and eating smart the total for all expenses for the six day ride was $392, and that included $62 for souvenirs.

Now, to beat the inevitable post-ride funk that seems to sink in after a return to everyday life.

To Spring Mill State Park
and Points North

According to my usual ritual for long rides, I would be getting up at four o'clock in the morning to head north on my Bonneville, en route to the Vintage Japanese Motorcycle Club's National Rally at Spring Mill State Park, near Mitchell, Indiana. I would be attending to cover the event for the club's *Vintage Japanese Motorcycle Magazine.*

I planned to take the shortest and quickest route out of Florida. That wasn't because I think Florida roads are all "straight and flat" and, therefore, uninteresting; because I knew that was a lie. I'd found that there is plenty of interesting riding in Florida. It was because I'd ridden this section so many times that I was thoroughly familiar with the territory and no longer felt like a trip was truly underway until the Georgia state line rolled under my wheels. By leaving at four in the morning, I could ride the usually crowded US 27 in almost zero traffic, jump across on the Florida Turnpike to I-75, and would be getting close to the Georgia line by the time the sun was lightening the eastern sky.

Earlier, I was worried I would not be able to afford to go on this trip. My business for the last few months had been abysmal. Although things had picked up recently, I would not see any income from those sales until about September. But it was important for me to go because our once a year face-to-face board meeting for the Vintage Japanese Motorcycle Club was held each year at the national rally and we board members were expected to be there unless it was absolutely impossible. I would have to scrimp on the trip to make it all work. I worked out the math and optimistically left my wife with a couple hundred dollars to keep her solvent while I was on the road. I nervously left with four hundred dollar bills in my pocket. That would have to do for gas, food, and accommodations for more than a week.

My target for the first day was a little town in northwest Georgia named LaFayette, where a fellow forum "inmate" from advrider.com lived and had offered space for me to pitch my tent for the night. ADVRider is an online community of adventure riders, some of whom wander the globe, while others glide back and forth in regions closer to their homes, with an occasional road, or off-road, trip thrown in once in a while. In the "Trip Planning" section of the forum was a thread that went on for hundreds of entries. In it any member could offer whatever they wanted to, be it backyard tent space, a couch or a spare bedroom, food and beer, motorcycle rescue, and mechanical tools and expertise for the passing moto-wanderer. All the places offered were pin-pointed on a map of the world. You could click the pins to get the original offer on the forum and the details of what the fellow member offered. I'd hosted riders before and had used the list myself when I was in the Ozarks. It never failed to be anything but a great experience and a chance to make new friends who had an interest in motorcycle traveling, too. This arrangement would help me a lot to keep the trip's costs down, saving me at the least the cost of one night's accommodation.

I headed out on my fully laden Triumph, on time for once, having packed the bike completely with all my riding clothes laid out the night before so that all I had to do was hop out of bed, throw on the clothes, and head out of the door. There had been talk recently between some riding friends and me about possibly doing a ride to Alaska next summer, so I had been steadily "ADV"ing my Bonnie, in case I could work it out to ride the 10,000 miles. So, not only did the bike have my usual assortment of traveling luggage, I had added a Roto-Pax one gallon tank that sat under my tail bag and had two MSR liter bottles, one on each side, mounted on the passenger peg brackets, holding another almost half gallon between them. The ride would give me a chance to test out the arrangement.

The now slightly heavier Triumph purred north on US 27 in the darkness until reaching the Florida Turnpike that cut diagonally northwest across the state joining I-75 at its terminus. I-75 would be my path all the rest of the way to the Georgia line.

Being late June, the night was cool but not frigid, as it had been on so many other northern treks I had taken out of state. Two hundred and fifty or so miles after departing, I left the Interstate at Exit 18 in Valdosta, and headed northwest on GA 133. Many times on my way back and forth I had stopped there at my friend's house, but this time I just waved as I passed her neighborhood on the south side of the highway and kept rolling towards Moultrie, then Albany as the day warmed and the pecan groves flew by. I turned north and continued past tobacco and cotton farms on US 19 and the ever present corn crop.

At Americus, I switched to GA 30 and then GA 41 north toward Warm Springs. This route kept me far away from the mayhem of Atlanta traffic and let me enjoy the Georgia farm country while watching the GPS's altimeter creep slowly upward. The predominance of pecan groves faded as the route headed ever northward on US 27 out of Warm Springs. That highway would take me to LaFayette and my stop for the night. I passed through Rome, where years before I had stopped at Panhead City on the First Motorcycle Kickstart Classic ride that had left out of Maggie Valley.

After a quick stop to make a phone call to my evening's host and to get final instructions for finding his place, I found the side road leading down to LaFayette City Reservoir, got lost, then found my way again, then finally rolled to a stop at Brent's place. I had avoided rain all day, but, now that I had stopped, the skies were darkening and threatening to pour. Brent said that rather than pitching my tent in the back yard as I had proposed, with the rain coming I should use his man cave above the garage/shop, where I would have a couch to sleep on and my own bathroom. I could keep my bike below in the garage, out of the weather. While I took him up on his offer and rolled the Bonnie into the garage, Brent got the grill going where he just finished hamburgers before the rain came down in earnest. I hurried into the house behind him and the platter of steaming burgers, and once inside we both commenced the formidable task of making a dent in the burgers and the food, including desert, that was overflowing the kitchen island. As we munched, we talked about bikes, riding, and woodworking, a hobby we both participated in. It turned out Brent often came down to fish in the area around Lake Wales, and we chatted about fishing in central Florida. I invited him to drop by or to stay with us when he came back down. After 580 miles, and now with a full stomach, my lids started to droop. I said good night, good-bye, and thanks to Brent and his wife (They would be gone for work in the morning by the time I got up.) and toddled off to the garage, climbed the stairs to the man cave, and hit the sack.

I had ridden almost 600 miles and only paid for gas three times at just over eleven dollars per fill up and had survived on an Egg McMuffin and a coffee until I arrived at Brent's. Brent didn't want anything for the dinner. While I didn't want to take advantage, this was good for my tiny budget, and I didn't resist much, knowing how far I had yet to go.

In the quiet of the next morning I repacked the bike. Brent had kindly offered the use of the extra gas he had stored by the garage door to top up, so I filled the tank to the rim which would allow me 140-150 miles before I would have to refill again—another budget bonus!

One reason I had planned my stop here was that nearby was Cloudland Canyon State Park, a place I had been wanting to see ever since I was tipped off about it by another ADVRider inmate. I was wandering around on the Triumph in the Smoky and Blue Ridge Mountains just over a year ago and had chanced to stop for the night at Vogel State Park, on US 129, just south of Blairsville, Georgia. Jeff was the camp host. It was after hours when I got in so I stopped to ask Jeff what the procedure was. He invited me to share his site and dinner with him. We hit it off and around a campfire we had talked into the night, when Jeff had mentioned Cloudland Canyon. He said some people called it the "Little Grand Canyon" and, although that was perhaps a little grandiose of a name, it was a truly impressive sight and something you would not expect to see in north Georgia.

Leaving Brent's I headed northwest on GA 136, intent on a visit to Cloudland Canyon, just a few miles away, even if it was only for a quick stop. Now the mountains started in earnest and I wound my way to the state park, where I paid a small fee for the privilege of viewing that work of nature.

When I parked up near the overlook and walked to the edge I beheld a truly awesome sight. Off to the left and right, directly below me, the gorge extended for miles. The stream at its bottom was only occasionally visible behind the trees and undergrowth that grew wherever the rock faces were not too steep to allow them to take hold. It was still early, and the morning mist hung light in the air, softening any sounds. With only a couple vehicles in the parking lot, I had the park virtually to myself.

After I had soaked in the scene from the overlook, I thought a quick hike was in order. I chose a trail to my left that meandered into the woods and along the north rim of the canyon. The greens of a mixed forest enveloped me in silence as I walked among sassafras, oak, hemlock, and hickory, eventually crossing a small brook on a little wooden bridge. I turned around and decided on a side trip when I spotted a sign to Hemlock Falls. I took the switch-backing path down a steep grade and to a huge overhanging rock, under which the trail passed. Beyond the boulder, the path dropped down wooden stairs for hundreds of yards. At the first level stopping place and with still no falls in sight, I decided my time was running out. I turned around to climb the steep stairs I had just come down, passed under the cave-like opening under the hanging boulder, climbed some more then turned back to my left along the rim trail to the parking lot, where the Bonnie was waiting. The day was now well underway, and I still had hundreds of miles to go before I would arrive at the rally in Indiana. I had seen enough to know that one day I would return to spend more time in this peaceful place.

Clearing the gates of the park, I continued on GA 136 away from Cloudland Canyon then onto GA 301 and toward the Alabama border. Beyond the state line the road became CR 90. I turned north on AL 73 and continued into Tennessee and onto TN 156. I was still trying to avoid busier highways so I stayed on 156 west then north through Franklin State Forest and to the junction with US 41A/TN 15, just west-southwest of Monteagle.

I hopped over to I-24 for a quick run up to US 231 where I would be getting off before I got into the Nashville traffic. Once across the Cumberland River, I ran west on TN 25 to US 31W, that runs beside I-65 into Kentucky. I connected to the William H. Natcher Parkway and rode it north to my exit at KY 69. From there all I had to do was stay on 69 until I reached US 60, which ran along the southern shore of the Ohio River, take a left, then a right again to cross the wide Ohio River from Hawesville on the south side to Cannelton on the north.

Once on the Indiana side, IN 237 continues straight on from the bridge, connecting to IN 37. I could have taken 37 directly into Mitchel and Spring Mill State Park, but now the riding was going to get good, and I wanted to avoid busy main roads until the last possible moment. Almost as soon as I hopped onto 37 I turned off again onto IN 145 into the hills on twisting tarmac through southern Indiana. I rolled and curved through the hills of the Hoosier National Forest. The National Forest is in two sections. The southern one, which I was passing through, stretched from the banks of the Ohio to just west of Mitchell. Here the twisties had their own particular flavor, with quick climbs over hills restricting views of the road ahead only to reveal as you passed the crests the need to turn, and turn quickly, into the next curve. I was used to the horizontally blind curves that I've encountered in the Blue Ridge and Smokies, where a cliff side climbing up on the inside of a curve hides the curve beyond, but this vertical blind corner was a bit unnerving at first. You would climb and hit the crest with your stomach still in the air, only to see a hard left or right teasing you and testing your braking and cornering skills. In other words, it was a blast!

Eventually, the roller coaster ride settled down into a more mild ride through rolling farming countryside, and I emerged at French Lick, where I jumped over to IN 37 via IN 56. Mitchell is at the intersection of 37 and IN 60, where I made a right on 60 for the final couple miles to the Spring Mill State Park entrance, just east of town.

As I drove down the wooded park drive, familiar sensations flowed through me. As a child, growing up just 250 miles north of here, my family had camped in this park on summer weekends. I have vivid memories of camping in our old canvas tent here, poking around the Pioneer Village and grist mill, and exploring the caves in the park. The rally would give me the opportunity to relive some of my fond memories in between what my duties as editor of the club magazine required. I parked up on the inn's circular drive and found the event team already on hand prepping for the upcoming rally activities. I stepped off the bike, said my hellos, and headed inside to check in. I had ridden around four hundred miles and had only stopped for gas and a quick coffee, so the budget was still under control. I would face my next monetary challenge when I went in to eat with my fellow members at the inn's restaurant.

I had paid the fee for the event a long time before and the evening meals would be covered by it, but I was here before the official start of the rally so this evening's dinner and all the breakfasts and lunches would be on my dime. It would be rude to ride out of the park to eat by myself at some cheap fast food joint while all the other members were gathering at the inn and sharing stories and laughs. I would just have to be cautious. I sat down to dinner with my fellow club members and this night blew the budget on the buffet, but this would be the last splurge. I would pace myself the rest of the time.

I rose early and once more joined my friends at the restaurant at the inn. I ordered coffee, then I perused the menu in search of something a bit less expensive that the full-blown breakfast buffet that sat tempting me with scrambled eggs, bacon, and hotcakes just a few feet away. For a measly couple of bucks I could have biscuits and gravy. I ordered that and coffee and drank enough refills to justify its price. It was great seeing old friends and making new ones and chatting about the club and old bikes.

Breakfast over, it was time for me to play photographer. I would write the article on the rally after I got back to Florida, but now I had to concentrate on getting shots of just about everything, and especially concentrating on getting some killer portrait-oriented shots. The story on the national rally would be the cover story for the next issue, and we would need a good choice of portrait photos to choose from for the cover image. I wandered around the grounds photographing the bikes that had already arrived and trying to get good images of the bikes with Spring Mill Inn in the background.

As I was shooting, a ride group formed up in the circular drive in front of the inn that was to be our meeting place, our bike show venue, and our general parking area throughout the weekend. I ran up to the room to grab the camera and GoPro, came back down, and mounted it to the mirror stalk on the Bonnie. I rode to the end of the line in hopes of getting some video of the group in the countryside from which I might pull some decent stills for the article. It turned out this was the "Long Ride" for the day and would not return for six hours. There was to be a lunch stop, so I crossed my fingers that we would make our stop at a modestly priced diner.

With me ironically following on my modern British motor bike, the dozen or so vintage Japanese bikes headed out of the park and zig-zagged through the southern Indiana cornfields over roads with hopeful repairs lumped over the many frost heaves left by the last winter's unusually severe weather. We passed through the northern part of the Hoosier National Forest, crossing Monroe Lake, and parked up eventually in Nashville, in Brown County, famous for its autumn colors which attract tens of thousands of visitors to the area each year. The dominating color, however, was green at this time of year but no less beautiful. Lunch was in a simple diner named Hob Nob Corner. I was in luck, as the burger option was not too expensive and really was delicious. With a couple more pounds on each bike after lunch, we headed back for the state park and inn, where we parked up on the circle again.

More attendees had arrived by the time we returned. I ran up to the room to get out of the hot Kevlar-lined riding pants and my boots, and returned in more comfortable street clothes. I resumed my photography duties and walked around the bikes and among my fellow members and shot until it was time for dinner. My wallet would get a reprieve at tonight's dinner and all dinners for the rest of the rally. All I had to pay for tonight was pre-dinner beers if I wanted them. This meal was the "Ice Breaker" for all the newly arrived members to get to know each other and start forming new friendships and renewing old ones. The buffet was extensive and, with no financial holds barred, I charged it as if I hadn't eaten for days. After dinner there was time for more conversation with friends as most of us drifted onto the patio above the steep hill, below which flowed the creek fed by Donaldson Cave. Offers of beer were frequent and no one was there waiting for payment and a tip.

By Friday morning, many more bikes had shown up and they would continue coming in all day. While the members unloaded bikes, registered, and started up conversations with each other, we board members gathered in a room off the inn's main dining room. We shared a breakfast of pancakes, sausage, and coffee, and soon turned to club business. A lot had been going on with the club and new challenges had to be managed. With more and more events popping up which were gathering increasingly larger crowds we had our work cut out for us organizing and planning. It was almost noon before we all emerged. I got back to my photography and soon I had enough photos for the time being, the rest could wait until the full contingent of vintage motorcycles had arrived.

The "Tiddler Parade" was just about to take off on a romp around the park before returning and lining up for the "Tiddler Bike Show," that I was to officiate. This was for all bikes under 200cc. The entries began at 50cc tiny Hondas all the way up to the limit at 200cc. Ballots went out and came back. I went inside to tally the votes, the winners to be announced the next evening along with the main bike show winners.

I ran inside to see what I might be able to manage for lunch and found a table with a couple friends already eating and decided a chef salad would be the easiest item on my budget.

After lunch was my chance to get away for a bit and try to relive some of those childhood memories I had made here so long ago. I remounted the Bonnie, but instead of heading out of the park, I went further in, stopping at a trail parking area with a sign pointing to Donaldson Cave. It was pleasant to be alone for a while in the quiet of the woods, no 865cc motor beating out its tune underneath me. Instead, all I could hear was the subtle crunch of my tread as I wandered into the woods along a small and gentle stream. The only sounds I heard to remind me of the rally were the voices above me on the patio at the inn, but soon they faded to nothingness. As I walked further, all I heard was the trickling water on my right and the quiet sounds of small forest creatures moving about, while the overhanging foliage filtered the light, leaving only small dancing patches of light here and there in the relatively dark forest. As I walked, the path started a gentle climb while the sound of the stream increased its volume, and the air took on a feeling of welcome coolness. As I walked, I tried to remember how it felt as a child to walk this same path, and attempted to put myself back in the shoes of that young boy. For a little while, fifty years didn't seem so long ago. Then a wall of rock stood before me with the water issuing forth from a massive entryway. I climbed on slippery rocks into the mouth of the cave as far as I could, feeling the air pumping out of the rock like a giant's cool breath, while mist rose from the surface of the escaping water. As a kid, we could enter these caves, but an outbreak of white nose disease, a bat malady, forced the park to close entry to the caves to prevent its spread, and so I was faced with the only option of turning around and walking back to the bike.

It was getting late in the afternoon, but I wanted to make a quick dash to the restored Pioneer Village to see if I remembered it accurately and whether anything had changed. I walked among the almost two century old log cabins, imagining how different it must have been here back in 1816 when this wasn't Indiana, but the Northwest Territory.

I wanted to get back before anything important happened at the rally, so I walked hurriedly, snapping photos as I went, but I couldn't resist heading up the trail that led to Hamer Cave. A short hike found me standing in front of another rock cliff with water gushing out, creating a stream. This, in turn, fed the wooden aqueduct that ran to the grist mill and spun the large wooden water wheel that drove the grinding stones.

My free time was up, but I was refreshed and rested. I scurried back to my duties at the rally. The circle was full now, and bikes overflowed into the parking garage. I resumed my photography and, between shots, sat and shared stories with friends. Soon it was time for the dinner buffet again and more camaraderie on the patio.

I rose early the next morning and, once again, ordered coffee and gravy and biscuits, then walked outside to continue my photography duties. By then the circle drive was buzzing with activity.

Another ride was queued up in the circle. This would be a shorter ride with a stop at a covered bridge. I asked if they would wait for me to grab my gear, thinking this would be a good opportunity to grab a nice group shot at the bridge. I ran to the room, threw on my gear, grabbed my camera, and hurried down to the waiting line of vintage motorcycles, now idling in anticipation. The line snaked its way out of the park and back onto the country roads through the endless fields of corn. I hadn't looked at the route on a map, but just followed along behind that buzzing line of motorcycles past iconic hundred year old farmsteads and through shady forests. We stopped for lunch at a very small country diner; hardly big enough to contain just our group. We ducked in just in time, as our bikes were pelted by rain, while we ate in the dry and cozy diner. Throughout the downpour the sun had never given up completely and by the time we exited, the bikes were already drying in the sunshine. My budget lucked out again here with my chef salad costing me little. We remounted and took off in the direction of the much anticipated covered bridge. There we had a look at the old wooden structure and gathered for our group photo before heading back to the rally.

By the time we arrived at the inn, the rain had returned. The show bikes were not spared a drenching. Some quicker thinking entrants had hurriedly thrown covers over their bikes, but most sat in the rain, with little beads all over the paint work reflecting the returning sunlight. The rain didn't last long, and out came the towels, while owners hurried to clean and dry their entries. Everything had almost completely dried by the time voting began. I took a ballot and wandered around making my choices for the several categories. After a few more photographs, I took the opportunity before dinner to go explore the park again and to get more photos of the Pioneer Village area for use in the article to give an idea of the setting for this event.

The grist mill had been locked when I was here the day before, but now I could enter. I took a look at displays on pioneer life and the wooden gearing that transferred power from the water wheel to the grind stones. Riding back though the park I had noticed a sign for Twin Caves, and so I stopped to take a look. This is the one cave in Spring Mill State Park that you can still enter. There is a large opening in a rock face on the left and a smaller one on the right. Water streams from the left and back under the hillside into the one on the right. Here, rangers manned two small aluminum "boats," which looked rather more like floating bathtubs, and rowed visitors 500 feet into the larger cave. The fee was an insignificant three dollars, but the tours were filled up for the day. Spelunking by refrigerator would have to wait for next time. I fired up the Bonnie and rolled back to the inn along the park road in the cool shade of the full June foliage.

I arrived in time for the Saturday evening meal, once again covered by my pre-registration fee. This was the big event of the rally. The buffet was huge, and, after all were full, awards were given out for the bike show winners and to members who had been valuable assets to the club. Afterward, it was back to the patio and more free beer. Most stayed late, knowing that in the morning everyone would be leaving for their respective homes scattered across the country, and it would be a long time before many of us would see each other again. I stayed long enough to not be rude, but I had to cross the state on a motorcycle the next morning and doing so with a hangover and bleary eyes would not do me any good on the trip, so I returned to my room relatively early.

Having enjoyed the rally, but also being a bit exhausted by all the activity, I looked forward to tomorrow and being back on the road on the Bonnie. I was to meet high school friends in Buchanan, Michigan, a little town just west of Niles, where I had attended school from the first grade to graduation from high school at Brandywine Senior High. Initially, I considered riding straight to Wheatberry's on Red Bud Trail, but with only a little over two hundred miles to run today, I reconsidered and decided to head for South Bend, Indiana, just over the state line from Niles, where my best friend from high school, Joe, lived. Because of the short distance, there was no need to hurry, so I avoided the straight and quickest route over to Indianapolis and on via US 31. Instead, I opted to head north from Mitchell and enjoy the ride through the farmland of western Indiana, where I had never traveled before, even though it was barely a stone's throw from my childhood home.

I headed north after a quick gas stop on IN 37, which would trend toward the big city of Indy. I turned off onto IN 39, before I got too close to the metropolis and swept west of the city, through the fields of corn and soybeans rooted in the rich, dark Midwestern soil. As I passed farm after farm, almost invariably of the classic type, with two-story white farmhouse, red barn, and tall columnar silo next to it, I began to notice I was passing old Japanese motorcycles on the roadside fairly regularly, each with a "For Sale" sign tacked to the headlight. I started to realize I had been seeing these occasionally all the way from Tennessee, but now the frequency surprised me. I started dreaming of traveling through the back roads of the Midwest with a pocket full of cash and a trailer behind a truck. I have no doubt filling the trailer with great old '70s motorcycles would be easy to do in just a matter of a few days. I would continue to see these old bikes for sale most of the way back through Ohio, and all the way through Tennessee.

At Delphi, I caught IN 25 for a short run northeast to Rochester, where I finally intercepted US 31, which ran north into South Bend. I was soon winding my way through the streets of the south side of the city toward Joe's place. It had been years since I last rode those streets, but I found myself recognizing turn after turn. I made my final turn into Twyckenham Hills and onto Woodmont where I spotted Joe in his driveway.

We went inside, had a bite and a couple beers, and got busy catching up. I was reintroduced to Sara, Joe's daughter, who was visiting from college. She was every bit grown up and I found myself envious of Joe with all his kids on their own and his freedom to go as he pleased. Yet, in spite of his seeming freedom, I was the one riding a motorcycle halfway across the country.

Joe and I headed out to catch up with our friends at Wheatberry's. One of my pals had said he was planning to ride his panhead up. I thought I would ride my bike, too, so I followed Joe in his car.

We made a stop at Joe's childhood house or, rather, lot. The old house had burned to the ground recently. His sister, Lisa, had been living in the house when something went awry in the attic, leaving nothing of the structure except the foundation. Lisa was rebuilding a new house on the same footprint as the old, and Joe gave me the tour. We also inspected the shed Joe's son had been living in and converting into a kind of Thoreau's cabin, while he started work to try to save the log cabin on Brandywine Creek below the bluff behind the new house that Joe had started his life in, but which now was in tumbling down disrepair.

My panhead riding friend didn't show, but the other five us had a great time and a great meal at Wheatberry's. Here started the strange phenomenon of my money not being any good. From tonight until I left the area two days later, I didn't leave more than a tip at any of the places I ate. I made an effort to pay my own way wherever I was, but every time I was turned down, but, honestly, this windfall probably saved the remainder of the trip.

After days of riding in the sun and heat, the night air felt good on the way back to Joe's, where I was staying the night in the vacant bed of one of his absent daughters. We had the bonus of watching a deer cross ahead of us, safely far enough away to not require a sudden stop. That was the first wildlife I had encountered on the entire road trip north, which surprised me greatly, as I had expected fairly frequent encounters on the back roads I had taken.

The next morning Joe was working, so I walked out into the kitchen to greet his wife, Jan, who graciously French-pressed us a couple rounds of coffee. Skipping breakfast I thanked her and said good-bye to Jan and Sara. Rolling the bike out of the garage, I carefully worked it backwards down the sloping drive and into the street.

I had called my uncle, Max, from Joe's and arranged to meet him and his new wife. On the way to his place I had a couple extra hours, so I decided to head toward Michigan and the old neighborhood. I headed north in a meandering track, choosing roads almost at random. Eventually, I made it to Redfield Road and the house and fields where I had grown up. Now the pasture where we had kept two horses was a part of the forest it used to front. The black walnut trees I remembered still lined the road side and the house looked the same. I thought about knocking on the door and seeing if I could take a walk behind the house to see if I could find the old trails, probably long gone, that I used to roam, but that would take time I did not have. Instead, I continued on toward the old high school, trying to see if I could recognize the route I used to take by bicycle. I went astray a bit, but it was not long before I found the school and parked up in front to take a long look and jot down some notes so I would not forget what was going through my mind.

Time was running out, and I would be late for the mid-morning meeting with my uncle. I headed back toward the east end of Mishawaka and found his place only a little later than planned. My aunt had died years ago, and my uncle had remarried only to have his second wife die. He had recently remarried for the third time, so this would be my chance to meet her for the first time. She was very pleasant, and I was glad my uncle had found someone nice with whom to share his remaining years.

After a short chat, my uncle suggested we go see my mother's sister's husband, Uncle Dick, who was in a nearby rehabilitation center. When I had called Uncle Max, I had also considered calling my aunt to see about visiting Uncle Dick, but had hesitated making the call, as I knew he had been in bad shape with an Alzheimer-like malady for quite a while. I settled for calling my cousin instead and asking about his dad's condition. I wasn't sure of the appropriateness of me just dropping in on my aunt and uncle under the circumstances, so I felt much more comfortable doing so in the company of Uncle Max. It turned out we had the bonus of seeing my cousin, Sue, who was there to help her mom with her dad. Although it was hard to see my uncle in a state that barely allowed him to talk or feed himself, Uncle Max said as we left that he was very surprised and happy to see how well he was doing, because during the last couple of his visits Uncle Dick just slept, completely unaware of Uncle Max's presence. While we visited, Uncle Dick was in a wheelchair and in the dining room, and even managed to feed himself a bit and respond verbally to us. I left hoping the trend continued and that he improved enough for him to go back home.

On the way back to my Uncle Max's, we dropped into a little neighborhood diner, where, once again, my paying was forbidden. Navy bean soup, a entree I had completely forgotten about and which I never see back home in the South, and a patty melt with fries completed our lunch.

I headed to Granger next to see a friend of my dad, who is also into vintage motorcycles and has a good sized collection ranging from an Ariel Square-Four, to a couple of BSAs,

Whizzers in different varieties, old Harleys in their own particular flavors of pan and flathead, to a couple little Honda Trail 70s, among others. A neighbor's Trail 70 was probably the first real motorcycle I ever rode, back when they were new models, and Hank had two in that Candy Gold I remembered so well.

At Hank's, after catching up over a couple cold beers, I was given the tour. Then Hank and his wife, Joanne, suggested getting dinner out. We loaded up in Hank's truck and headed up IN 23 into Michigan, where its name changed to MI 62, to Edwardsburg, for a bite. Tacos were on special and sounded like just the ticket. After three each and a beer, we headed back into Indiana the way we had come. Not long after we returned I got a call from my cousin, Denny, Uncle Dick's son, who had to deliver something from his work to the area. He was going to drop by. He had known Hank for years, too. We all talked well into the evening. Denny left and we turned in. During my good night call home it was revealed that Andrea had pneumonia—not good news and a reason to not dilly dally getting home. I went to bed anxious to start back.

Rain and gusts up to a hundred miles an hour were forecast for the evening, and soon the rain began, and the promised wind arrived as the night wore on. I was glad to have the Bonnie safely tucked inside beside Hank's row of rare bikes and to be in a bed, instead of on the ground somewhere watching my tent billow around me while waiting for it to become airborne, me an unwilling passenger inside it.

By morning, the winds and rain had abated. I woke first and took a walk outside. Large limbs were down across the street but Hank's trees were relatively unscathed, with just a few small branches scattered around the yard. I found a burn pile in the back yard and piled up the debris I had picked up during my stroll on it, while the world came awake. Hank and Joanne insisted on taking me to breakfast, their treat, of course. My budget looked ten dollars better. The diner was only around the corner and my hosts, of course, were well-known there. The food was good and our coffee cups never stayed empty for long. Hank and Joanne admitted to me they were trying to hold me up, at least enough so that I would not be running into the backside of last night's storm as I proceeded east, the same direction the storm was moving.

I was itching to leave, but to defer me a bit longer, they dropped by their daughter's natural foods store on the way back. The selection was top notch and the ambiance was nice, with even a wine room with non-sulfited wines to choose from. Sometimes living in a metropolitan area has its advantages, and I wished we had something like that in Lake Wales, where "health foods" consisted of light beer and barbecue.

I really had delayed my departure too long, so, while politely turning down invitations to stay a couple more days, I rolled the Bonnie out of the bike barn, across the lawn, and waved good-bye as I rode onto the street. I pointed the bike northeast on 23 toward Michigan, once more.

Once across the state line, in Edwardsburg, I caught US 12 and headed east. I went north to go east because along this stretch of highway there is a little town named Sturgis. I'd had a silly idea for a while to get a picture of my bike in front of the Sturgis sign as a kind of lame joke about having ridden to Sturgis, while all my biker friends back home would instantly think Sturgis, South Dakota, the location of the famous motorcycle rally. It was a bit of a lark, but not far out of the way, and I had to ride east anyway. I found a suitable Sturgis sign, snapped the photo, and headed back out, bound for southern Ohio.

I turned south at Sturgis onto MI 66, which becomes IN 9 at the state line. At the intersection at Howe, I turned left onto IN 120. As I passed out of town I searched the roadside for the house of a girl I once dated in this little town, possibly the first girl I had thought I'd "loved"—Gloria, but that was all of her name I remembered. I failed completely in my attempt to identify her house, seeing nothing I recognized as familiar at all.

I followed 120 parallel to the state line, and as I moved along I could see massive trees down along the roadside, obviously just removed from the road, a result of last night's wind. When the Michigan state line made its southward bump, just past Clear Lake, I rode briefly through Michigan again, until I caught MI 99 south into Ohio, where it was renamed OH 15. Continuing south until Bryan, 15 then made an abrupt change of direction to the southeast. All this time I was watching the sky ahead of me. Surely, I could not catch up with that storm from last night, but the sky to the east was cloudy and seemed to be getting darker. A few sprinkles fell on my visor, but at OH 65 the road and I turned south and the clouds sped east without me, the sun eventually brightening the sky and slowly heating the Ohio countryside and drying the roads. I began to swelter, and the rain proof liner in my mesh jacket went into storage.

As I buzzed along the country roads of Ohio, I caught sight of an Amish buggy, a sight I recall seeing often in the northern Indiana countryside when I was a kid. I hadn't thought about it as I was passing through Indiana, but now wondered how I had missed seeing buggies there, in what I thought was a more likely location. Now that I was seeing them in Ohio, I determined to get some video to show the kids when I got home. That would be something so strange and foreign to them, having never been exposed to such a contrast of cultures before. I mounted the GoPro in preparation for the next sighting. I rode on and on and thought I had missed my chance when I sighted another one. I pushed the on button on the fob around my neck, but nothing happened. I had put the GoPro in the tank bag to charge, but hadn't thought of the batteries in the remote. By the time I had fumbled around trying to start the camera manually, I had missed my chance and the buggy had disappeared into the countryside.

I made my way to Lima, where I got confused and took the wrong road. It seemed major enough and was going east, the direction I wanted to go, so I stayed on it, passing a large reservoir and then farm after farm until I finally decided I had to be running parallel to the road I had meant to take. I took the next major crossroad south, and, within a couple miles, I was back on track, eastbound. Crossing OH 696 I turned south and soon was on OH 117, heading into Bellefontaine.

My brother had moved to Bellfontaine years ago, after marrying a seemingly nice girl from there. When he got to Ohio, the truth came out about her, and I cringed to think of the misery Bob had suffered there and the stuff he had left behind when he bailed and ran for his life, back to Florida. Passing through gave me a funny feeling, but soon I was out the other side and on US 33, heading for Columbus.

I approached Marysville on fumes and pulled off the highway to refuel. Relieved to have a full tank, I moved out again passing the huge Honda plant and soon was at the Columbus by-pass. I entered southbound and was soon bound up in bumper to bumper traffic moving a hundred feet at a time at five miles per hour, then stopping, then repeating the whole dance time and again. It took over an hour to get past the city, but then the traffic eased, and I was moving south on US 23, bound for the Ohio River and Shawnee State Park. The landscape started to roll, and by Cillicothe I was in small mountains strikingly similar to the Ozarks.

The late start and the delay around Columbus put me way behind where I wanted to be as the afternoon faded and evening came on. I began to worry that the state park would be locked up by the time I arrived. At Portsmouth I got a quick look at the Ohio River. The park was not far to the west, along the river, and I wanted to get gas and something to eat for dinner before getting there. I putted around town looking for a grocery where I could pick up a cheap sub and a beer to bring with me to the park, but the town seemed devoid of anything resembling a grocery. I gave up and backtracked up US 23, pulling into a gas station to fill up. I went inside to buy an overpriced and lower quality sandwich than I had hoped to find. The day was waning fast, and I headed out of Portsmouth with my fingers crossed that I could still get into the park, even if I had to enter after hours and settle the fee in the morning.

I followed US 52 west, mirroring the curves of the big brown river on my left, and found OH 125 and the entrance to the park. I was in luck. It was still open and the light had not faded completely. I was able to ride the campground circuit, pick my spot, go back, pay the eighteen dollar fee, and set up before darkness. As I was pitching the tent, I realized my mistake of having chosen the site while riding the bike. Now that the Bonnie was quiet, the whir of a generator nearby could be heard clearly. Still, it was not obnoxiously loud, so I decided to live with my choice.

I tried to call home, my usual evening ritual to let everyone know I was stopped for the day and out of certain danger, as envisioned by my worrisome family. No signal. Nothing. I had never been anywhere where the phone didn't even attempt to ring out; but here it simply said "No Service" and threw up its hands. I would be in hot water if I failed to report in, so I went back to the ranger's post and asked about calling out. "You can try riding up to the lodge; I can usually get out there." I asked how to get there and rode back out of the camp and further up the mountain until I saw the sign for the inn. Following a short but steep driveway I arrived in a large parking lot in front of the inn. "If I can get out at all, I ought to be able to here. It is higher than all the surrounding hills," I thought. Still astride the Bonnie, I punched in the numbers. Nothing. "No Service." I was about to give up and just take my licks the next day, when I should be able to contact home, when my phone rang. It was Mom. I don't know why that one signal got through, and at the very moment I was in the only place it probably would have had a chance to. The signal was shaky, but I managed to let her know I could not call out but was safe and sound for the night, and asked if she would call Andrea and let her know. I also got an update on Andrea. The diagnosis had changed from pneumonia to acute bronchitis, and the kids were with my parents.

Back at camp I devoured my sandwich, which in spite of its gas station origins, was pretty good. Not having eaten anything since breakfast clearly contributed to its flavor, and it was gone in an instant. I cracked the quart can of beer I had bought along with the sub, took a sip, then looked around camp for twigs and small pieces of wood for a camp fire. The pickings were slim, but I didn't need a fire for long, just until total darkness fell, when I would crawl into my tent to sleep.

I unstrapped one of my MSR bottles of gas from the bike, removed the cap, and poured what I thought was a little fuel on the dry twigs. I pulled out the only lighter I had, one of the short cigarette types that has to be held close to whatever you are going to light. I held the safety and flicked the wheel—POOF! I had fire...and singed hair on my hands, but no burns. I settled onto my little three legged stool by the crackling fire and finished my quart of beer next to the fire ring. Once the can was empty and the fire had died to almost nothing, there was not much more to do but hit the hay. I crawled into the tent and listened to lightning far off in the distance. Surely, that was the tail end of the storm from last night and it was moving away from me to the east. I should be OK. I drifted off to sleep.

I woke to heavier thunder and rain pattering down on the tent. Soon it was pouring, and drips started finding their way through the fly, which I had noticed had started peeling its seem tape the last time I had pitched it. Luckily, I was on my sleeping pad and would not be lying in any water that might make its way in, unless it really came down hard and for a long time. I climbed out of the bag and, instead, laid under it, using it to intercept the drips before they got to me. Soon the rain diminished, and I managed to fall back asleep. I didn't wake until early morning and was only slightly damp. I crawled out in the semi-darkness and packed the bike. With the rain hopefully behind me, I was looking forward to a great day of riding, if the mountains I could see on the other side of the Ohio were any indication of what I had in store for the new day.

I crossed the Ohio back at Portsmouth, crossed into Kentucky, and continued on US 23. The highway followed the south shore of the Ohio River to the east and then south, passing through the industrial town of Ashland, where coal was loaded on barges bound for downstream ports on the Ohio and Mississippi Rivers. Soon I had the Big Sandy River as my new companion, with West Virginia on the far side of the river dividing the two states.

I followed the river until Louisa, where the highway veered inland into the mountains and eventually crossed Pound Gap and entered Virginia. US 23 continued south then southwest, following the southern contour of the Jefferson National Forest. The road eventually took an eastern turn toward Kingsport, just over the Tennessee line. I opted to go west on US 58/421 before I reached that point, in order to catch an alternate, wiggly route south on VA 70 into Tennessee. Almost as soon as I got on 58, I regretted it when I caught up with a line of vehicles jammed behind a heavily loaded truck that was trying to negotiate the increasingly extreme grades. Luckily, it was only a few miles before the truck turned off and I had unfettered riding into the western Virginia mountains. US 58/421 eventually wound its way to Cumberland Gap National Historic Park, but about halfway there I spotted my turn off at VA 70 and headed for the state line, where the road's name would change to TN 70. I would be on this roller coaster ride all the way into North Carolina and to just north of Asheville.

As I was enjoying the winding road, I rounded a sharp curve, almost a switchback, to the right, with a stream on my right and hillside climbing up on my left. After negotiating the apex of the turn I straightened up and squeezed progressively harder on my brake lever as I watched a black bear walking nonchalantly across the road thirty feet in front of me, on its way from the creek up the hill. I paused a while longer, considering my good fortune and with the idea in mind, given this was a fairly small bear, that if there was a mother following it, I would not want to get between the two. The Bonnie sat idling in the middle of the road while I watched the wild creature saunter off. A minute later, I eased out the clutch, released the brake, and moved on.

I twisted and turned, climbing and descending my way through Tennessee when at a particularly tight hairpin realized I was a bit out of practice. As I made the tight right, I felt my right foot peg digging in and found myself crossing the yellow line. Luckily, I had a clear view ahead and nothing was barreling down on me, so I did not fight it but casually completed the turn and got back in my lane, while considering what I had done to make it come out wrong and telling myself to keep my head in the game from then on.

I came to an intersection where a road came in on the right. I continued on straight, but something didn't feel right, so I U-turned and headed back to the intersection. There, a man with a stringer full of trout was climbing up from a creek to his pickup that was parked in a small gravel pull off. I asked him about the turn and he told me, yes, I needed to turn right, confirming my instincts were correct. I thanked him and tore off south toward North Carolina.

The plan was to make it to my brother's in Inman, South Carolina, for the night. I knew he would have a houseful for the night, with an old Navy pal of his with his entire family visiting for the week of the Fourth of July, but all I needed was a small spot on his backyard grass for my tent and I would be set. I decided to take the Interstate from Asheville. Tim's exit was just off I-26, just inside South Carolina, so it made sense to just jump on and make some time toward his place, so I would have more time to visit before pitching camp. I knew his friend, too, from a time long ago when I had sailed my boat up to Virginia Beach to stay with Tim for a while after a long jaunt in the Bahamas. It would be nice to see Steve again and share a beer or two with him and Tim.

It was about sixty miles from my entrance onto I-26 to my exit at Inman. I gathered speed and tore down the highway with the rest of the crowd and soon was out of North Carolina, crossing Lake Bowen, and exiting at Inman. Almost as soon as I exited the Interstate, I made a hard left and negotiated the now familiar back roads to Tim's, nestled just above a creek in a little cove defined by the treeline at the back side of a clearing.

Steve and his family had not arrived yet. Tim and I sat on the back porch, having cold beers, and watching the wooded background fringing the edge of the backyard. I had been here many times, and it was a home away from home of sorts and a comfortable spot to relax. Soon, Steve and his family arrived, and more beer followed. We all walked down to the creek and got reacquainted, and I got to know Steve's family members. Everyone got on great. We walked back up to the house, pizza was ordered, somehow the delivery person found the hideaway, and we all dug in while the beer and conversation flowed into the night. Knowing I had to get up early and hit the road, I eventually said my good nights and left the group, headed to my little tent pitched on the back lawn. The continuing revelry on the porch didn't affect my attempts to go to sleep at all after the long ride I had that day, and soon I was fast asleep.

I woke up early and was glad to have cut myself short on the booze the night before. I felt good and started gathering my things while the rest still slept. By the time I got things packed, Steve's wife had gotten up, and we chatted a bit before I got on the bike to go. Just as I was about to roll up the drive, Tim showed up, and I was able to say good-bye and thank him for the hospitality he was always ready to show.

I jumped back on the Interstate and headed south through the quiet morning. Soon I was past the bottleneck of I-26 and I-85 between Spartanburg and Greenville, but at this hour I barely noticed any congestion, and kept barreling toward my exit at Clinton, where I would leave the Interstate and start my trek home on back roads. I stopped at a Hardees at my exit and had coffee and a cinnamon roll.

That was the first food I had paid for since Kentucky. The budget was looking good.

I aimed south for Augusta, the only large city I would be passing through all the way south until home. I first rode SC 56 then veered right onto SC 39 which took me into Saluda. I turned on to SC 121 and about halfway to Augusta joined US 25.

Having ridden this route several times before, there was no need for stops to map check or ask directions. I made good time on the mostly empty country roads. I like this route. If you draw a line from Lake Wales to Inman the route came very close to following that straight line. Others usually take I-26 to I-95 to I-4 to US 27 home. Perhaps, they can get there in less time because of the higher speed limits, but I-26 veers toward the southeast to the coast before intersecting with I-95, which then veers southwest, making a huge elbow that juts out of the way. Going the way I did actually saved miles and forfeited only a little extra time. The biggest advantage of my route was the chance to see beautiful farm country drift by at a more relaxed pace and to pass through small towns that are mirrors of the past.

At Augusta, I hopped on the I-520 loop, once again catching US 25 on the south side, inside Georgia. From here, I followed 25 south into the land of pecan trees and yellow pines. Those familiar Georgia smells returned as I rode south. At Jesup, I chose US 301, leaving 25 to wander off into the southeast and to the coast without me. 301 shot straight for Florida. I rolled onward on quiet roads in the hot Georgia summer sun, crossing into Florida just past Folkston at the incursion Florida makes into Georgia's territory north of Jacksonville.

I had gone a week without any more rain than the single sunshower during my ride with the vintage motorcycles during the rally, so it was about time my luck ran out. Looking ahead to gathering clouds, the future looked darker and darker. Not far before my planned turn off on 301 to jump over to

FL 21 a virtual night was falling, although it was midday. I could see lightning searching out the ground on both sides of the highway dead ahead as the rain came on. I had seen the sheet of rain coming a while back and had stopped to don my rain pants and slip the rain liner into my mesh jacket. When the rain hit, it was a monsoon, and I struggled to see ahead. Soon, bolts of lightning were on both sides of me and the Bonnie, and flashes overhead coincided instantaneously with their loud booms of thunder. The lightning was directly overhead. I wondered what the chances were of a bike and rider being struck. In a car with its metal shield, if lightning hit, the current would run on only the outside of the metal, protecting the passengers inside, but I felt like a sitting duck with nothing but the top of my helmet between me and any mischievous bolts. There was nothing else to do but keep rolling. I'd lived in Florida for a long time and knew that these storms, while intense, often were not wide, and, eventually, I would pop out on the other side. I kept heading south as the trickles of water began their relentless pursuit of every chink in my "waterproof" layers. I could feel the water wick into my boots, and soon my feet were sloshing inside both of them.

By the time I exited the storm, I was soaked inside my outer clothing. I hoped the wind would start the drying process, although I knew my feet would be wet from then until I got home. I made it to 21 and then switched to FL 315. That took me to the north end of the Ocala National Forest. I reached the Cross Florida Barge Canal, an alternate route to the Okeechobee Waterway, that never was quite completed and fell just miles short of its intended connecting waterway of the Saint Johns River. Here I turned east on FL 310, headed for US 19, which cuts from north to south through the heart of the National Forest. At 19 I turned right and ran south as the clouds gathered in front of me again. By midway I was, once again, in a virtual night of rain and accompanying lightning. Vehicles in front of me slowed to a crawl as their flashers went on. I could see their tail lights and the white edge strip on the road, otherwise I might as well have been blind. But this storm was short lived, and I left it behind me as I emerged from the forest.

At Eustis, it was relatively clear, and I continued on. I slipped onto CR 561 toward Astatula and hoped I could get through to US 27 before dark. The light faded as I chased a couple slow cars through that section, where they robbed me of the fun of taking some great curves at more spirited speeds. I successfully arrived at US 27 before daylight was gone and turned south.

I was then just one county away from home. I sailed down the familiar stretch of highway, passing though Minneola, then Clermont. The pace picked up as the speed limit rose to sixty at Lake Louisa and I flew south in light traffic. As I approached Four Corners, where Orange, Lake, Osceola, and Polk Counties all met, the traffic increased and continued, as I passed west of Orlando and over I-4, the main corridor into the city Disney built.

At Davenport I normally bail off 27 and take FL 17, but I recalled that south of Haines City the highway was torn up for construction, so I stayed on 27 all the way to Dundee, south of the construction zone, and then finished my ride into Lake Wales on 17.

It was about eight o'clock when I pulled into Fuzzy's for my celebratory beer. I wondered if anyone would notice the five days' growth of beard that had developed over my features. I got the usual "Howdy Ozzy!" welcome and sipped the beer slowly, savoring the first thing I had put to my lips since breakfast. The budget was sufficient, barely, and I had less than ten dollars when I left Fuzzy's for the two mile ride home.

I dragged the bike into the garage and removed the bags to haul them into the house with me for unpacking in the morning. I walked into the house to find a still sick Andrea asleep. It would be another two weeks before Andrea would be out of that bed for good. I dumped my baggage and soon joined her for a solid night's sleep, comfortable at last in my own bed. I would now leave my traveling self behind, exchanging it for the role of caregiver.

I had traveled over 2,900 miles and covered eleven states. In spite of the responsibilities of family, I managed to stay on the road for eight days. I reconsidered my envy of Joe's freedom that a childless house offered him, and realized that being free means being willing to embrace adventure when the opportunities come along, even if that means shouldering responsibilities at the same time.

COLD RIDE TO CAROLINA

Maybe I should have seen the signs, but, then again, I am not a believer in signs anyway. But it is creepily eerie the stuff that was conspiring to mess up my perfectly planned trip to see my brother in Inman, South Carolina, just fifteen miles shy of the North Carolina state line, and to hunt deer for a couple days with him.

It had not been long since my return from a trip that had taken me from Lake Wales, in central Florida, to Barber Vintage Festival near Birmingham, Alabama, to northwestern Arkansas and southwestern Missouri, and back. During that trip I had worn out my rear brake and rotor, and the miles ticked over 12,000 on my Bonneville, which meant maintenance was due. That trip had also seen the last of the middle tread on my rear tire, so that had to be replaced before much more riding.

I tackled the brakes first, then turned my attention to the 12,000 mile scheduled maintenance, which included new air and fuel filters, and valve check and adjustment. I pulled the cam case cover and dutifully checked the valve clearance, hoping with the short time I had before leaving for Inman that I would find them all in spec, and all I would have to do was simply replace the cam cover and stick the filters in without further fuss. I was not so lucky.

The exhaust valves were all out of spec, loose from where they should have been. The intakes were spot on and needed no work. The Bonneville uses "shim and bucket" valve adjustment; where a "bucket" sits atop the valve stem and on top of this, inside a short lip, resides a "shim"—a 25 millimeter disk of varying thickness. By changing the shims to thicker or thinner you adjust the gap to be within specification. Which means you have to pull the existing shim to see what you have installed already, so that you can determine what you need to create the correct gap.

To get the shim out you have to remove the camshafts. With the camshafts out, of course, the bike is disabled until you can get new shims and reinstall them. I didn't have another bike to ride while the Bonnie was down because the CB350 was disassembled for restoration, and its parts were scattered around the small garage. While at home I could, if necessary, borrow my wife's car, but, of course, to get to Inman I would need my bike. I couldn't take the car, our only four-wheeled form of transportation, for that long. Time was ticking, and I had to get this job finished.

I pulled the camshafts and exhaust shims, measured them and calculated what I would need in new shims, and put my order in at my dealer. Meanwhile, I changed the oil and filter. When the shims arrived, so did the fuel and air filters. The filters went in without a hitch. Then I measured the shims I had received; none of them measured what I had requested and were not close enough to do a proper job. I knew the dealer was going to send me what they had on hand, so I was not surprised that a couple were used and one was rusty. That would not affect their utility at all, but what would was the thickness, which just didn't measure up.

I had already waited a few days, with the countdown clock ticking away for my departure for Inman. Now I was back at square one. The bike wasn't going anywhere without the proper shims. I had always had good luck ordering from Bike Bandit and generally received my stuff lightning fast, so instead of trying the dealer again, who had already disappointed me once, I went ahead and ordered new shims from Bike Bandit. However, I had missed that fine print on the web site saying that parts for Triumphs may take up to ten days. I didn't have ten days. I crossed my fingers and hoped for the best. Time crept on, and, panicking, I started calling other Triumph dealers. None had the shims I needed.

I ordered a new rear tire and waited some more for the shims, but as time passed with no change in the "On Order" status, I grew more frustrated. I vented my frustration on the Triumph Facebook page about what I thought should be a standard part that dealers should have on hand, being a regular maintenance component, being checked or changed every 12,000 miles. Soon, a representative of Triumph replied and offered to help out. We talked on the phone. I told him what I needed, and the next morning four shiny new shims, unused and in the correct sizes, arrived at my front door. I went back on Facebook and gave kudos to Triumph for their great customer support and got back to the job at hand, two days before the appointed day of departure for Inman.

The bike was done. I buttoned her back up and hit the starter button. I could hear the fuel pump re-priming and watched the gauges go left to right then back to left again, then thumbed the starter. The bike roared to life. Success. I turned it off, and then turned the ignition back on and went through the ritual again of waiting for the gauges before starting it again. I could still hear the pump. with its raucous re-priming sound, but when I hit the starter the bike lit right up. No engine light was on and no unusual sounds were coming from the engine. The next day the tire arrived, was mounted, and I was ready to go. The following morning, before light, I would head north for a one day ride of close to six hundred miles.

Or so I thought.

Friday morning at five o'clock, I drug myself out of bed and into my riding clothes and out to the garage to release the waiting bike, already loaded with baggage the night before. I rolled the bike outside into the cold and climbed on board, turned the key, and hit the starter. To my surprise, I saw the ominous orange "Check Engine" light glaring back at me from the speedometer. That wasn't there before! I turned the bike off, and what followed was hours of pulling the tank and looking for loose hoses, reinstalling the tank, and trying the motor, only to see that hateful light glowing on the speedo again, pulling the tank again, trying something else, then getting the same results. The bike seemed to run fine, but that little light kept telling me something was wrong. I rode the bike to the gas station and filled up, thinking perhaps the tank was not full enough for the pump to fully prime properly, but the light keep glaring back at me, defiant of everything I tried. I called the dealer for ideas at nine o'clock and got nothing I could use. By ten o'clock I gave up. The bike was still under warranty, and if I had ridden the bike in spite of the light's warning and something serious would have happened on the road I could be sure the warranty would be voided. I reluctantly called the dealer again, telling them I would be there in two hours.

I pulled the trailer around to the garage and loaded the bike, then headed southwest the hundred miles to the dealer.

Arriving at the dealer just before noon, the bike was unloaded and rolled into the shop, where the computer was hooked up to it. The bike was powered up and we waited for it to warm so the diagnosis could begin. The engine light was reset and now stayed off, but the computer gave no clue of what had happened. The mechanic and I tossed around ideas, and I settled on the idea that when I had first started the bike after installing the fuel filter and putting gas in the tank, that the pump must have not fully pressurized the fuel system and had sent the error message to the ECM. I knew to always let the gauges cycle before hitting the starter, because not doing so could cause electronic errors, but apparently waiting for the gauges to cycle was not enough. I should have waited for the buzzing and rattling sounds from the fuel pump to stop before starting the bike. Come to think of it, when I did start the bike the second time, I recalled hearing the pump still priming, which is a different sound than the pump normally pressurizing the fuel system. Why the light didn't come on then is still a mystery, but that diagnosis was the most logical.

Now the bike was ready, but I had another two hours to get it home, and then I would have to reload all the gear before leaving. I almost abandoned the idea of going, but I figured I could still salvage the ride by going as far as possible that day, and making the Saturday ride short. That would still leave me at least three-quarters of the hunting time I had planned on.

My departure time had changed from five AM to three thirty PM, when I finally I rolled out of the driveway with a new route planned to make up for lost time. I would head up on the turnpike and Interstates, instead of the more direct country road route I had planned through Ocala National Forest and southeast Georgia, and into South Carolina near Augusta. Going up I-75 gave me the option of crashing at my friend's house in Valdosta if I was exhausted by then, or, if not, I could roll on to Macon, where I could easily jump off in the morning and make Inman by mid-morning.

I was only two hours into the ride when darkness fell. I roared on in the darkness at more than seventy miles per hour on I-75. As I rode, the temperature kept falling.

By my dinner stop at Valdosta, where I would eat and decide if I could continue or needed to stop, I was freezing. I had my regular underwear and T-shirt on with thermal long underwear over it, followed on the bottom by leather-lined riding jeans and on top by sweatshirt, fleece-lined nylon shelled jacket, and thermal liner in my mesh riding jacket. Around my neck was a fleece hunting gaiter.

By the time I had eaten a hearty dinner of stew, cornbread, and coleslaw, I felt sufficiently warmed and called my friend,

Julie, and told her I was going to be continuing. Figuring that along the freeway I could easily stop from time to time and grab a coffee to rewarm myself, I pushed on.

I raced north on I-75 through the dark Georgia countryside. Normally, I would not ride after dark in Georgia, because the likelihood of deer strikes in Georgia was second only to Pennsylvania out of all the states in the US. On the Interstate I felt relatively safe, however, and I could stay on that until Macon, then look for a place to stay the night—a mere 216 miles from Inman. With luck, I could do that distance in four and a half hours. If I left Macon around five in the morning, I could make it by mid-morning to Tim's and our hunting grounds behind his house.

I got to Macon late in the bitterly cold night and took a jog onto I-16 exiting almost immediately onto US 129. I had been telling myself that surely I could find a place to stay where US 129 and I-16 met, which was the intersection of two major highways, after all. I took my exit and within minutes was in the countryside, but with nowhere to stop for the night. There were none of the expected Interstate exit motels, so, with no other choice, I moved through the night, expecting any time to have a deer jump into my path. My eyes darted left and right watching for my deadly enemy and for any sign of a motel at which I could stop and rest for the night. I had come on a mission to get a deer, but now the tables were turned and I feared that, instead, the deer would get me.

As I sped through the night, I realized a couple good things about riding in the cold. The first was that when you are freezing to death it is hard to get sleepy. I rode through the frigid night with eyes wide open. The second good thing was that when your core body temperature has fallen below the ambient air temperature your visor doesn't fog up anymore. So, wide awake and seeing clearly the road ahead, illuminated by my headlight, I kept on until, thankfully, spying a Days Inn in Gray. I pulled in, unattached my frozen limbs from the motorcycle, and stumbled in to request a room.

The room arranged, I walked back out and lifted the luggage from the bike and drug it with me to my second floor room. It was now a half hour past midnight, and the plan was to go right to sleep, bypassing the niceties of a shower that such rooms provide and, instead, just passing right out. In the morning I'd throw everything back on and get out as quickly as possible. Still shivering from the evening ride, I climbed under the covers.

I think I fell asleep before my hand reached back from turning off the bedside light. I woke a few times in the night, each time feeling itchy all over. I was too tired to care and each time fell back asleep. In the morning, in spite of the bed looking nice and clean when I jumped in it last night, I expected to find other hotel guests peppered across the sheets, but they were still spotless. Then it hit me. It wasn't bed bugs; it was probably my frozen skin cells returning to their normal state last night that had made me itch.

I had the television on just long enough to catch the temperature the night before. The local channel said it was 41 degrees, but I had my doubts, unless they meant 41 degrees below absolute zero. They said the temperature would be the same that morning. As I rode in the pre-dawn, the frost was on the fields, grass, and cars I passed parked beside the road. For water to freeze like that it must have been less than 32 degrees. As I rode away, I wondered what the wind-chill would reduce that to at sixty-five or seventy miles per hour.

I was back in the saddle again, riding once more on the Georgia back roads in the dark and the cold. I tried to stay behind occasional cars, using them as a kind of shield against deer strikes and also utilizing their headlights as an auxiliary to mine, which, in spite of being adjusted time and again, generally lit the cloud bottoms when turned on "bright" rather than the road ahead, and on "low" illuminated the tarmac a few feet in front of the bike.

Eventually, the sky lightened, and I was struck by how long at these higher latitudes it took to go from pre-dawn glow to full sunshine, compared to the off-on semi-tropical dawns of Florida. With the light I would have thought would come warmer temperatures, but, of course, as the day progressed I was progressing northward and to cooler climes, negating any increase in warmth the rising sun might have imparted.

It wasn't until north of Athens, Georgia, that dawn finally became day. I rode the loop around the city and out the other side onto US 441. Within a half hour I had come to Interstate 85, which aimed me northeast toward Spartanburg, South Carolina, and my turn-off toward Inman.

Crossing Lake Hartwell and entering South Carolina brought traffic, which thickened as the day went on. It was now Saturday, however, so I was spared much of the normal traffic around Greenville and made good time, spying my exit onto I-26 North soon after. I was almost there, with only three exits to go. Finally, I turned onto Asheville Highway and immediately took a left on a small side road, finishing the 620 mile trip with a two mile ride down the winding dirt road, arriving at Tim's place in a little clear pocket among the woods at around quarter 'til ten.

After a quick hello, I pulled my camo over the clothes I had ridden in. I assembled the shotgun I had strapped behind me on the back of the bike, and off into the woods behind the house we went. Tim took the ravine to the east that followed the creek, and I walked downhill to the north, climbing into the tree stand Tim and I had built a few months ago on an earlier visit that looked down across the creek and up the wooded hillside toward the house. Then it occurred to me that I had ridden exhausted in the cold to get here and then climbed exhausted into the stand to sit for hours in the cold. Now, *that's* a vacation.

Tim and I used to hunt deer in Florida, but I gave it up after hunting for seven years and bringing one deer home about the size of a greyhound, and then Tim had moved away. All we had to hunt on was public wildlife management areas, and they were under such pressure that it was rare to even see deer, let alone put some meat on the table. Tim now, however, had bought some acreage that included woods and a stream. The first day he hunted here he bagged two deer, and another followed not long after that. So, as I sat and shivered in my tree, I had high hopes of finally having some venison for the freezer. If I was successful, Tim could haul my bounty down in a few weeks when he came south for his daughter's graduation from the University of South Florida.

Hours passed, then a walk back to the house for a quick lunch of venison barbecue, which was followed by a climb back into the tree until evening. The wind blew chill, and the temperature fell again as night came on. There were no deer today, but we had the consolation of a fire in the fireplace and a venison tenderloin on the grill for dinner. Tomorrow, we surely would have better luck.

In the morning, I woke to deer sausage and gravy with biscuits, and then, once again, we were in the woods. We sat until noon, went in for more barbecue, and then out again until nightfall, seeing nothing but squirrels. The hunting gods were not smiling on us, and my time had run out.

The next morning, I left before light, heading south now on the route I had intended to take on the way up. Google Maps estimated 557 miles, compared to the 580 miles an Interstate route via I-26, I-95, and I-4 would yield, and I would be able to ride on back roads, which I vastly prefer to freeway travel. My desire to have venison in our freezer now depended on my brother getting another deer before he came down in the middle of December.

In the dark and cold once again, I headed south on I-26, crossing my previous route and getting off at Clinton, South Carolina. From here my route was south on SC 56 and SC 72 to SC 39, as the light crept into the eastern sky. I was supposed to follow 39 to Saluda and SC 121, which would take me to US 25 just past Trenton and on to I-20, just east of Augusta and the Georgia state line. Instead, I missed 121 and kept following 39, which eventually dumped onto I-20, but much farther east than I had intended. I reestablished my bearings and soon was heading toward Augusta where I was to take 415 around the city and join US 25 in Georgia. Again, I zoomed right past my exit and pulled off at the next one to get fuel. I swore I had not seen a sign for the by-pass, the same for 121 back at Saluda. I began to have little faith in South Carolina road signs, which must be on the bottom of the budget list of things to do when maintaining roads in that state.

It turned out I had exited onto US 25, so after gassing up and getting some calories in me by means of some toast and hot black coffee, I got back on 25 and headed south into Georgia. Luckily, this route did not pass through too much of the city as I had thought it would, and soon I was back in the Georgia countryside among cotton fields and pecan groves.

US 25 flowed through the east Georgia farmland, through Statesboro, Jessup, and on to Folkston and US 1, just north of the Florida border.

By now I had been able to remove the gaiter, but that was the extent of my disrobing. I was glad to be rid of it as it had caused my neck to become stiff by not allowing my head to tilt backwards, being bunched up under the back of my helmet. The air was still cold, but bearable without the gaiter, and with my inner jacket's collar zipped up under my neck.

I was back in familiar territory for a while, having ridden US 1 through Georgia more than once before on my way to the Blue Ridge Mountains on other trips. I again split from the familiar road at Callahan, continuing on to Jacksonville and the I-295 by-pass. Back on the Interstate, I sped south only as far as US 17, and, after passing Orange Park and Green Cove Springs, I was out of most of the traffic all the rest of the way to Palatka.

Palatka is the northern gateway to the Ocala National Forest, and, checking my fuel to be sure I could come out the other side not walking instead of riding, I got on US 19 for the ride through the forest.

It was now late afternoon and still chilly, with clouds blotting out the sky and a frigid breeze working its way under my clothing. I wanted to be sure of being out the other side of the forest before darkness fell. I succeeded and even made it through Eustis, Mount Dora, and out onto US 27, by way of County Road 561, before the light faded completely.

Now back in the dark, I was on the lookout for some food. I knew I would be home too late for cooking dinner there, so I was thinking a small steak would fit the bill nicely to finish up the trip. I kept an eye out for a place to procure one and soon came across a Santa Fe Steakhouse. I went inside, took off a couple of layers and started the rewarming procedure while enjoying my last meal on the road. A sirloin and more coffee consumed, soon I was back on the road with only one more stop to make before riding into the driveway.

I had a traditional stop at my local hangout, Fuzzy's, which was only a couple miles from the house, for a single celebratory beer before returning home from my trips. This is a place where I feel like Norm of *Cheers* fame, where I was usually greeted by warm shouts of "Ozzy!" when I walked in. The moniker "Ozzy" was due to a likeness I am supposed to have to the Black Sabbath singer. I don't believe more than two of the patrons know my real name.

I arrived at home about seven PM, about thirteen hours and 580 miles after I had left my brother's place, making the total mileage 1,200 miles. I learned something on the trip: I do not mind riding in the cold, and I do not mind riding for hour on end, but it would be a long time before I would combine the two.

To the VJMC National Rally in North Georgia

1,365 more miles have just passed beneath Old Faithful, my venerable 1968 Honda CB350. I had only recently finished putting the scattered bike's pieces back together after a year of disassembly, following the discovery of a cracked frame. The bike was finally started and running correctly just three days before leaving for the 2013 Vintage Japanese Motorcycle Club's National Rally at Helen, Georgia

The Ride North

The computer calculated that the rally was 553 miles north from my home in central Florida. What the computer doesn't know is what it is like to sit on one of these motorcycles for over twelve hours and that mortals need a break from sitting on the hard metal seat pan, covered by the thinnest of foam every couple hours, at least. Not only that, but the buzzing and whirring of those 325ccs of sheer power at 6,500 rpm on the Interstate is not conducive to an enjoyable ride. So, I recalculated via less trafficked roads with this information in mind. The route only stretched to 568 miles in length, but running this new route would extend the ride from about twelve hours to fourteen because of all the passages through small towns along the way.

I had planned on heading out at about four in the morning on Thursday, the 20th, in order to get past the traffic and interminable stoplights in the stretch of US 27 between Leesburg and Ocala that cause this area to be like a long thin parking lot at any time between sunrise and sunset. The night before my departure, I whisked the kids off to their grandparents, who would watch them until my wife came home from her business trip, went home and packed up the bike, set my cell phone alarm for four, and went to bed. I slept fitfully and woke before two, unable to get back to sleep. With the kids gone and everything sitting on the bike and ready to roll, I decided that two was as good as four to leave, so I threw on my riding clothes, all laid out the night before, opened the garage and rolled "Old Faithful" out into the drive in the dim light, climbed on board, and, just for kicks, jumped on the kickstarter and fired her up.

This trip was like every other one I had taken on the CB350; the beginning filled with worry about the bike and its ability to drone on as long I was going to be asking it to. Every noise I couldn't immediately identify became cause for concern and every gust of head wind causing a drop in momentum was interpreted as an engine problem. But, as always, as the miles added up, my confidence grew in the little Honda. By the time I would park the bike for the night in the little north Georgia town of Helen, Old Faithful would have lived up to her moniker, once again.

I rode north past sleeping houses and honked when I passed Fuzzy's, my local biker bar, as they were closing up. In spite of the ninety-five degree afternoons we had been having already, the night air was cool, and I was glad I had zipped in my liner in my mesh riding jacket for the ride north. I turned north on US 27 and flew along the all but deserted four lane.

Before I knew it I had passed Interstate 4, then Clermont and Mineola, and then Ocala. With Ocala behind me the road passed increasingly through blackened countryside.

US 27 veered west, and I left it, veering north on US 41 at High Springs. I passed under 1-75 and rolled toward Valdosta as the sun was making its way over the horizon. US 41 and US 129 had been sharing the road since just south of Jasper, Florida, and at Jasper they again parted ways with me buzzing into Georgia on 129 as the eastern sky lightened. As morning progressed I approached Macon, and, by clever use of US 129 Alt, I bypassed the city and rejoined US 129 north of Macon and I-16. I could have followed 129 almost all the rest of the way, but that would mean a transit of Athens on the Interstate-like by-pass. So, at Gray, I split off to the north and west on GA 11 aiming to miss Athens and its traffic completely, joining back up with US 129 just before crossing I-85 north of the city.

High clouds had kept me pretty cool while I passed dormant cotton fields and bright green pecan groves, but, on 11, Georgia did what Georgia does in the summer—got hot—and I removed my jacket liner, letting the air flow through the jacket and across my T-shirt. In the mid-afternoon I passed under the last of six Interstates and rolled into Cleveland, Georgia. Here 129 went on without me, and I turned right for the final nine or so miles into Helen on GA 75.

It was scorching at four when I entered the parking lot at the Helendorf Inn, where I would be glad to step off the 350, strip off the jacket, and have my butt anywhere but on the saddle of that bike.

In the parking lot, I found a parking spot amid the hundreds of both vintage and modern motorcycles, many parked, and many buzzing here and there like excited bees. I climbed off the Honda and looked around to find Peter, my friend and organizer of this big event, who could fill me in on check-in procedures. I was keen to rid myself of these hot riding clothes and get into shorts and a T-shirt and out of my boots. I found

Peter quickly—with his larger than life presence he stands out in a crowd—and after answering in the affirmative the many "Did you ride up on that thing!?" queries from other members, I got my instructions and walked off to check-in, returning to the bike, room key in hand. I found a shaded spot, nearer the entrance to the hotel, and moved the CB there.

Unloading the bike, I once again was glad I had shelled out the money for the Cortech soft sport saddlebag and top bag system. These bags are held to the bike with simple frame-attached straps with quick disconnects, so getting them off-loaded took mere seconds, and carrying them to the room was easy thanks to the built-in carrying handles. My old First Gear magnetic tankbag was even easier and I wandered up to the third floor taking all my kit at one time, opening my door to the most welcome seventy-three degree, air-conditioned room.

I laid my bags out on the low bench just inside the room and started digging for cooler clothes to wear, then jumped in the shower for a refreshing cleanse.

The Rally

Back outside, I now could enjoy wandering around the many bikes, taking photographs of the crowd and the amazing examples of like-new classic bikes, while bumping into old acquaintances and making new ones. This was one of the main reasons for me being here, to get acquainted with the many members I would soon be working with as a new member of the board and editor of the club's magazine, *Vintage Japanese Motorcycle Magazine*. The sudden departure of the former editor had left the club in the lurch, and with my experience with designing and publishing books I had been asked to fill his shoes.

Being a loner and social wallflower, I took my time wandering around but made an effort to start meeting other members, while taking in the festive atmosphere. The first night's club dinner was not until six o'clock, so I had a couple hours to take it easy, look at the bikes, and ease myself into this social situation. I wandered from bike to bike, greeting those I already knew and making small talk about bikes with those I did not. I eventually made my way to the back side of the inn and watched the many tubers float by on the river that was situated just outside the shaded hotel patio.

Once I had taken in most of the sights at the inn, I realized parts of me were still buzzing from the road, so I decided to walk around the corner into town and find a cool corner where I could enjoy a cold beer and relax while my body and mind made the transition from the road to the pedestrian life off the bike. Literally around the corner, I found a spot at a Mexican restaurant. I sat in the cool air-conditioning watching the parade and ordered a beer: "¡Dos Equis, por favor!" and was asked, "Large or small?" "Large, of course!" To my surprise, large was thirty-six ounces. I thought, "I would make a great first impression at the dinner if I showed up drunk!" so I sipped on the first twenty-four or so ounces, snacked on tortilla chips and just enough spicy salsa, then headed back to the hotel and dinner, leaving a full regular bottle worth of beer in my glass to be wastefully poured into some sink.

When I arrived at the meeting hall below the hotel and adjacent to the river view patio, people were already in line for their food, the line starting, apparently, a few minutes early. Attendance had exceeded expectations and the room was full of members and their friends and spouses. The large hall was filled with over a hundred and sixty people, and I was told attendance broke all records for the club's national rally, not to mention any of the regional ones.

I sat with Peter and, between mouthfuls of pulled-pork, talked to him and the other table mates and got the lay of the land and the schedule. After dinner, over cold beers and conversation and tales of one restoration after another with other members, I continued to get to know my vintage motorcycle peers, while my eyelids slowly dropped lower and lower. When the talk started coming through in little snippets of "...the carburetor wasn't the problem..." and "...the camshaft was out by three one-thousandths..." without the accompanying context to make sense of it all, I told everyone I had to call it a night. I left them to their verbal wanderings while I drug myself upstairs to my waiting bed. I stripped out of my clothes and crawled into the clean cool sheets. I had forgotten that I had been up since two in the morning racing though the darkness on my way up to Helen, but my body hadn't forgotten and took quick advantage of my prone position to send me into a solid unconsciousness, unbroken until my cell phone alarm roused me the next morning.

The board meeting was planned for early this morning. I was to meet fellow members for a ride to a local restaurant for breakfast, followed by a half-day long board meeting. I bypassed the snooze button and hopped out of bed, threw a coffee packet in the machine, dashed into and out of the shower, wolfed the coffee down, and made my way downstairs to the waiting group of vehicles. I climbed in Tom's and made the ride over an exercise in getting to know another member. The ride was short and at the restaurant, sitting around a acre-worth of tabletop while devouring eggs and drinking hot coffee, I got a better chance to learn names and roles and find out how the organization worked. Before the abruptness of the appointment to the editorship and resultant board member standing, I had not fully understood the organizational management and how it all worked together, and now I was in the middle of it. For getting a start on understanding the organization of the club of which I was now a managing member, the meeting was very helpful. As a result, I finally had a fundamental working flowchart of the club management, which would be crucial as work at my new duties got underway.

The meeting ended just after noon. Returning to the inn, we were on our own for lunch. I opted for a quick salad at Wendys, directly across from the inn. I wanted to get back to the staging area to join in a ride planned for the afternoon, following twisting and windy roads to Suches and back. There had been four different routes planned for the rally, each one catering to different people's skills and riding preferences. I had chosen one that was more technical in nature, with more twists and turns, and which required more advanced skills to ride it safely. I got back just in time to roll my CB350 up to join the four other riders—a nice size group for the more challenging ride we had in store. I had been in the area a few weeks before on my Bonneville and rode roughly in the same area we were heading to, so I knew the route would be my favorite kind of riding. I would not be disappointed.

As we rode along, me trailing a fellow member on a CB450 and being tailed by a Honda NX650, I started recognizing the route from my ride here not long before. There was a double curve that gave me a fright before, while riding on wet pavement, when I found myself in a bit too hot. I had trail braked through the very short straight between the initial right and second left turn, and my rear wheel started to step out. Gentle easing of the rear brake as I entered the second curve kept me upright that time. This time it caught me again, although not so bad as before, but enough to startle me. While my entry speed was fine for the first curve, the second was much tighter, turning ninety degrees left across a bridge, with not enough straight between the two to slow sufficiently and I found myself flying through the second, leaning for all I was worth, and, thankfully, not dragging hard parts as I went. I was smart enough this time, however, to ease off the brake well before entering the second curve and had no rear end slide. I made a mental note for the future to not only calculate speed into each curve but also to take into consideration what might happen after that curve. What doesn't kill you makes you smarter, right?

After a mid-ride break, we continued and eventually rode back toward Helen, taking GA 348 southeast and up one of the steepest grades I think I have ever ridden, requiring wide open throttle in fourth gear on the little CB350 to climb it at a modest, but ever diminishing speed. We stopped for a quick photograph of the group three-quarters up the grade at an overlook, and, upon leaving, I opted for higher revs in third gear, which made the rest of the climb more manageable.

Back at the inn, there was time for taking more photos, hoping to get something useful for the upcoming, and my first, magazine issue, which I had been told must have an article on the national rally in it. Soon, Friday's group dinner was ready and we all started filing back toward the meeting hall on the river. At the board meeting we were asked to sit at tables at dinner where there were others not on the board and who we didn't know, and to try to encourage talk about the members' impressions of the rally, to act as receptive ears to suggestions that might improve event in the future, and to generally get to know more of our members. For me, doing the new editorial work posed its own challenges, but making myself into a social and outgoing person was going to be the hardest part of my new role. I found the way to get myself over my shyness was just to throw myself into the new scene, so I did just that, sitting down at a table filled with unfamiliar faces and throwing out immediately a "How do you like the rally, what would you change, and what would you like to see in the magazine?" question to the group. The group I was with responded positively and offered ideas toward improvement, and I was glad I had found the courage to jump right in.

After dinner, we sat back nibbling on leftovers, sipping drinks, and listening to a talk about the history of Yamaha motorcycles from a fellow who had been with Yamaha for thirty-five years. He started with the early '60s and, by the end of the evening, finished up in the '90s, illustrating his talk with projected images of just about every model Yamaha had dreamed up during those years.

As the crowd cleared out, some of my fellow board members and several other club members found ourselves once again sitting in the hall and shooting the breeze about this or that old bike and the differences between that year's model and the next, while downing ice cold beers. Eventually, a new friend, Jack, suggested we go out and have a couple beers somewhere in town, so we made our exit and headed onto the main street, searching for a place to sit back, chill, and talk.

The first place we found had a cover charge and we, feeling indisposed to pay to get in, went on to the next place, where music could be heard floating out onto the street from a balcony. We shouted up to a few people gathered on the balcony and asked if there was a cover charge. "No, no cover charge here!" So, we made our way up the stairs to the awaiting bouncer, who then asked us for the cover charge. Rats; we were there now, what the hell; so we paid the charge and went into the noisy bar. Inside was a scene I recalled from when I was young and single, with a darkened space punctuated with flashes of intense light and booming, modern "disco" music, for lack of a better term, while young girls lined up on a miniscule dance floor in their miniscule dresses to shake their nubile bodies to the boom-boom-boom. Not that I was adverse to watching those young girls dance, but it was the kind of place I had assumed in my long absence would be as extinct as a pterodactyl. We decided the way to have any chance of having any kind of conversation was to step out on the balcony with our beers. Out there we could still get a look at the crowd, while still being able to hear each other and possibly return home with some hearing left. The night air was pleasant and we talked about the club, about money and women, and what it took to get by or ahead in this world, while the forthcoming beers lubricated the conversation. After adequate imbibing, and with more in store for tomorrow, we both returned to the hotel and hit the hay. I was surprised at myself when I realized I had exceeded the midnight hour, considering at home I am often snoring by ten o'clock. I made a point of drinking a couple large glasses of water before retiring, in hopes of staving off the effects of dehydration my beer drinking might bring on in the morning.

The water did its trick. I woke up and rolled out of bed after only a couple bumps of the snooze on the alarm, feeling no worse for wear. Jack and I had made plans to get together for breakfast, but after the appointed hour had come and gone and a half hour extra had expired, Jack was not to be found. No harm done, I figured. Jack was a big boy and either we got our times mixed up or he simply decided to sleep in. I bumped into another friend and went to breakfast with him at a Huddle House, a couple buildings away, filling up on coffee, eggs, bacon, and sausage gravy.

With a full stomach, I grabbed my camera and headed over to where the bike show would be held that afternoon to take a look at the gathering crowd of contenders and to take more photos for the magazine. There were classes for Yamahas, Hondas, Suzukis, café racers, competition bikes, and "modern classics." Many bikes would be entered, among them a collection of pristine Honda six-cylinder CBXs, old Honda Dreams, two-stroke dirt bikes, a rare rotary-powered bike, a collapsible motorcycle not bigger than a suitcase, CB450s, CB and CL350s, a Kawasaki W650, and many more.

My photo duties accomplished, I decided to try and fit in a quick, solo ride somewhere. While I enjoy the dynamics of a group ride, I wanted the freedom to choose my own route and speed while I had the opportunity in these Blue Ridge Mountains. I headed out of Helen by way of GA 75 north. Brasstown Bald was not far, and it has the distinction of being the highest point in Georgia—as good a destination as any other. At GA 180, I pointed the little CB northwest and started climbing. Soon I was at 180 Alt, the entrance to the park, where I discovered the climb had only just begun and a grade that challenged GA 348 for steepness. Shifting down into second gear now, I started my ascent, twisting and turning my way to the parking lot at the base of the bald, paid the modest fee while chatting with the attendant about how his first bike was a CB350, parked Old Faithful, and climbed off the quiet, panting bike. The little Honda had developed an oil leak, probably originating under the tach cover, and, although it was minor, not even requiring me to add oil on the trip up and back from Florida, it did make a bit of a mess. Getting off her now at Brasstown Bald, the beads of oil on the engine, I imagined, were the motor's imitation of sweat, a result of her exertions getting up here. With an appreciative pat on the tank, I turned and walked up the hill to the area where people waited for the tram to the top, leaving Old Faithful to rest. I glanced toward a trail on my right and noticed a sign that said 0.6 miles to the summit. "Heck! I walk about that same distance every day back home to pick up my daughter at the school crossing to walk her home. How hard can it be?"

My confidence resulted in a quick pace, and I thought I would soon be on the mountaintop looking down on the surrounding countryside. That initial pace did not last long, as I realized what the climb I was in for was going to be like. I quit passing other hikers and found it necessary to rest every once in a while on the way up the difficult grade. Not willing to be defeated, however, I finally found the top and climbed the flights of stairs to the observation deck, atop the visitors' center. My breath slowly returning, I walked the perimeter of the circular deck, trying to see if I could identify what I was seeing in the distance haze with a town here, a lake over there, while the blue ridges of the mountains rolled away like ocean waves to the horizon all around.

I took more photos and looked at my watch. I was running out of time before lunch and a meeting I had set up with an author who lived in the area near Helen, who I was hiring to write a new teacher's guide to an English textbook I was republishing. At this rate I was going to be a minimum of half an hour late for our meeting. Should I take the tram back down or the path? The tram would have to be quicker, but after what seemed like a very long time, with no tram in sight, I headed back down the trail. As I was hoofing it through the tree-lined walkway, my phone rang with a text message. Cathy had arrived early. I texted her back and told her I was on my way but running behind. Luckily, she had some shopping to do and would wait to hear from me when I got back. Being mindful of the severe grade I had ridden up, I took it easy on the way down in a lower gear, not wanting to wear the brakes out keeping my speed in check. At the bottom, I turned onto GA 180 west. I knew this road connected to GA 348 and its challenging grade that would lead me back to Helen. I managed the mountain climb much better, this time in third gear most the way up.

More than a half hour after our originally scheduled time, I found Cathy sipping a drink and snacking on chips at the Mexican restaurant where I had ordered the jumbo beer on my first night in town and that we had chosen as our meeting place. No harm done, Cathy assured me, and we ordered lunch while we discussed the guide, and I handed her the textbook manuscript and the original teacher's manual that I had brought with me in a saddlebag. I wolfed down my meal, while we made sure we both understood each other and what needed to be done with this project. I was already late for the start of the bike show, so we said our good-byes and went our separate ways—Cathy back to Murphy, North Carolina, and I back to the hotel and bike show.

The bike show area was now filled with more than seventy motorcycles. I once again took photos for use in the magazine and for the club's website. Once I had gotten what I thought were sufficient numbers and varieties of shots, I checked the rally schedule again and decided I could get one more ride in before tonight's banquet and the bike show awards ceremony.

I pulled out my Georgia map once again and studied it for possibly interesting routes. This ride would have to be a shorter one, so I chose GA 356 north and east to GA 196 and toward Lake Duncan. I had planned to explore some smaller roads south of the lake, but blew past the turn and continued north without realizing what I had done. Finally coming to US 76 I could see that it would take me east across the north side of the lake to Clayton, where I could head back south on

US 441 and take the same roads back west across the south side of the lake that I had intended to take east, completing a loop back to 196. From there back to Helen I would return the way I had come. Once off 441 with all its traffic, the ride back was a pleasant run along gently winding roads through green countryside, with lake houses punctuating the roadside.

Arriving back in Helen, I was ensnarled in the bumper-to-bumper weekend tourist traffic, and it took me almost as much time to get three blocks across town as it had to get to the lake. The day had become hot, and I was broiling in my jacket, sitting still in the sun in the traffic, and was relieved when I finally turned into the hotel parking lot. A shower was required by now, so I headed up to the room to cool down and clean up before the banquet.

Dinner was just beginning to be served when I entered the hall from the river entrance, camera hanging from my neck. That night it was important to get good pictures, especially of each bike show award winner, along with general images that were representative of the event.

I lined up, picking up plate and utensils, and loaded up on a little bit of everything, ending up with a heaping plate. I decided to once again join a table of members I had not had much interaction with so far, and we all made small talk and bike talk throughout the meal. It turns out I had chosen a seat with the crew from Atlanta Motorcycle Works, who were the generous donors of the show trophies, and who were dedicated to making a living bringing all sort of vintage bikes back to life, either as restorations or customizations. We all decided the desert was too good to pass up, even already being stuffed by the evenings victuals, and hot black coffee sealed the deal.

The meal over, attention turned to the bike show. Award winner after award winner walked to the stage to receive their trophies, culminating, of course, in Best of Show. I stood dutifully near a column at the front, hoping not to block too many members' views and clicked away at each winner as they shook hands with Tom, our president, and Gordon, another board member. Thank yous went out next to all the various people who's hard work had made the event and club a success, and the evening ended with a blitz of door prizes handed out to many members. Donors had been so generous in fact, that you were the odd man out if you walked out without winning something. As the gathering came to the end and before everyone would wander off to fulfill their independent plans for the rest of the evening, the crowd was asked about the rally and how they felt about it. When asked if they would like to see another major event hosted in Helen, a unanimous raising of hands in approval let the board and volunteers know they had done a good job. That was the best reward possible in return for all the hard work putting the rally together.

As the crowd filtered out, our after dinner group once more gathered around in the emptying hall and, between gulps of cold beer and chasers of Crown, chatted about motorcycles and the event, now successfully completed. We all stayed way too long, considering the early departure most of us had in mind for the morning.

For the last time I climbed the stairs to my room to get some sleep. After taking a quick, final shower before climbing into bed, though, I made sure all the bike's bags were packed and ready to go, with only my riding clothes laid out for the morning. I had been riding in the one and only pair of riding jeans and jacket I own for the entirety of the trip, so perhaps that shower was wasted as I would, for the last time, pull on those unwashed jeans and jacket and hit the road through the sweltering Georgia heat.

Riding Home

I had gotten up early, but was not in a hurry, having decided already that I was not going to chance riding through the Georgia countryside in the dark morning hours. If I was to ride in the dark it would be on the Florida end of the ride, where deer strikes were much less likely. I threw the Cortechs over the saddle and snapped them to their frame-mounted buckles and the top bag onto the saddlebags. The tank bag went on, and I once again Velcroed the GPS to the handlebars, just in case, even though my speedometer had started working steadily again. I said good-bye to the few other members milling around the entrance, getting their own things together for their return trips, threw my leg over the top bag, turned the key, kicked the start lever, and rolled out of the Helendorf Inn parking lot, this time bound for home.

The few days I had at Helen with only occasional rides had given my butt a chance to recover, but I knew on the ride home the pain returning was inevitable. The day before I had talked to my wife, hoping to get an approval to split the ride into two days, making the seat time each day much less. Fortunately for Andrea, but unfortunately for my butt, she had started a new job the week before. Part of the job requirements was traveling three out of five days a week to meet agents with whom she hoped to do business, and Monday was her first day on the road. The kids were out of school and could not be left without an adult for the day. I had to be back Sunday evening, so I could be daycare for the kids.

With this news, I decided to minimize, as much as possible, my time on the road and headed back by way of US 129, this time circling Athens on the by-pass to save time. Arriving at what I thought was Clermont, I turned left at a sign pointing to US 129 and dutifully rode on. It was not long before I knew something was wrong. After that turn, I had not seen another US 129 sign. I thought about turning back, but took a look at my map after spotting a sign to Lula, a small community east of US 129. I had to be on GA 52. Then I saw a sign for 52 pointing left. I turned expecting this road would reconnect to US 129 further south, so there was no need to turn back and waste miles when all I had done so far is taken a small detour. Arriving back at US 129, I thought it was odd that the sign for 129 South was to the left, but there it was, clear as could be. I turned left and immediately was plunged into déjà vu. I had seen all that before. As I passed my original errant turn off US 129, I realized I had not left at Clermont, but at Gainesville, several miles south of where I thought I had been. I had run the 52 loop detour backwards and ended up well before where I had started. As I whizzed past the spot I had mistakenly turned, I saw, once again, a clearly marked sign to turn left for US 129; this time I ignored it and kept going straight. The time I thought I had saved by heading straight toward Athens instead of around it was lost I thought, but at least I was back on track now. There was nothing to do until I was in Florida but to follow US 129, the only exception being US 129 Alt to by-pass Macon.

I negotiated the Athens by-pass with no trouble and was soon scooting south toward Macon. The little 325ccs I often have misgivings about upon my departure on these trips had not let me down once and had proven perfectly capable of running Interstate speeds. As I neared the Florida line, I decided to make up for lost time, so once I got on US 41 and crossed Interstate 75, I would take 75 south and eventually jump over to US 27 via the Florida Turnpike, south of the Ocala and Lady Lakes area. This would save me from riding through that area during the day time and in typical heavy traffic, with stop light after stoplight requiring me to bake in my jacket.

I-75 shot relatively straight south through the heart of Florida. This part of the ride I knew by heart and there was no need to replace my Georgia map in my tankbag with a Florida one. Before I knew it I had passed the Wildwood exit and arrived at the Florida Turnpike, which veered south-southeast toward a meeting with US 27 south of Leesburg and the worst of the US 27 traffic.

A dollar and a quarter and twenty-five miles later, I rolled onto US 27, the main north-south route that passed through the western edge of Lake Wales. From here it was an easy ride with moderate traffic. I left US 27 a few miles north of Lake Wales and got on FL 17 for the rest of the way into town, so I could stop in at Fuzzy's once again for my traditional, celebratory single beer before gliding into the driveway at home.

The return ride was 556 miles, and, even with my detour on GA 52, I had beat my outgoing time by an hour. I rolled into the drive and did my usual circle across the grass, parking the bike nose-to-nose with Andrea's car, so I could roll the CB backward into the garage next to my sleeping Bonneville, with it parked facing the street, ready to go the next time.

The Trip I Didn't Take

As you get closer to the end of life than the beginning, you tend to look at things differently. You no longer dream of what you can do in the future. Instead, you contemplate the dreams you have and wonder how many of them you can fit in the time you have left and how to do that.

Fifty-six years had come and gone, and, although I'd had adventures in my youth, sailing boats and visiting exotic places, I now realized how many places I have not visited and how little I'd done. Although time had always been ticking away, I was suddenly, it seemed, acutely aware of it. What seemed could be put off forever, didn't seem so anymore. I calculated how many years were left, and, even more importantly, how many *good* years were left—years when I would still be able to physically do the things I would like to and ride the places I'd dreamed of.

After my adventurous youth, I settled down to home and family life, fitting in a riding trip now and then for a few short days, perhaps a week, then quickly returning. As my kids grew along with my love of riding, so did my dream ride list—one of these days, when the kids can be left alone, after school has

181

started. When the kids are in college, I thought, "How old will I be?" The answer came back, "Sixty-two when my son goes; sixty-five when my daughter does." "When they are out of college, I'll be close to seventy," I told myself. "When was I going to ride those dream rides, if I didn't start now?"

With the truth of my mortality vividly in mind, I finally decided to take a stab at whittling down that list of rides. "This one is going to be epic," I told myself. Even though it would be only a bit over two weeks long and not across a continent, it would be a start. As the kids grow older and I could be away longer, I could slowly stretch out my wanderings, but, for now, this would do and start shortening that list.

Just after I graduated from high school, I had taken a trip with my dad. It was a journey I would remember bits and pieces of for years. Those fond traveling memories would prompt me later to set out on other adventures. We had not really travelled far, just a few hundred miles from our home in southwestern Michigan to the Upper Peninsula and Mackinac Island, to Tahquamenon Falls, then along the south shore of the peninsula to Wisconsin, and concluding with a ferry ride across the great Lake Michigan and the final drive south to home. I had always wanted to return and recapture at least some of those memories of misty fog and pine trees, long stretches of deserted beaches, cold air rustling tree limbs, tannin tinted waterfalls, and glacier deposited boulders.

I now had a suitable bike for a lengthy journey, having outfitted my Triumph Bonneville with a touring saddle, a tail rack and bag, a tank bag that doubled as a map holder, and a versatile set of soft panniers with top bag. I even had rigged my automobile GPS onto the handlebars to back up the paper maps. While not capable of super long stretches without refueling, the Bonnie had much longer legs than my old CB350, which required fresh fuel every hundred miles. On the Bonnie I could stretch that out to over a hundred and forty, if need be. I had also mounted two MSR fuel bottles, thirty ounces each, one on each side of the bike on the passenger peg struts, giving me an emergency supply for another twenty miles or so, and doubling as a fuel supply for my miniscule camp stove.

As I planned my escape, studying map after map, the ride grew. Instead of heading north-northwest to Michigan, I would make this a multiple destination ride. If you drew a line due north from our home in central Florida, you would eventually pass very near my brother's place in Inman, South Carolina, just fifteen miles south of the border of North Carolina with its magical roads. Tim had just bought a new bike, too. I could ride up and join him for some spirited riding north and slightly east across North Carolina, into Tennessee, sweeping through the western tail of Virginia, and into West Virginia, taking US Route 52 along the east side of the Sandy Rider that, flowing north, empties into the Ohio. That would be a fairly easy day's ride, and we could camp just before the Ohio River crossing. The next day Tim could return home, and I could cross over, finishing phase one of the three phase ride.

After a short ride along the Ohio River, I would head northeast across the farmlands of Ohio and northern Indiana arriving at the start of phase two, at South Bend, Indiana. This would give me a chance to meet up with old high school friends. From there, I would have to go north to get to the Upper Peninsula, so what better way than to make phase two a scenic ride along the eastern shore of Lake Michigan? I would camp two-thirds of the way up, near Traverse City, before a final run hugging the coast to the Mackinac Bridge via the "Tunnel of Trees," also known as Michigan Route 119. A ride across the big bridge and arrival at Tahquamenon Falls State Park would complete phase two and be the jumping off point for phase three—the main event.

Phase three would not follow the south shore, as the trip with Dad had, but would run as close as possible along the north shore, with a first day stop in Houghton, on the Keweenaw Peninsula. From there it would be a quick hop up to Copper Harbor at the tip of that peninsula, a run west to Duluth, and then northeast to Two Harbors, where camp would be made, on the north shore of Lake Superior. From there I would run into Canada, stopping at Nipigon for the night, then on to Wawa for the next night, crossing back into Michigan at Sault Saint Marie. With Lake Superior circumnavigated, the third and last phase would end, and I would high tail it south to Florida over the next couple days.

This ride would only last fourteen days or so, not epic by many adventure riding standards, but a launch on the way to filling the rest of my life with bigger and better adventures. It would be my longest ride so far and pass through three areas I had wanted to explore for a long time. For me that would be epic, and I would pass from being an observer of other true adventure riders' ride reports, which I had followed so many times on advrider.com, to being an adventure rider in my own right. It would be a great beginning.

But then it all went to hell. All along I'd been plotting and planning, working out when the income would be coming in as a result of some good business months during the first part of the year. My target was mid-May. This would enable me to get back, with a couple day buffer in case I was delayed, before the kids got out of school, and I went into my annual daycare duties period, which would last until mid-August. As the time approached, finances improved. After a long period of poor sales, a much better stretch of months followed. With time from sale to payment stretched out a hundred and twenty days, in the midst of good sales our income was miniscule, but it was improving as May approached, and the good months finally should pay off. I figured up bills for the time I would be gone and estimated what would come in to cover them. It looked good...until the last moment, when I realized I had estimated inaccurately, and, although the funds would cover bills, there would not be nearly enough to cover fuel and expenses for my two week ride.

Depression set in. I felt trapped without some kind of release before the hassles and stress of managing our two children for the summer would begin. Even in bad years, I had always managed to get some kind of extended ride in before summer. I had always managed to arrange a fall ride after the summer had passed and a ride in the spring before summer arrived, but now my long anticipated, epic ride was not going happen. The dream was dead.

I stewed as the time I would have left came closer. I took a deep breath and weighed my options. An epic ride was now out of the question. It would not be same, but I could manage a frugal week on the road. I had already promised my brother that we would ride together and, with him being only six hundred miles away, that could still be done. I could be there in one day. Staying at his place would not cost me anything. Tim, being informed of my situation, offered to pay for our night together while riding. Now that I was not heading to Michigan, there was no need to follow my original plan. With the Blue Ridge almost at his back door, we could explore any of it we wanted without having to travel far.

So, disappointed in my plan's failure, I packed the bike knowing I would at least get some good mountain riding and camping in before heading home for the summer. The Bonnie and I were ready for leaving by my original departure date. Early in the morning darkness we rolled out of the drive. With the headlight and new LED auxiliary lights parting the darkness in front of us, we rumbled northward.

The plan was to get north on US Highway 27, past Ocala, and onto US 301 into the Florida countryside long before all the traffic was on the roads, that usually made passing through Lady Lakes and Ocala, so slow and difficult. The plan was successful, and 301 was clear as I sped through the flat north Florida landscape and into Georgia's piney eastern woods onto US 1, where the usual woodsy smells of Georgia bought back memories of earlier trips through this quiet corner of the United States. With only an occasional car or logging truck as company, I avoided all but the smallest towns and eventually reached US 25, which I would follow to Augusta's by-pass and into South Carolina. There I took familiar country roads, zipping north on an intercept course with Interstate 26. From there, the ride on 26 was fast and brought me to Exit 15, just short of the North Carolina border. Turning west on Asheville Highway, recrossing I-26, and taking the second left onto a small side road, I wound my way to a dirt road that ran across an incredibly steep railroad crossing followed by a hard right. From there the little path curved left through the woods and into an opening ringed by forest. At the back, in a small bay in the woods, lay Tim's place, perched above a forest stream.

I had been up there before, by car, with the entire family. The kids could not be dragged from the creek in which they incessantly panned for gold, which turned out to be mica. It was a little bit of heaven, not far from his and his wife's employment with all the conveniences of larger cities like Spartanburg and Greenville close at hand, but also minutes away from the expanses of the beautiful and quiet Blue Ridge Mountains.

I was early, so I took the short hike to the creek, hoping I might scare up a deer on the way down the wooded, shadowy path. The recent rains had swollen the creek to about twice the depth it had been last time I was here, muddying its usually crystal clearness with the load of foothill mud it was carrying. I made my way back up the hillside to the house. It was not long before the crunch of tires on the gravel road told me Tim and Pam were on their way home from work. Hellos were exchanged and cold beers were opened.

Over steaks on the grill, the planning began for the next couple days' ride, with Tim on his new Star Stratoliner and I on my Bonneville. It was now Thursday night, and Tim had a friend coming on Sunday. Together they were flying to Chicago on a business trip with an early Monday morning departure, so Tim had to be back by then. We could ride out for a day, camp somewhere, then he would return on Sunday morning, while I would ride on alone. There was no need to ride to West Virginia as originally planned, so we studied our options. I had ridden a lot west of a line drawn between Inman and Asheville, so we looked further east for interesting destinations. I had ridden east on the Blue Ridge Parkway one time on the second Motorcycle Kickstart Classic out of Maggie Valley, ending at Denton for a huge Antique Motorcycle Club of America meet. It was glorious riding among the seventy-five running antique examples of the best two-wheeled transportation America, Europe, and Japan had ever produced. On the way, we had passed Mt. Mitchell, the highest point east of the Mississippi, but had zoomed right by the access road winding north from the Blue Ridge Parkway. Mount Mitchell looked perfect as a first stop for us, and we could ride the area east of Asheville on side roads on the way up, past impressive Chimney Top Mountain and around Lake Lure, which is tucked neatly among the surrounding mountains. The route chosen, we hit the hay, but there was no need for an extremely early start, with the mountains so near. That was a luxury for me because I was accustomed to leaving in the darkness of early morning on my other trips from home, with usually hundreds of miles before the next stop.

Upon waking, fresh coffee was waiting along with a hot breakfast. We said good-bye to Pam as she left for another Friday at work, while Tim and I remained behind to load the bikes and get ready for our ride.

Tim took the lead back down the dirt road, across the tracks, and out of Inman. Within fifteen minutes we were in the open countryside rolling toward Lake Lure, with the mountains looming ever taller as we sped north. Following NC 9, soon Chimney Top was visible ahead as we veered west around Lake Lure's water, twinkling in the early morning light. We passed through the little town in the shadow of the towering mountain and its rock pillar, looking like a sentry post overlooking the valley. Now the rolling countryside was behind us and we were climbing in the mountains. On one of the first curves, I eased the throttle, slowing in an attempt to catch a better view and to point out to Tim the wild turkey scrambling up the side of the hill through the trees, trying to escape us. Throttling up again we continued, turning east at US 70, and found our way to NC 80, our connecting road to the Blue Ridge Parkway. Route 80 rivaled many of the other highly touted riding roads in the area, but escaped the crowds many of those roads attract. Also known as "The Rattler," the twists and turns of 80 provided the kind of riding I revel in and they didn't let up until we were deposited onto the Blue Ridge Parkway. This was a great start to the trip, and, instead of regretting what I had missed, having had to dump my epic ride plans, I started to appreciate the pure pleasure of the present.

We backtracked west on the Parkway for the few miles to NC 128, the access road up to Mount Mitchell, and wound our way north into the clouds and thinner air. We stopped at the parking lot just below the summit and dismounted to give our legs a workout on the walkway to the peak, at 6,684 feet. With our eyes satiated by the views of the surrounding mountains, it was time for our hunger to be treated likewise. We had followed a group of bikes on our way up. They had turned just before the peak into a parking lot of the State Park restaurant. On our way back down we decided to give it a try. I expected the fare to be uninteresting and overpriced, given the location, but was pleasantly surprised by the reasonable prices and fair selection, not to mention the spectacular view out the wall of windows, apparently perched in space, with nothing but air and mountains far below in view.

We hadn't planned what we'd do after visiting Mount Mitchell, so over lunch we discussed our options. When Andrea and I had been visiting Tim before with the kids, we had run over to Devil's Fork State Park on Lake Jocassee, in the northwestern corner of South Carolina. I remembered the unique camp sites there, set up on mini terraces in the woods overlooking the lake. We could head west from where we were and come down the west side of the lake through an area filled with waterfalls. I would be quite a haul to get there, but plenty of other opportunities were on hand along the route if we would decide to stop short of our afternoon goal. At Brevard, was Davidson River Campground, where we had camped with the family, in a perfect spot for us should we halt short of Devil's Fork.

Now with a plan laid and our energy replenished, we headed west on the Blue Ridge Parkway, past Asheville and on to the southern dip the Parkway makes before heading northwest to its terminus in the Smoky Mountains National Park. Just past the southern point we turned south on NC 215, a road both of us recalled riding a couple years earlier which had provided some of the best riding in these mountains. Taking 215 south would get us to US 64, where a turn west would take us in the direction of Lake Jocassee, or a turn east would take us to Davidson River.

We would need food for the evening at camp, whichever destination we chose. Studying the map, it did not look likely we would find a food store on our way to Lake Jocassee. We decide to run into Brevard, where we knew we could pick up the evening supplies, then head west again and go on to Devil's Fork if we had time. At Brevard, we found the large Ingles we remembered from our previous camping trip there, and filled up on stuff for dinner, snacks, and beer. Then, estimating our remaining time until dark, we retraced our route west passing NC 215 and continuing to NC 281 south, which led to the South Carolina line. From there, the route was renamed SC 130 and wound south to the Cherokee Scenic Foothills Parkway, or SC 11. On 11 we headed just a few miles east before turning north again, up into the hills surrounding Lake Jocassee and to Devil's Fork State Park. We pulled in, only to find out there were no camping spots left, this weekend being one of the first nice weekends of the camping season. Disappointed, we turned around but remembered a sign on the way in saying, "Camping." Not far from the park entrance, we spotted the sign again and rolled onto the gravel parking area. There were bunches of travel trailers in the park, apparently parked there year round as vacation homes for the summer season, but almost all seemed vacant now. We were the only campers it seemed, and we were offered a spot for a whopping eleven dollars. We were sold. We remounted our bikes for the descent down the steep rutted dirt road to our site, which was luckily near the top of the hill and surrounded by tall hickories on a more or less level terrace set above a wooded hillside.

We got to work setting up camp. It wouldn't be camping without a camp fire, so Tim gathered deadfall while I pitched the tent and, by the time I had finished, he had built a fire which was soon blazing. The tent was set quickly, then filled with our sleeping bags and pads and the stuff we might need overnight, while we enjoyed our first beers of the day and the darkness settled over the woods. I covered my bags on the bike in case of overnight moisture. Tim pulled up a log and I mounted my handy, tiny hiking three-legged stool, and we sat in the glow of the fire, breathing the smell of the woods and the smoke of the fire while Tim dined on his fried chicken and I on my Italian sub we had picked up back in Brevard, washing it down with more beer. The fire slowly died and night soon enveloped us, as we shuffled off to the tent.

In the night rain came, tapping on the sides of the tent beside my shoulder. I moved so I would not touch the inside wall and get wet myself from the moisture wicking through the tent fabric and was glad I had a inflatable pad under my bag. If rain made it into the tent, even a little, there would be no joy sleeping in a bag while the water saturated it. The Thermarest pad ensured that would not happen. I drifted off to sleep.

In the dim light of morning, I woke to continuing rain. We were in no hurry, so I rolled over to rest a bit longer, listening to the tap, tap, tapping of the rain dripping from the sky and off the leaves overhead onto the tent. I heard Tim stir, unzip the tent door, and step outside into the rain for his morning smoke. I closed my eyes hoping to get more rest, if not sleep, and hoped that soon the rain would be gone.

It wasn't long before most of the rain I could hear was only dripping from the trees, so I, too, shed my sleeping bag and stepped out into the still early morning. The sky, seen through the trees, was overcast with gray and it was looking like the rain was only taking a break and would soon be falling again. To my surprise, when saying good morning to Tim, he told me that when he had gotten up out of the tent he was greeted by a very large brown bear twenty yards from the campsite, down the little wooded valley, coincidentally the area where he had been tossing his chicken bones during dinner the night before. I was disappointed that he had not gotten me up when he saw the bear. He had thought I was still sleeping and had not wanted to disturb me, but I would have liked to have gotten a look at that big visitor. By the time I had popped out of the tent, though, he was long gone.

I got out my Dragonfly camp stove, for the first time, other than its test run. I got one of the two MSR bottles I had mounted on the passenger peg brackets, removed the cap and replaced it with the stove valve, pumped up the bottle, let a little flow into the burner, then lit that, allowing it to heat the burner. A moment later I open the valve, got a working flame, and placed the little pot of water on top in preparation for a breakfast of tea bag coffee and instant oatmeal. This little stove was very practical, set up easily and stowed small. It produced a flame that would boil water at least as quickly as the burner on the kitchen stove back home. It ran on unleaded gas, allowing the fuel canisters to do double duty as both cooking fuel and spare fuel for the Bonnie.

Hot food inside us now, we packed up camp, stowing all our gear in the big bags. I rolled up the wet tent and strapped it fore-and-aft along the shelf formed by the intersection of the top and side bags. The three legged stool was secured the same way to the opposite shelf. All packed and ready to go with the rain covers still on the bags, we weighed our options.

Rain looked certain for most of the day, and Tim had to return to Inman at the end of it. We decided to head back towards Inman, but first going north back into North Carolina, then east toward Tim's place by way of US 64. If the rain relented, there were plenty of interesting side roads to explore, and, if not, we had a fairly straight and quick shot back to Tim's, where I could stay another night avoiding camping in the rain if it continued.

We rode east first until we spotted US 178, where we turned north toward the state line, just before which was Bob's Place, a little bar on a hairpin Tim and I had visited before because it reminded us, more or less, of Fuzzy's back home. We zipped by Bob's this time and entered North Carolina again. At US 64 we headed east, passing through Brevard once more. We were right about the rain and it came and went all day. We stopped at a McDonalds to get some food and to take advantage of the free Wi-Fi to check the weather radar. After watching the animated radar that offered no good news to us, we made a decision; we would ride directly to Tim's and get out of the rain for the rest of the day.

We found US 176 in the road congestion of Hendersonville and peeled off to the southeast toward Inman. After a few miles we were riding through quiet mountain countryside again. After passing US 25, the highway began to twist and turn its way southeast and the sky lightened a bit. Soon, after a long downhill grade, we crossed a river and could see to our right an old, no longer used bridge crossing it beside the new one, with a turn off and a parking spot on the far side of the river. We took advantage of this spot and rolled up just short of the old bridge, parked, and dismounted for a short break. We walked around the large concrete barriers, intended to keep vehicles off the bridge, and wandered out onto the span. To the right was the modern bridge we had crossed over and to the left was a marvelous gorge with stair-step pools of water being fed by the river above, and in turn feeding the pools below. We imagined what a spot for a swim those pools would be, if there was some way to get to the bottom. It was steep all around. If it was possible, it was not something that could be accomplished quickly, so we satisfied ourselves with the view from above while we explored a short way from the bridge along the ridge above the gorge.

Refreshed from our short walk, we remounted our bikes and headed out onto US 176 again, passing though Saluda, then Tryon. At Tryon, we took a short detour, looking for the road to an interesting campground Tim had found on a previous ride in the area. We weren't stopping this time, but we wanted to know exactly how to get there, in anticipation of a future camping trip. Tim soon recognized the turnoff, making a mental note to remember it, and we returned to 176, continuing southeast into South Carolina. We passed Landrum, Campobello, and Inman. Tim made a detour here before heading home saying he wanted to show me "his country club." Soon, we were at The Country Club, which turned out to be a local biker bar. We climbed off our bikes, and, still dripping from the rain, we headed across the parking lot toward the bar. Before we could cross the parking lot, the owner came out to meet us, shaking our hands and looking back at our soaked bikes and baggage. It happened to be bike week at Myrtle Beach, which explained the absence of bikes in the usually crowded parking lot and our warm welcome. I've found the more tired you are and more travel weary your bike looks, the more other bikers take to you; this fellow was no exception. On the way into the bar, he showed us his cherished panhead in the room next door, then once inside we found it hard to pay for anything. Before the warm welcome had a chance to inebriate us, however, we said our good-byes, promising to return, and rode the last few miles back, finally finding the dirt road that wound its way over the steep railroad tracks and through the woods to the little clearing where Tim's house waited for our return.

Tim's guest wasn't to arrive until the next afternoon. I figured this was a good place to get out of the rain, and the next morning I could start out on my own to places yet undecided. Food on the grill and cold beers from the fridge only steps away would not be a bad way to spend my last evening with my brother and, in spite of my comfortable sleeping bag and Thermarest, a real bed with clean sheets and inside, out of the rain, would be welcome.

The only glitch to me leaving in the morning and getting out on my own was that my cell phone had quit functioning. I don't mind being out of touch, but a cell phone is a good safety device to have on you, especially when riding on your own if you happen to break down, or worse, wreck. In the morning before his guest would arrive, we made a plan to find the nearest Verizon office and replace the phone before I took off.

Morning came with a clear sky and sunshine. There was no need to get out the Dragonfly today to enjoy hot, black coffee and breakfast. Googling Verizon and making some calls over breakfast revealed the necessity of waiting at least until noon, when the local Verizon store would open, it being Sunday. We killed some time by hanging a couple ceiling fans my brother had bought, and, at the appointed hour Tim and I drove to the phone store. I could not swap out my phone for a new one without penalty because I was a month from the expiration time on my contract, and replacing the phone using my insurance was not practical, as it would take fifty of my dollars to pay the deductible, and I was already on a super tight budget to do this trip in the first place. Plus, a replacement phone would be a few days wait and I did not have the time, either. Luckily, Tim had recently upgraded to an iPhone with the same company I used and remembered that he that he still had his old, deactivated phone. He offered the old phone to me, which was almost identical to my non-functioning one, and the phone company swapped out the contacts from my old phone to his, along with my number, for no charge. I was set, but by the time we left and had gotten back to Tim's the day was shot. If I left then, it would have been a short while before I would have to find a spot to camp for the approaching night. Instead, I gave in to my brother's and sister-in-law's invitations to stay one more night. On a previous trip I had met Tim's friend and coworker who was staying tonight, so there would be no awkwardness of meeting and trying to get to know a new person. I passed another night eating grilled food, drinking Tim's beer, and chatting with this small crowd of friends and family, with an aim for an early departure the next morning.

I was up not long after light. While Tim and his friend prepared to leave for the airport, I packed the bike, said my good-byes, and left on the dirt road, crossing through the woods and across the tracks for the last time.

I had been riding in this area before and had always wanted to hop across the Smokies on US 441 to see what it was like on the north side, but always somehow bypassed doing that. Now I was on my own, and I could take my own path. I headed back out on 176, stopping once again at the bridge to take some photos of my bike on the old bridge, then continued to retrace our route from that rainy Saturday a couple days before. At Brevard, however, I turned off our route and onto US 276 north toward the Blue Ridge Parkway, zooming past the familiar Davidson River Campground and Sliding Rock, a place that last time I had visited had turned me into a little kid again, with countless climbs and slides back down to the frigid pool of water at its base. This time I didn't stop, but kept climbing until I got to the Blue Ridge Parkway, where I turned west toward the Smokies.

I was now on familiar ground, having ridden this part of the Parkway several times before, with Tim and on the Motorcycle Kickstart Classic Ride. Soon, I would be passing the highest point on the Parkway, where Tim and I and most every new rider of the Parkway stop to have pictures taken of them and their bikes, in front of the big sign at the turnoff. Before I got that far, I noticed a series of mountains to the north with relatively smooth, unforested tops. I thought to myself how one could simply walk up those mountains if one could get to their bases. Suddenly, I came across a sign for Black Balsam Trail, part of the Art Loeb Trail. I turned off, wanting to see if the trail went out to these mountain tops. Climbing the narrow trail of a road I soon found cars and SUVs parked on the roadside where a path scrambled off to the right. I noted this and continued to the end of the road which changed to gravel, but soon ended in a small empty parking area, devoid of vehicles. I turned around and went back to the populated roadside, which obviously was the main trail head, and parked the Bonnie among the other hikers' vehicles. Grabbing the camera from the tail bag, I started up the trail on foot.

It felt good to stretch my legs after the last several days of sitting in one place on the back of the bike or in a chair at Tim's. The trail climbed, and I climbed with it. Soon it disappeared into a thick copse of trees, that shaded the needle laden ground beneath them, creating a kind of outdoor cave, with only dapples of light moving here and there among the shadows. While thick and shady overhead, the clump of pines was not big and light filtered in from the sides, with the indirect lighting giving it a tranquil feel. The trail was lost here, so I simply walked through the open spaces under the branches until reaching the top of the tree filled area where I broke through into sunlight again. I could now see the trail in the open, not far from me. I followed it ever higher across the open hillside, some times walking in the water eroded dry-stream-like path and sometimes walking beside it on the short grass. At bigger elevation changes, exposed rocks made stairways, and I climbed on, passing an older couple on the first crest. Exchanging hellos, I continued down a hillside ridge between the first and the next peak, eventually trending again uphill to the next mountaintop, strewn with boulders and rocks. While taking in the view at the third peak and getting my breath back at what must have been close to an altitude of 6,000 feet, I noticed a small burned area among the rocks. I thought how glorious it would be like to camp up here, sitting around a small fire as night came on and millions of stars revealed themselves. I also thought, in this exposed place, how quickly a night up here could turn unpleasant, even dangerous, with no protection from the rain or wind, which I supposed could whip up furiously in little time and with little warning. Still, I'd take the chance for that night view.

Now, fully recovered from the climb, I started down and soon found myself passing through the dark shadiness of the trees again and emerging back at my Bonnie. I was glad and strangely satisfied with myself for having stopped and taken the time to explore.

I literally rolled back down the hill to the Parkway, and headed west, flying past the marker for the highest point, this time not pausing to take another picture. The Parkway now turned northwest and I continued following that dark ribbon through the spectacular scenery all the way to its terminus at US 441 at the edge of the Smoky Mountains National Park.

I turned north on 441, finally on my way to crossing the Smokies to the other side. Unfortunately, here the traffic was slow, clogged with tourists obeying the twenty-five mile per hour speed limit religiously, while we passed beautiful riding curve after curve that begged to be ridden, if not aggressively, at least spiritedly. Still, the surroundings were beautiful, shady, and green and the climb into the park even at this slow pace and among these other vehicles was pleasant. Reaching the crest and before starting down the other side, I stopped at the Appalachian Trail crossing at Newfound Gap. Here, at the border between North Carolina and Tennessee, I parked, took a break from the traffic, and stretched my legs. I grabbed the camera and took photos of the valleys that stretch both north and south from there, and one of the Appalachian Trail for the benefit of a friend at home, who dreamed of walking it some day.

US 441 wound down the mountain in a series of abrupt twists, turns, and switch backs, as I headed north toward the edge of the park and Gatlinburg. Knowing Gatlinburg to be a tourist Mecca, I opted for the by-pass to Pigeon Forge, which was itself a tourist destination, but unavoidable. Passing through Pigeon Forge, I took a break and had a cheap meal at a Taco Bell, remembering to re-lube the chain before going in for my burritos. I needed to make a decision here on where I was headed for the night, even if it was only a very loose plan. I decided to follow the backside of the mountains toward Tellico Plains, where I could either take the Cherohala Skyway back into North Carolina, or continue south to find a place for the night. US 321 would fit the bill.

At Maryville I could catch US 411 to Madisonville and from there it was simple business to take TN 68 into Tellico Plains. There I would consult my maps once again to decide how to proceed with an eye on how much riding time was left by then.

On my way, I passed the turn to US 129, the famous, or infamous, depending on your point of view, Tail of the Dragon. I have always resisted running this, not because of the many twists and turns, but because of the many tourist-riders negotiating the stretch, turning it into either a race track or a parking lot, depending on your luck. But still, it is one of the roads that is nice to be able to say you've ridden. Maybe on a weekday, early morning, or at the very start or end of the riding season, when many riders have not started to ride or have already put their rides away until spring; maybe then. But today, no, not on a sunny afternoon in the start of the peak season for riding up here. I let the intersection whiz past, as I continued on toward Tellico.

I saw the sign for 68 and got off the main highway and back into rolling countryside. Arriving at Tellico Plains, the signage confused me and I pulled off and parked at Tellico Motorcycle Outfitters, where the owner came out to greet me and look at my Bonneville. I asked him about a good route south towards North Georgia, and he confirmed my choice of continuing on TN 68, which looked sufficiently twisty on the map. I'd heard of Tellico Outfitters on advrider. com. It is almost at the doorstep of the western end of the Cherohala Skyway. Many had proclaimed the helpfulness and friendliness of the owner of this gear and supply shop catering to motorcycle adventurers, and I was happy to confirm this in person. I took a look around the shop while the owner chatted with a couple who had come in. It was the end of cold weather up here and the start of a sweltering summer, so winter jackets of very high quality, the only kind they carried here, were drastically reduced in price, making me wish I was not on such a frugal budget on this trip. I knew I would pay much more, eventually, for a new jacket of perhaps not as high quality. Sometimes, though, the best choice is not the possible choice, so I left the shop empty-handed, but with clear directions and refreshed from even this little break from riding. Waving good-bye to my host, I headed back to 68 and on toward the Blue Ridge countryside.

Traffic was non-existent on little 68, and I motored south unmolested through lovely rolling mountains. I turned off 68, onto TN 123 east, which became NC 294 when it soon crossed into North Carolina. I wound my way east and south and found US 64, the main east-west conduit through this mountainous region, and followed it east only a little way until I spotted US 129, the other end of "The Dragon," where I turned south toward Georgia.

On one of my very first trips, again with my brother, we had taken this route south on our way back from Michigan, I on my little CB350 and Tim on his Kawasaki Nomad 1500— an oddly matched couple of motorcycles. We had taken this route because when we looked at our map it looked fairly straight, and we were in a bit of a rush to return home to Florida. We had found that, in spite of the less-than-squiggly line on our map, the road had its share of challenges, and we wound ourselves down this stretch minding our brakes and trying to estimate proper entry speeds before being swept around one curve after another. This time, after a few years' experience, it was less of a challenge, but still a lot of fun, and I reveled in what I thought would be my last stretch of this kind of exciting riding.

It was late in the afternoon when I crossed out of North Carolina and into Georgia, and I needed to start watching for a cheap place to throw my tent down for the night. I continued twisting down 129, without any luck on the camping spot search, when just after Blairsville I spotted a small sign for Vogel State Park. I slowed and turned right onto the gravel road into the park, passing a lake, which had an impressive swimming hole on the far side that my kids would have been crazy about. I crunched up to the visitors' center only to find it closed, so I asked a woman walking nearby what the procedure was for a late camping arrival. She said she only knew that there was a self-service station where you paid a parking fee, deposited half of a form, and took the other half to hang on your bike. I filled out the form and was glad I had the five dollars in cash to drop in the box. I remounted and rode to the end of the lake, then turned left into the camping area.

I had barely entered when I caught sight of another rider with his BMW GS Sertao adventure bike parked in the first camping spot. He waved at me, motioning for me to stop. He walked over and said he was the campground host, so I asked him what the after hour check-in routine was. He noticed my ADV sticker and said I could camp with him, just to pull in and I could set up next to his tent and share his fire. He said to not worry about checking in. If anyone asked, he would just let them know he had a friend visiting him. The thing is when traveling by motorcycle fellow riders are friends simply because they ride motorcycles, too. It's hard to not find friends among fellow riders when traveling by bike, and Jeff was also a fellow advrider "inmate," so that sealed the deal.

I pulled in and backed the bike next to his, then lifted it onto the centerstand. Jeff asked me if I was hungry and offered to cook up some spaghetti, which I gratefully accepted. Jeff cooked, while I set up my tent and stowed my gear. Over dinner, I found out Jeff was a photographer, among other things, and was riding and hosting at state parks for a while—a cheap way to ride and see different parts of the country. We finished dinner and moved to the fire, which Jeff already had burning, and chatted on into the darkening evening about High Dynamic Resolution photography, which I had been dabbling in, and other riding related subjects. Jeff had mentioned he had a bear visitor recently, and as we sat telling lies around the fire, we heard a crash just several yards away in the woods. We were blinded to anything outside the ring of light created by the campfire, so whatever made the noise could have been anything—a falling branch, a clumsy raccoon—but of course, to us it was a bear. Jeff jumped up blowing his bear whistle and yelling and waving his arms. We did not hear anything more and soon turned back to conversation. As the night wore on, Jeff faded into sleep in his chair by the fire. I debated whether to wake him up so he could take to his tent, or leave him to the bear. The bear won out, and I left Jeff snoring in the ring of fire light, while I told myself that if it was a bear it would be long gone by now and crawled into my tent just a couple yards away.

Morning light began to filter through the trees, and I woke to the sounds of Jeff shuffling around camp. So, he made it through the night without becoming bear food. I climbed out of the tent, and Jeff greeted me with the suggestion of taking a ride back up 129 to Blairsville for breakfast. I was not in a hurry now that my truncated alternate trip was much shorter than my planned trip to Canada, so a day or two more would still mean I would return home many days earlier than I had previously planned, plus one of my favorite things when on the road is discovering little out of the way, non-chain, local restaurants for breakfast fare. I told Jeff I would enjoy a run to the diner. He suggested we could take another way back to the park, so I could have a little taste of the local riding. Even better, I thought. I finished rolling up my wet tent and strapping it and my camp stool on the luggage "shelves," and we shoved off for Blairsville, breakfast, and a morning of riding mountain roads.

Breakfast at "Hole in the Wall" did not disappoint my taste buds or diminish my desire to visit another truly local diner. Refreshed after eggs, bacon, and plenty of black coffee, Jeff took the lead out of town. We headed west on Blue Ridge Highway, until we picked up Skeenah Gap Road, which headed southwest toward Georgia 60, also known as Morgantown Highway, and the roller coaster ride began. Highway 60 twisted and turned, climbed and fell toward Suches and Georgia 180. At Suches, we dismounted for a short break at a former motorcycle hangout, where a couple other riders had stopped. We dismounted in the gravel parking lot and chatted with our fellow riders and watched the activity at the restaurant that was being prepped to reopen soon and once again takes its premier place as the area mountain riders' rest stop. On the adjacent corner was a gas station, where other bikers were fueling or taking a break. Jeff took advantage of it by filling his BMW Sertao one-lunger. Just down the road the Appalachian Trail crossed 60, just miles from its beginning point to the southwest, but instead of crossing the Trail we rolled out of the station heading northeast on highway 80, also known as Wolf Pen Gap Road, back toward US 129 and Vogel State Park. The wild ride continued on 180.

When we approached Lake Winfield Scott, a combination of wet pavement and a blind right turn, followed immediately by a left across a short bridge, caught me off guard. Coming in fast for the first right, I rounded the curve only to see the hard left turn. While the entry speed for the first turn was manageable, it was instantly obvious that I was in too hot for the second, with little straight road before I would be in the middle of the left. I laid on the brakes, but the curve was coming up fast. I drug my rear brake too long and too hard for the wet surface, then I felt the back wheel start to slide. With visions of a high side flitting through my head I unconsciously rejected the idea of letting go of the brake completely. Although the reaction was accomplished in a blink of the eye, I somehow released the brake gently as I completed the turn, and felt the rear get back in line and comply with the request to follow the curve. I shot out the other side unscathed, but with my heart beating violently. While telling myself how stupid I had been, I slowed the pace for the rest of the run to US 129, where a right, followed immediately by another right, put us back in Vogel State Park. By then I had calmed myself down, and when I stepped off to say good-bye to Jeff I was relatively my old self but, hopefully, a bit wiser.

Leaving Jeff at Vogel, I turned right out of the park and moved south on US 129, headed for Valdosta where I would see my old high school friend, Julie, who lives there working at Valdosta State University, teaching art and managing the gallery. There was a small group of us in high school that claimed to be artists. Julie was the only one of us who stuck with it and made a career out of fine arts. A couple of the group, Joe Frucci and I, managed to incorporate art into our work over the years as graphic designers, but Julie paints today as she did back in the 1970s, not bowing to someone else's need to sell something.

Because Valdosta is at the gateway to just about any part of the country I may travel, being 280 miles from home, I often stop over for a night to see my old friend and spend the night, in anticipation of a short ride home the final day or an easy first day as I set on to places farther north, east, or west. This time I was not pressed for time, so I thought I'd spend some more substantial time with Julie, instead of my usual one night stand. I moved south with the mountains around me slowly diminishing and into the softly rolling hills of north Georgia around Athens. From Athens I stayed on US 129 into the ever flattening and agricultural heartland. At Macon,

129 intersected with Interstate 75, and I jumped onto the Interstate, following it into the afternoon sunshine toward Valdosta and Exit 13. Heading west a few miles, I pulled into Julie's driveway minutes before she arrived home from the university. After Julie and her dad, Jack, and I finished our initial hellos and I was asked, "How long can you stay for?" we made plans for the evening. Julie's brother, Danny, who I had also known at school, had moved to Valdosta, so we made a night of getting to know each other all over again over steaks and beers at a local eatery. Once back at Julie's we settled in for the night, and, although I had only had an easy run of around three hundred and forty miles, it was not long before I was yawning, saying goodnight, and crawling into my already prepared bed in the spare room.

I woke early and decided it would not be a breach of etiquette to start the coffee myself. While it gurgled, I checked all things electronic in my world and found that it did, indeed, still spin without me. Julie soon joined me and we savored our laziness in the cool morning, sitting outside and talking about nothing in particular and sipping our hot coffee while we watched the birds and squirrels in the feeders and the relative wildness of the space behind her back fence. We roughly formed a plan that would include either canoeing or hiking, with Julie as passenger on the Triumph. Eventually, we procured a friend's helmet for Julie, and off we rode. With hiking having won out, we set our sights on a ride through the farmland to the west and northwest, ending at Reed Bingham State Park. With the whole day before us, we took our time. When railroad repairs held us up at a crossing and we backtracked looking for a detour, and getting lost in the process, we didn't care. We calmly took a break, rechecking my on again off again GPS and her iPhone to find our way to the park. We parked among the long leaf pines and were glad for their dappled shade, now that the day had taken to heating up in earnest. We wandered in the shade along the river, where I was tempted to strip and dive in to cool off, if it wasn't for the idea of the ever present alligators possibly taking an interest in me. Eventually looping back to the bike, we picked up some more water at the visitors' station and headed back the way we had come, with the anticipation of ice cream at a peach orchard stand we had visited together on a previous stay. The fresh churned ice cream was just the thing for cooling us down for the last leg of our ride back to Julie's in the now sweltering Georgia afternoon heat.

Back at the house we took to the cool of the air conditioning until the sun got low in the west, taking our time to enjoy each others' company. Julie fired up the grill as evening crept in. A mutual friend, Steve, dropped by, and we all ate and talked as darkness fell over the south Georgia countryside.

By Valdosta, I had reached ground I had covered many times before between the Georgia line and home, so rather than taking back roads this time and to avoid the daytime traffic around Ocala on US 27, I took the ramp for Interstate 75 South and within a few miles was speeding through the Florida landscape on my way to Wildwood, where I could jump over using the Florida Turnpike to US 27, south of all the traffic, and then zoom home. The other reason for taking the Interstate and Turnpike was that I had a plan.

I usually walked the half mile to the school crossing to meet my daughter and walk her home, and I wanted to be there when the bell rang at school. I made good time on this route and parked the bike in our drive just in time to start my walk at the usual time and surprise her at the crossing.

I was home. There had been no epic, border crossing travel, no alone in the wilderness camp outs. I had ridden one day's distance from home, albeit a long day's ride, then puttered around the area, half of which I had already traveled, then rode home. I had only camped out twice.

Part of me was disappointed in my failure to pull off the Lake Superior ride, but part of me was grinning from ear to ear having just completed a refreshing and rewarding open-ended trip. Other than getting to my brother's to meet up, the entire week's time I was bound by no schedules and went wherever looked interesting to me at the moment. Each day's ride was as long or short as I wanted it to be. There were no endless stretches that I had to span to stay on schedule. Added to that was the fact that the weather had been cold and wet the entire time I would have been in the Upper Peninsula, which partly vindicated my altered plans.

No, it wasn't the epic ride I had envisioned. I know time is fleeting, but I still have a little time to live the dream. One day, sooner than later, I will see that Superior ride through, but until then I am not sitting still, either. Once more, I'll get out the maps and trace the route of the next epic ride, but if, when I am set to leave and life gives me lemons again, I'll make lemonade, although I prefer limes.

FLORIDA TO THE OZARKS

Morning couldn't break too early. It was once again time for my annual pilgrimage to the Barber Vintage Festival. The antique bike festival is held yearly at the Barber Motorsports Park, nestled in the hills east of Birmingham in the western tail of the Appalachians. After the Kickstart Classic Ride up last year for my second visit, this would be my third year attending.

It was early October, and I needed a break after a summer of being alone in the house with our two kids, who had been out of school since June and had only returned in late August. I am a bit of a rolling stone and being stuck at the house to be the daycare provider for two children for three months with the constant whining and tantrums had worn on me. A road trip promised to be a welcome break from the kids' incessant bickering, constant struggles to get them to do homework now that they were back in school, and an escape from the wreck of what used to be our neat home, now littered with toys, discarded wrappers, dirty clothes, and scattered dishes.

I'll admit it, although I feel a twinge of guilt to say it, I have no illusions that I am the greatest dad. My patience had left me years ago and readjustment to having children later in life and the requisite forbearance required had not been easy with my temperament. I often prefer to be alone—a condition usually denied to a father of young children. And I know, and have been told numerous times by well-meaning people, that "...they are only little once, spend as much time with them as you can. Soon they will be grown," but I find it hard to deny following that urge to get out, and get out alone. As much as I admire the parents who do everything with their kids and who seem to enjoy, no, live for that experience, I just feel something tugging me away.

I have had an internal conflict with how to balance the time I need to spend with my kids and wife and the time I need for myself. One one side, the kids needed a dad around and Andrea needed support, too. On the other side, this wanderlust seemed to be an innate part of me. Would I do my kids service by example, showing them to deny their dreams by staying home when their dreams called? There must be a healthy balance, but I've struggled to find it.

Ever since I left my parents' home, I had been on my own seeking adventure and new experiences, first moving to the Great Plains to work after a stint in college; then a tour of Mexico, Guatemala, and Belize; from there it was a move from Michigan to Florida; next sailing a small boat, mostly solo, around the Bahamas, the US East Coast, and the Caribbean; with other jaunts thrown in here and there, finally ending with riding motorcycles. I blame my parents for this. They used to pack us in our 1960 Volkswagen Beetle, or various other vehicles, and haul us Midwestern kids to strange and exotic (to my young mind) places like Colorado, Pennsylvania, West Virginia, Florida, or the caves in Kentucky. Those trips generally took us not to major tourist attractions, but to small town America, often on back roads and usually camping in a musty old canvas tent. I don't know if it was the places or the people, like the beautiful young West Virginia coal camp girl I fell in love with for the first time on one of those trips, but those trips and experiences stuck with me and gave me an appetite for more. I find it strange that my mother has always hated the idea of me out traipsing about, whether it was on a boat or a bike, yet part of why I do it is because of the traipsing we did as a family when we were younger.

In spite of all that, I have tried to be responsible and do all the fatherly stuff—I held my temper, doled out what I thought to be judicious rewards and punishments for good and bad behavior, took them to their appointments, and endured their continual raids on my office and all it contained. I know I am supposed to say how much I was going to miss the little ones when school started again but really, by that time, school could not start soon enough for me. I would still have them after school until their mom came home from her "real job" in an office, but during school I could enjoy the quiet of the house inhabited only by me and our house cats and settle back into my work routine uninterrupted.

Now that the kids had settled into their school activities, I could think about relieving a little of that wanderlust that always is floating around in the back of my head. Because of Andrea's flexible work schedule at the time, she could come home when the kids got out of school and work from home for the rest of the day as needed. That set the stage for the opportunity for me to make my escape, while I would have to shove the guilt I felt for leaving her alone with the kids for a week to the back of my mind. Besides, we had a clever plan that we hoped would make the time alone with the kids easier for Andrea. She had decided to go to the beach with the kids and a friend of hers, who adored the children, and spend the weekend playing in the waves and sand. The kids can't get enough of the beach and the promise of them getting to go would hopefully curb their tendencies to misbehave before the weekend and the constant physical play over the weekend the beach would provide them might make it easier to keep them in hand. That, at least, would ease the burden of child care at for about two and a half days.

Beside the joyful release of fulfilling some of my lust for the road, the trip also would provide benefits for my business, publishing and promoting books on motorcycling. Books were shipped ahead for me to sell at the festival's swapmeet area, but the really important advantage of going was the opportunity to network it provided. I could talk face to face with magazine representatives about future advertising and marketing plans and offer review copies to people in the position to review and promote the books. I also figured in a stop on the return trip to visit my website host and discuss some issues that had developed with the websites.

As I looked over maps preparing for the trip, I was struck by how close to Arkansas Birmingham was. Heck, I would already be two-thirds of the way to a place I had read about riding in, but had never been to. As long as I was that close, I figured I might as well add a couple days and ride some new mountains. Besides, one of my best friends from high school lived just outside of Little Rock, and I had not seen her in over thirty-five years. I owed her a visit.

Usually, I rode alone from home in Lake Wales to Pinetta, Florida, where I joined a group of friends, riding the rest of the way up with a small group of four or five bikes. This year, however, I would be riding up with a partner. Roger and I had ridden up to the second Motorcycle Kickstart Classic ride in the Blue Ridge Mountains the May before and we had found a nice balance between us on the road, so I knew riding with him on this trip would add to the camaraderie that riding with a fellow biker contributes, without the hazards of possible catastrophes that riding with an unknown rider could bestow on a ride.

The day before we were to leave I loaded enough gear and clothing to last me a week, more or less, and provide something for both hot and cold weather, both of which I could expect at that time of year, leaning more toward the cool side for the Ozarks part of the ride. The tail bag was expanded to its maximum and contained all manner of electronic gizmos I might need on the road—my netbook, Kindle Fire tablet, camera, and a waterproof box with my air card and all of the gadgets I would need to keep all that stuff charged. I installed a double USB mount on the handlebars, next to the GPS holder mount and so could run the GPS while charging my phone or other electronics while stowed in the tank bag. The tank bag sucked itself down onto the tank with it magnets mounted underneath, and I added extra security by clipping a tether from it around the handlebars. Soft saddlebags were thrown over the rear portion of the saddle with a convenient top bag made to clip to the saddlebags underneath. The whole thing then clipped to the frame. On the little shelf formed between the left side of the top bag and above the left saddlebag I strapped my tent. On top of all this I bungeed a large dry bag filled with sleeping bag and mat. The whole mess was reminiscent of a camel with an abnormally rear-shifted hump.

It was a chilly morning for early October in central Florida as I made last minute adjustments to all the bags and camping gear strapped on the back of my Bonneville T100. Roger arrived minutes before the departure time we had agreed on. We had decided on a back roads route to the north and rolled out of the drive about eight AM and headed north on FL 17 to Haines City and our first fuel stop before continuing west into the Green Swamp via Deen Still Road and FL 33. At Groveland, we headed west and north to Bushnell and then Floral City, where we picked up US 41. Once north of Dunellon we had the highway mostly to ourselves all the way to US 27 at Williston. At Chiefland we turned north on US 129 to US 90, then west to Madison, where FL 145 took us on into Pinetta, a quiet little village with nothing to denote its presence but a scattering of houses and a blinking yellow light.

Even though as time passed the air warmed, the chill that had started the day stayed with us in a small way all day. It grew warmer, into one of those days where you are warm when standing and chilly when moving at highway speeds on the bike—perfect riding weather. There was just the smallest hint, almost a ghost, of the chill throughout the day. I started with my jacket liner in, and it stayed in all day, but I was able to remove the sweatshirt I had underneath my jacket and never quite needed to change from my vented gloves to the heavy winter ones stowed handily in the outside of the left saddlebag.

Luis, Debbie, and their daughter Elizabeth met us at Luis's closed shop soon after we called them. We followed them east on county roads and down their enormously long dirt-road driveway. At their house was a new, gigantic, motorhome they had just procured for stationing at their newly purchased north Georgia mountain land. Although I had come prepared to tent camp each night of the trip, there was no need to unload the bike here, with the motorhome hooked up to power and the air conditioning cranking. Roger and I unloaded what little we needed, considering the luxurious accommodations, and "made camp" in the RV while pizza was ordered for everyone, provided by our hosts. The rest of our time in Pinetta was spent helping Luis load bike frames and parts into their trailer for sale at the festival swapmeet and chatting about bikes over beers.

I made a call home before turning in and found out things were not going well on the home front. Jacob had been promised the beach weekend with the provision he got his book report done and handed in. That day he had lost it, a very common problem with my son, and was beside himself with the thought he might be left at home with the grandparents while Mom and his sister, Tess, trotted off to the beach. Now when I say Jacob "was beside himself," I mean he was making life a living hell for Andrea. I was already 280 miles away and in too deep to head back. Andrea would have to deal with it, and then I would have to deal with her ire when I got back. I hoped for the best.

Bedtime was early, soon after sundown, and it was not long before we were asleep in our comfortable accommodations.

Morning dawned cool and foggy. We hastily drank coffee in anticipation of an early start, hoping the fog would not be an impediment. The trailer loaded, we followed it and Debbie and Elizabeth in the van out and back to the shop where a few more things were loaded while we waited for the other two riders to join us.

Soon Kevin's silver Dyna rolled in, and we got acquainted while waiting for Chuck, our final rider, to arrive. The wait was short and soon we could hear Chuck approaching on his Honda Valkyrie long before he appeared into view, with his exhaust howling like a banshee in heat or a Ferrari under a green flag.

Once all together, we roared out of town following the van and trailer, Harley Ultra Classic playing lead, followed by the Dyna, then my Bonneville, and Roger's Shadow Phantom, with the screamer tagging behind and sparing our eardrums, along usually quiet country back roads and to our breakfast stop in Thomasville, Georgia. We all were fairly experienced riders and in this small of a group we rode well together, considering our relaxed pace, with a minimum of sling-shotting. As we rolled along, in spite of the fading fog and increasing sun, there was still a chill in the air. I was outfitted the same as the day before, in T-shirt and sweatshirt under my jacket, with thermal liner installed and my perforated leather gloves covering my hands. Whizzing through the countryside brought alternating chill and warmth as we passed through sections of shaded road, then sunny patches. I began to consider whether I should have dressed more warmly and was eagerly anticipating our breakfast stop. After a hot breakfast and more coffee, once back on the bikes, thoughts of cold faded as the day warmed, and soon I was comfortably moving through the south Georgia landscape along with my four riding brethren.

Soon we were past Camilla and on GA 37 to GA 41 to GA 520 riding towards Fort Benning and Columbus, where we crossed into Alabama on US 280. On the way, we took a break next to a shady pecan grove and snacked on fresh raw pecan meat that was almost as sweet as candy.

I made a quick call home to Andrea to see how she was faring. She and her friend, Leah, were leaving work early and picking the kids up from school to get to the beach as early as possible. Luckily, by the time I called, Jacob had regained his composure and buckled down and redid his report and handed it in on time after all. He would get to go to the beach. I breathed a sigh of relief and hung up feeling better and a bit less guilty for having left Andrea to be a single mom for the week.

The hills began to grow as US 280 rolled further northwest into the Alabama heartland. We were finally entering the margins of the tail of the Appalachians. Not far past Talladega National Forest we stopped for lunch at the AL 25 turn-off that would take us towards what could finally be called mountains.

I had ridden AL 25 before. It was also sometimes called "Mini Tail of the Dragon." While in all honesty Dunnavant Road couldn't hold a candle to the famous road in eastern Tennessee, it did have welcome twists and turns and was a tree-lined mountain pathway to Leeds with a hairpin curve thrown in to keep us on our toes. It was a fitting entrance into Leeds, Barber, and the surrounding mountainous countryside we had finally reached after the flat fields of cotton and grove after grove of pecan trees we had sailed by during our ride north.

25 came to an abrupt halt at US 78, which would take us west to Rex Lake Road. A final right turn off Rex Lake, less than a mile from where we had turned onto it, took us into the heart of Barber Motorsports Park and the Eighth Annual Barber Vintage Festival.

Once inside the park, we headed for the swapmeet area, where Luis and Deb would be selling their wares. Luis had gotten a bunch of Norton frames in various shades of condition. One, in particular, that he called a "fastback," was a factory café-style bike with gold rear cowl and tank. It sold for a tidy sum before the trailer was parked. The other Norton frame, a Honda Dream 250, complete except for side covers, and most of the parts were sold by the end of the weekend.

I unpacked the Triumph as the rest went off in search of their hotel rooms or camping spots. I was going to camp in the middle of the swapmeet and thereby provide a guard dog presence again, just in case anyone got more than curious in the contents of the trailer after hours. These were rather luxurious accommodations as far as I was concerned. The grass at Barbers is like a soft carpet or putting green and sleeping on it would be a dream compared to my usual sleep-on-the-rocks routine, especially this year because I had finally broken down and bought a self-inflating sleeping pad to go under my bag. These were not cheap, which explains my long reluctance to buy one, and mine never really "self-inflated" as promised, but it took me perhaps six breaths to have it tight and ready for duty and the comfort it provided was worth every bit of the seventy dollars I had paid for it. I won't camp again without one.

The tent was pitched at the back of one of our three lots and, after running out for a bite in Leeds and to pickup an evening beer, the rest of the evening was spent getting to know our neighbors directly behind us.

Tony and Nathan had come down from Tennessee to try and sell a pair of CX500s that together might almost make one whole bike. They also had a variety of parts and pieces they hoped to send to better homes. They brought a portable fire pit, and we sat around the fire talking bikes. It was their first time to the festival and they were suitably impressed, and the real show had not even begun. Having a fire completed the experience and now I felt like it was really "camping." But it had been a long day, and it did not take long for us one by one to wander off from the fire to our sleeping places. The night air moved in, perfect sleeping weather, in the low 50s, and soon I was asleep.

I woke to the sounds of scores of vendors un-tarping and setting up their display areas. The first order of business was, of course, a quest for black coffee. I had spied the day before an official looking trailer promising food and went to see if they offered coffee, too. They weren't open but would be soon, so I ambled back to camp to watch the early shoppers strolling by and stopping to pick up this or that rusty piece of invaluable metal. My neighbors were awake, too, and we chatted about the coming day. I noticed some passersby holding coffee cups, so I turned my steps back to the trailer and was greeted by an open window. Coffee cost two dollars a "large" cup, but I wasn't going to argue. I am used to my morning pot and knew I was not really going to be awake until some of the hot goodness had settled in my stomach. Eventually, the rest of our group straggled in, and I set out to walk at least half of the swapmeet area.

The Vintage Festival at Barber Motorsports Park is something every motorcyclist owes themselves to attend at least once. There is continual activity for three days, with racing of all classes of vintage AHRMA bikes all day long on the GP track. For those who grew up on dirt bikes or who simply have a passion for that kind of riding, the festival offers dirt, trials, and scrambles races where you can get up close and personal to the racers and their bikes, which makes for great action photography.

Of course, there is the swapmeet, but this is not an average weekend swapmeet; it occupies a large area near the southeast corner of the track with row after row of vendors. Not only can you find aftermarket and original parts for Evo Harleys, but also rare and exotic hard-to-find parts for makes such as Montesa, BSA, and Norton. Vintage bikes from the '60s and '70s such as Triumph, Honda, Suzuki, Kawasaki, you name it, are there along with every part an old bike wrencher might need to finish an authentic restoration. For those who love old bikes, but don't have the time, experience, or inclination to rebuild a bike, there are finished restorations for sale, ready for the street or the dirt. If you are really on the hunt then you must leave yourself most of one day just to rummage through what's offered in the swapmeet.

While wandering the grounds, I strolled to the Vintage Japanese Motorcycle Club's area, just inside the entrance gate. As the owner of a 1968 Honda CB350 who has succumbed to the charms of this old metal, I am a member of the club and had to take a look at row after row of meticulously restored Japanese bikes. I am a rider of these bikes, fixing and riding and doing the minimal of cosmetic work in order to just enjoy the experience of riding bikes that in my youth I was denied the pleasure of owning. So I am always amazed at the care and attention to detail put into these bikes, down to original, period-correct screws and small fittings. I had been in on the planning of the first state-wide Florida Rally of the group and stopping here gave me a chance to check in with other people involved in the rally. I also was able to finally meet Bill Silver face-to-face, also known as "MrHonda," who I had been helping with a book he had written on the Honda Scramblers, but whom I had only known online.

Below the hill from the VJMC tents was the vendor area where Triumph, the festival sponsor, had a huge tent filled with gear and "Trumpets". In this area, too, were *Motorcycle Classics* magazine, with its own bike show; Erik Buell, formerly and famously or infamously, depending on your viewpoint of Harley-Davidson, who had now gone on his own; and numerous other specialty vendors.

There is a perimeter road circling the entire track and scattered along it were visiting motorcycles, most of which were vintage examples of both rare and common makes. One of my favorite things to do at the festival is to walk along this smorgasbord of bikes, looking at the clever or unusual modifications the owners had made and watching for unusual marques.

Just before I had left home, I received an email from a magazine I had written for in Florida before asking me to do a story on the festival, so I was wandering, camera in hand, snapping away in search of scenes that could be used along with the story. I went down to "Ace Corner," a café racer specialty area that was supposed to have good inside track views and snapped some pictures of the bikes whizzing by, only to find blur after blur when uploading the photos to the computer later. I did the same thing at the track-side forested hillside, so popular with race watchers. I obviously needed more time training myself with my DSLR. I took picture after picture as I strolled along of the swapmeet area, the bikes parked along the snaking perimeter road, the bikes at VJMC, and the air show over the track at midday. The auction bikes, too, were captured in my flash as I wondered what kind of prices such priceless motorcycles might fetch when the gavel went down.

Friday, after a quick run out for my evening dinner, I came back to camp at the swapmeet. A couple spaces away and across from our spot was a group that drove in with a large motorhome, equipped with fold-down handrails and a roof deck. When I returned to my tent the whooping and hollering had just started. I sat down at the fire with our neighbors, and we chatted as the night began to cool down from the sunny 80s that had baked us all day. During the day, I sold a book at a substantial discount to Tony, with an agreement for him to provide me coffee for the rest of the weekend, solving my expensive coffee situation in the mornings. During the evening conversation, I found out that Nathan had lived in my town for a year "back in the day." After swapping Lake Wales stories of "Is this still there?" and "Do you remember..." we each wandered off to our tents as the volume from the sky-deck club climbed louder and louder. Surprisingly the tumult had little effect on my passing into sleep.

Saturday was the busiest day at the swapmeet. During the day, Luis all but emptied his trailer of goods. I wanted to get as much of the magazine photography out of the way early so I could head out with my Florida riding partner, Roger, into the mountains northeast of Leeds. I continued my wanderings, winding up the picture taking in the morning, sporadically stopping back at our swapmeet spot to check in and to enable some of the others to wander off on their own quests.

By three o'clock Roger and I met up and headed out on our search for twisties, with a vague idea that most of the mountainous area appeared to be to the northeast. We left Leeds behind us and headed north on US 411 through Leeds and north past Interstate 20. After I-20 we continued on this road northeast until AL 174, which looked like our best bet for putting us in the mountain ridges that ran roughly parallel to the north side of I-59 and, hopefully, into some twisties. 174 would become County Road 9 just past I-59 and would start climbing. As it was about to crest the ridge, it made a hard left and ran just south of the top until turning back on itself in a tight hairpin that put us on top of the ridge at an altitude of 1,800 feet. Here we took a quick break in a gravel pull-off and overlook where we could look a thousand feet down into the valleys we had crossed.

The plan was to follow County Road 27 north across the convoluted landscape and join US 231, which we could take back southeast to US 78, completing our loop. Instead, we got off 27 somehow and found ourselves running the crest of the ridge on rural and scenic County Road 24, which ended up emptying us back where we began, at the same overlook. It was now late afternoon, and we decided instead of trying to find our original route and continue, we should high tail it back the way we came. The added bonus was we could run that hairpin again in the opposite, downhill, direction.

We retraced our path and arrived back at Barber at six o'clock. I had put off going to the museum until after our ride, but as we pulled into the parking lot the visitors were being shooed out and the doors locked. Luckily, I had been in the museum twice before and the pictures for the article of the collection would have to be selected from the previous visits. This was a small price to pay for the fun of getting out and riding in the area, and, for the purpose of giving the readers an idea of what the museum was like, the older pictures would serve just as well, and I had many of then from which to choose.

Roger and I had chatted on motorcycleforum.com about meeting up with other members who might be going to attend the Vintage Festival at a restaurant in Leeds where 441 crossed I-20. One member from North Carolina had stopped by the swapmeet booth earlier with his friend, and others indicated they were attending, but after riding up to the meeting place, Roger and I ended up eating alone. While it would have been nice to meet face-to-face with some other members, we weren't really surprised. With so much going on at the motorsports park it would be hard, especially for first-time attendees, to tear themselves away. We enjoyed our meal together and talked about plans for the next day. Roger thought he would ride back with the Pinetta group and then take to the Interstate to get back the same day. I, on the other hand, was heading on alone to the Ozarks. I had received more good news of a great weekend had by Andrea, Leah, and the kids, which further relieved my guilt for abandoning Andrea and the kids while I went off touring.

My destination was in northwestern Arkansas, near a little village called Wesley, a little east of Fayetteville. If I was going to make it before dark I was going to have to leave well before dawn on Sunday morning. I settled down early for my last night camping at Barber after a bit of chatting and a shot of bourbon enjoyed around the "camp fire" of my new friends, Tony and Nathan.

Tomorrow would start the part of the trip I was looking forward to most. As much as I enjoyed riding with a few friends, I would be back in my element from here on, riding solo into new lands. Nothing compares to the experience of riding solo and becoming one with your bike in a way that is impossible when riding in groups, where an eye must constantly be watching the group and trying to stay in synch with it. Now, all I had to synch with was myself, and I had all day to think about whatever came to mind. It was during this part of the trip I quit thinking about each thing I did, and I just let it happen. It is a kind of synch between bike and rider that is similar to what I had experienced in my days as a solo sailor where all the tasks aboard my boat to get her from one place to another were done competently without consciously thinking about them. It must be akin to what an athlete feels when he or she is in the groove and the body does what it has been trained to do without conscious effort. In a way, this part of the trip was the real start of the adventure for me.

In the chill of the dark morning, I broke camp and reloaded the Bonnie. Birmingham traffic is awful, but I figured I'd be safe at five o'clock on Sunday morning, so I passed through downtown in the predawn darkness on empty city streets, following US 78 to the far side and into the countryside northwest of the city. It was cold, but I had taken precautions and broken out my winter gloves, reinstalled the liner in my jacket, and donned a sweatshirt under that. 78 was a wide and empty divided four-lane highway rising and falling over the diminishing foothills of the end of the Appalachians. It was soon to be upgraded to Interstate 22, as the signs along the side and on the overpasses attested.

Halfway between Birmingham and the Mississippi line, with my reserve light on, I left the nascent Interstate for the little town of Eldridge just as daylight was about to break and filled the tank. I took the opportunity to go inside the little combination gas station, convenience story, and restaurant to grab a large cup of coffee. The early-rising locals were scattered about the seating area doing the same. We sat while we drank and discussed the hunting season and the prospect for deer this year, with the inevitable deer strike story thrown in, and perhaps embellished. The shot of coffee had revived me and I went outside to lube the chain before chucking the bottom of the cup, remounting the bike, and heading back up in the growing light to US 78 and continuing west to Tupelo, Mississippi, on the still deserted highway.

Not one to savor the experience of riding through big cities, to avoid Memphis I took US 278 west from Tupelo on good two lane pavement, heading for the Mississippi River and the first crossing south of Memphis. Soon after my departure from 78, I could see a bank of ominous, dark clouds gathering up ahead. I passed another motorcyclist going the same direction as he pulled into a small parking lot. A mile or so further down the road as I watched the sky get darker, I realized he must have pulled over to put on his rain gear. When I saw an empty, covered fruit stand, I turned off the road and pulled under its metal roof, as the sky grew wilder, and did the same. I had my rain jacket on, and the pants on one leg when the sky let loose and poured its wet contents onto the shed roof. I finished dressing in a cacophony of pelting rain, and, still under shelter, I remounted the Bonnie, negotiated the now wet gravel entrance, and returned to the road in the midst of the downpour, relatively safe from being drenched. My rain jacket caught the wind up the sleeves and billowed out, making me feel like the Sta Puft marshmallow man. I'd need to do something about that once I found a lull in the rain, but for now I puttered along trying to see the best I could through my rain splashed visor under a dark gray ceiling. The wind had picked up tremendously from the west-southwest and made for a turbulent ride when combined with the wind caused by my forward motion as I rode into the teeth of it.

Soon I could see what I thought was the edge of the front, a tranquil bright blue spot to my right. But the front was teasing me and the clear spot stayed just out of reach as I apparently paralleled the front, and I stayed tucked just inside its northern edge.

The rain continued as the land grew flatter, and cotton fields appeared around me as I approached the Delta area of Mississippi. I was looking for a small road to the right, MS 3, at Marks, but blew right by it without a clue and ended up at US 61/49. I turned right and rolled north to a place where

49 would split off and continue to the mighty river and my crossing to Helena, Arkansas. Finally, the blue sky was close to floating overhead, and the rain had tapered off and almost completely stopped as I crossed the last levee. I pulled to the paved shoulder just before the bridge across the Mississippi, next to an Indian casino, to take off my rain gear and to grab a photo of the bridge ahead that would be my gateway to Arkansas and the first time I was to ride in the West. Rain gear stowed away again, I rode over into Arkansas.

On the other side, I continued to follow US 49 out of Helena and to Arkansas 1, which led me north to Wynne and US 64. Heading almost due north, it was nice to finally have the wind more or less behind me. Unfortunately, the front had not finished toying with me, and, not long after my entrance to this new state, the blue hole in the clouds closed up, and the rain began again. At least this time it rained with less authority, and I was able to keep rolling and did not have to stop to re-don my gear. The rain came and went, but the skies slowly started to improve, and each rain shower was lighter than the previous one had been. Somewhere around my turn to the west at US 64 the rain left completely, and I regained the sunshine. Then, all I was left with was the terrific wind blasting me from the front and left side, or forward of my port beam, as I would have said so many years ago when I depended on the wind to sail from one place to another. The land opened up and gave encouragement to the wind, which now fairly howled across the farm land, as the flat fields rolled quickly by, and I struggled to keep the bike on the road as gusts roared in.

US 64 moved me west and turned into a Interstate-like four-lane for a short while heading southwest, where it joined US 167, then a short time later split off again to continue west to Conway and Interstate 40.

It was getting well into the afternoon by then, and I was starting to have doubts about my arrival time. The wind was still blustery and threatening to knock the wheels out from under me. I hopped onto I-40, the first real Interstate I had ridden on the trip so far, with the intent to haul ass and get to Wesley before dark. But there is a time warp in Arkansas, I swear, or some kind of space-time distortion. Anywhere I pointed my front wheel toward took me fifty-percent longer to reach than even my unoptimistic estimated forecast. This phenomena followed me for the rest of my time in the Ozarks.

I continued west, and, as the afternoon was waning, I found my turnoff at little AR 23. This was my first chance to be riding in the Ozark mountains, and this road did not disappoint, but with darkness falling quickly and having quite a way to go I could not relax and enjoy the ride as I should have. I sped on 23 through marvelous hills and mountains, into and out of the rapidly cooling shade cast by their flanks, with plenty of twist and turns on my way north to the junction with AR 16. I turned left on 16 and went a short distance to where 16 met AR 295. 16 went northwest here, and 295 went northeast then north. If followed far enough, 16 would take me into Fayetteville, but I knew that was further than I needed to go and Wesley, where my camp was waiting, was east of 16 on AR 74, where it joined for a while with 295, forming a circle with me at that moment at its southern edge. Light was fading fast, the sun having set behind the mountains quite a while earlier. The cold was coming on, chillier than it had been even on those cold mornings at Leeds. It was time to make a call. Stopped on top of a concrete divider at the 16 and 295 junction, I took out my phone and searched my contacts list for my host for the evening. No "Doc" listed! I was sure I had entered the info into the phone before I left, but what I was seeing was telling me otherwise. I was in deer-infested mountains and would be riding in the dark soon. I scrolled back through all my old called or received numbers, hoping Doc would be there, but apparently we had not talked on this cell phone. Then I remembered that initially he had texted me. I looked over those old texts and, luckily, found my host's number there. I texted him and told him I was lost. We agreed I should ride up 16 to where it joined 74 and then text again when I got there. I hopped on the bike, mindful of his warning to "watch out for deer!" and, when I could, I stayed behind cars so if something jumped out the car would take the brunt of it instead of me. I got to the intersection without incident and texted again. Doc gave me final instructions and I picked up a sandwich for my evening meal, threw it in the baggage, and hopped back on the Trumpet for the last short stretch of the ride. Doc would be waiting for me at his "road" on an ATV.

In all fairness, Doc did say in his invitation post, "OFF ROADERS ONLY," so I was not surprised when I spotted Doc's headlight on the right side at the start of a dirt path. We said our hellos, and Doc informed me that the road was rough and there was a little water crossing on the way to his place, four miles or so up. "Up" was right; the road wiggled its way across the Ozark landscape across a valley and up a mountain. I had ridden on dirt roads, usually clay grove roads, before. In fact, I had at times purposely searched them out just for practice, so I was not too concerned about having to ride a mere four miles on dirt. As we rode on, at times the road was smooth and comparable to a graded gravel road—not bad. At times, though, it turned into a passage across exposed rock, albeit more or less flat rock. The "gravel" was a collection of round rocks ranging from the size of golf balls to baseballs. A little momentum got me through the water crossing with no surprises, even on this "street bike," and soon we arrived at Doc's mountain home, perched on the crest of a ridge and with a view through a gap in the trees down into the now dark valley we had ridden through before our ascent. There was a roaring fire already blazing in the area in which I was going to pitch the tent. After a little chewing the fat at the fire, Doc left me alone to eat my sandwich and call my family. I got about a half minute of clear communication with Andrea then lost contact completely. I was not to get through again at all while there, but at least I was able to let her know I got in safely.

Tomorrow, when I was out exploring the Ozarks, I would be able to check in again. I crawled into my bag dressed in my sweats, exhausted from the day of fighting wind gusts, and soon was asleep in perfect camping weather, the wind having dropped at sundown and the temperature falling.

I woke to the view of the valley, now in sunshine and illuminated below, and climbed out of the bag with the promise of coffee wafting in the air. The Ozark Mountains were in full autumn color under a blanket of reds, oranges, and yellows, with spots of green from the pines counter-pointing the riot of colors. I found Doc and the coffee, up on the wide veranda jutting out from his house, on which we could sip the hot brew and watch the glory of an fall Ozark morning develop around and below us. I had carried up my maps, and Doc and I set to work figuring a doable day ride from here to the outskirts of Little Rock that would give me the best riding roads northwestern Arkansas and southwestern Missouri had to offer. I had only a day to get in some just-for-fun riding, then I had to meet my friend and, afterward, start the long trek home.

Doc suggested he take his dirt bike and we could go out the other way together, completing the loop his trail made back to the paved road. I rolled up the tent and had the Bonnie loaded almost instantly, having had plenty of experience by now loading and unloading it. We rolled away from the house and up the trail. Doc, on his more capable dirt bike, would ride up ahead and wait for me on corners, so I could take my time on the Triumph. This was ideal so that we could each ride at our own pace , staying within the capability envelope of our bikes and experience. Doc moved ahead, but the Bonnie did well, and Doc didn't have long to wait at each stop. I found standing on the pegs helped a lot in the rougher patches and soon got the hang of riding over rock and loose rubble. We stopped for some pictures and then at the end of the dirt, we said our good-byes, and I rolled onto the pavement and back to AR 74.

I headed northeast and rolled along in the still early morning light on a quiet country road among hills and pleasant valleys. Passing a large golden field on my left, I saw what I had hoped to miss the night before—four large does racing across the field toward the road. There were two cars in front of me, and they barely slowed. I was not willing to take any chances, and I rolled to a stop. The group saw me ahead and heard my motor growl and with one jump changed direction and bounded off in the direction from which they had come through the field flood lighted by the morning sun.

After admiring that spectacle of nature, I moved on and came across the little village of Huntsville, where I spied a pastry shop. I stopped for more coffee and a taste of a delicious, freshly made poppy seed muffin while I jotted notes of things I wanted to remember about the ride and took a rest before my day long adventure got into high gear.

I have done my share of riding in the Blue Ridge and Smokies, so I did not expect the Ozarks to be very impressive. After all, mountains in the Blue Ridge are four or five thousand feet high, with occasionally higher peaks; the Ozarks, on the other hand, are in the neighborhood of two thousand feet high. However, in the Blue Ridge the valley floors may be at three thousand feet, where the valley floors in the Ozarks may be one thousand, or even five hundred feet, so the change in elevation you see in the Ozarks is still impressive. Admittedly, they are not as dramatic as the Smokies, but all that we love as riders—all the twisties, elevation changes, beautiful views, quiet valleys, and, in the right season, the glory of autumn—are offered by the Ozarks. Of course, the Blue Ridge Mountains are taller, but unless you just want a higher drop from which to fall to your death, the Ozarks have all a rider's heart desires.

After breakfast, I found AR 23 and took it north twisting my way into Missouri where 23 changed to State Highway P, which landed me at the junction of Missouri 86. Continuing, I turned east and followed 86 as it meandered just above the Arkansas line until I reached US 65, which is the major southern route into Branson, Missouri. I turned toward Branson and there found a Taco Bell, which I had been craving for days and which, apparently, were all but absent from the state of Arkansas or Mississippi. I called Andrea from the restaurant, letting her know where I was and what my plans were for the rest of the day. It sounded like things were going well on her end, too, which was encouraging. After lunch, I found Missouri 76 that took me away from Branson and the traffic and landed me on US 160, well east of the city.

I buzzed along this road running parallel again above the state line north of Bull Shoals Lake, which is really a dammed up river that flows from Table Rock Lake, a similarly dammed river turned lake that lies west of Branson. The plan was to follow this road until I came to State Highway M, which should have ended at a ferry that would take me back to Arkansas. Fifteen or so miles, indeed, took me to the river, but the road dead-ended with no ferry. I was hoping to find fuel on the other side of the ferry crossing, and my reserve light had been glowing orange for a long time by then. At least the Bonneville still had nine-tenths of a gallon left when that light came on. Back to 160 I flew, enjoying the twists and turns again M had offered on the way south. The detour and worry about running out of fuel was a small price to pay for some good riding.

Once again on 160, after checking my map, I headed east to MO 125 and turned south, with the miles now racking up since that light went on. Luckily, in a few miles I spied a small gas station, where another bike was stopped, and able to replenish my fuel supply and end the worry. Not far beyond the station the road ended at Peel's Ferry, which at the moment was docked a half mile away on the far landing. I was once again in Arkansas, as the border doesn't follow the river course as is often the case, but is an arrow-straight line running east and west intersecting the lake in various places. I took the opportunity to stretch my legs and take a few photos before the ferry returned. The sportbike from the station and its two riders joined me and one car for the ride across. We parted ways on the other side, and I headed south on 125 to AR 14, then west to AR 7, famed for its excellent riding. I had the joy of riding 7, but only as far as US 65. My error on M and the Arkansas time warp had me running late again, and, if I was going to see my friend in Bryant early this evening, I needed to make up some time.

Although 65 was a busier road, punctuated by a few small towns, it was still a lovely ride, and I enjoyed it as the day grew late. At Clinton I veered south-southwest, then south on AR 9 all the way to AR 5, also known as Hot Springs Highway, which I followed into Benton. By then, it had long since turned dark and cold. I had called my friend, Brenda, to let her know it was not going to be a dinner meeting but a mid-evening one instead, but by then it was late enough to call it off for the night. We arranged to meet for breakfast at a Cracker Barrel restaurant, which was almost across the street from my hotel, the first hotel I had stayed in on the trip. I wasn't happy with myself because a morning meeting would mean a late start after breakfast, and I had wanted to run straight through to Dothan, Alabama, in one day, where I would have a place to stay at a relative's home. But there was nothing to be done. I had not seen Brenda since high school over thirty years ago, when our close group of friends were as thick as thieves, and I was determined to see her again, so I made the best of the luxurious room and bed.

I was packed quickly in the morning and met Brenda at the restaurant while the sky was still pink from the newly risen sun. She had just had an operation as a result of a serious illness. When I had talked to her three weeks ago it was questionable whether she would be up for a visit, but the operation had gone well, and she was able to drive to meet me. Over breakfast I found out that her prognosis was excellent and her recovery was swift, and she should soon be back in the best of health. We discussed old friends and lost friends, as old pals usually do, and made plans to meet up with each other again, at least on Facebook, when she finally moved into the twenty-first century, got an account, and logged on.

For the previous day or so, I had been hearing an ominous sound emanating from the rear brake. It started quietly, but, as time went on, the sound increased, and I became concerned. In my rush in the dark to get to Benton, I let it go. I don't know if it was my hurry or just the reluctance to prove to myself what I already knew, that I had a mechanical problem, but by the time I checked the brake in good light on the morning I was meeting Brenda, I had worn the rear pad completely out and the rotor, too. This was an inexcusable maintenance failure on my part, and I felt guilty for letting it go this far. I should have known better and checked sooner. Now I would be riding with only a front brake from Little Rock to home in Florida, almost a thousand miles away, where I would change the brake pads, and unnecessarily spend more money, which was in short supply at that time, on a new rotor.

It was ten o'clock by the time I rolled out of the parking lot—not a good sign for making it to Dothan at a reasonable hour. I headed southeast, hoping for the best, but then it occurred to me that I had not bought the kids' souvenirs, a big transgression in daddy-land. As I moved southeast I watched for any sign of somewhere I might find something, at this late time almost anything, that said "Arkansas" somewhere on it. I made several false stops, coming up empty each time.

I headed out on AR 35, hoping to see another side of Arkansas and to cross the Mississippi further south. I followed 35 into the Delta area across some of the flattest land I had ever seen. On riding forums, Florida is often ridiculed for being flat, and the section for Florida riders is called "Flatistan" at advrider.com, but whoever laid that name on Florida must have never ridden through southeastern Arkansas. As I moved east and south my GPS often told me I was at an altitude lower than my driveway in central Florida.

Cotton reappeared and stayed with me to the Florida line. The harvest was underway and I got to see the crop in all stages of growth and from picking to loading to baling into truck-sized bales, which then were slid into the back of special trucks and hauled away to mills, I suppose.

I followed 35 to US 278 turning south toward Lake Village. I stopped at a station there to fill the tank and get some food at the next door McDonalds. As I was pumping, a lovely woman walked up to me to look at the bike. We struck up a conversation, and I learned that she was about to buy a bike herself. We chatted about bikes, and I suggested taking the Basic Rider Course, which she told me she planned on doing. It's funny how sometimes these kind of things happen; I had never met this woman, but I instantly felt a connection, and I think she did, too. Talk moved past bikes, and she said she left New Orleans after Katrina and moved to Benton, Arkansas (where I had stayed the night before), and that her daughter had stayed behind in the Big Easy. She was driving down to help her with some project. It was a pleasant break from the solitude I'd had riding alone for the last two days. We exchanged numbers and promised we would meet up someday if our paths crossed again. It's curious how you never know how many people you pass by each day that could have ended up being friends if you had only taken the time to speak up and talk to them. It's a little life lesson that can enrich us if we take the leap of faith to connect with others.

After a quick bite and more coffee, I crossed back over the Mississippi River after tracing the contour of the ox-bow Lake Chicot. Not far into Mississippi, I made a last ditch effort to secure souvenirs at a little tourist shop at Leland, on US 82. The shop turned out to be a museum dedicated to Jim Henson, who had been born in this small Delta town. The lonely attendant tried hard to follow her much-loved script as I looked around, but the gift shop section turned up nothing not Henson related, and, as interesting as the place and the man was, neither of my children had been fans, so I got back on the bike and kept on my way toward the east, passing Indianola, made famous by B. B. King, this area being the heart of the Delta Blues. I wish I had not been short on time. I saw signs for the B. B. King Museum, the Blues being one of my favorite kinds of music and King being, well, the King of the Blues. I would have enjoyed visiting it.

Now devoid of hope for picking up souvenirs and contemplating the fate that awaited me as a failed father to my disappointed children, I continued on as the day grew late and I grew tired. I had talked to Andrea and asked her whether my being a day late would be all right with her. I was exhausted, the day was winding down toward darkness, and Dothan was still hundreds of miles away. She was more worried about me riding tired than any complications my arriving late would cause her. I thanked her for understanding, and close to sunset I stopped in Columbus, just inside the Mississippi state line that separated it from neighboring Alabama.

I spied a Best Western, which generally were biker-friendly and at which I received an AMA discount, so I rode up and checked in. The price was reasonable and included breakfast, which made departure in the morning much easier for me. Also, stopping here early would give me the opportunity to shop for those pesky souvenirs where I might have better luck, now being in this bigger town.

I asked at the desk, and the clerk told me Walmart had all sorts of stuff with Mississippi written on it, or Georgia for that matter. She was talking about universities, of course, but the kids only care about their gift being from somewhere else, and a state name other than Florida written on it sealed the deal. Besides, my son is a football fan, so when I saw a cooling towel with Mississippi written across it, I knew he would be happy. Among the other school spirit stuff, I found a cheer bracelet with that desirable state name on it and threw in a nice soft throw I found covered with peace signs for my daughter.

That task completed, I relaxed and had dinner at a conveniently located restaurant in the hotel parking lot. The only other souvenir I wanted to pick up was a bag of shelled pecans for Andrea and I, but I was too far north for that item yet, and, besides, I knew where to find that, as the road between Dothan and Valdosta would be lined with pecan groves. I headed back to the hotel room, tried to watch part of a presidential candidate debate, but couldn't stay awake. I clicked off the light and was soon asleep.

I had been able to park right outside my door the night before, so packing went quickly. Soon, I was partaking of the breakfast inside the hotel lobby. Word was another front with rain was coming through from the west and heading southeast, and I wanted to stay ahead of it and beat it home, if I could.

I aimed my wheels southeast on US 82 and was soon back in the State of Alabama. I flew through the heartland of Alabama, passing through Tuscaloosa, then Montgomery. At Montgomery, I switched to US 231 and rolled past cotton field after cotton field until I got onto Rose Clark Circle, which encloses Dothan, about mid-afternoon. I stopped in an empty car lot and called my father-in-law's nephew, Lloyd, who owns the company that hosts my websites and e-mail. We had gotten to know each other over the years on family fishing trips when kingfish were running out of Panama City, where he kept his boat.

Lloyd gave me directions to his office, which, happily, was just a bit farther down the highway I was already on. I pulled up to Lloyd's office and found him in his office, where his wife, Kay, joined us. Lloyd had just bought himself a Harley Dyna, and we chatted about bikes and family and then about a minor issue I was having with the websites, which he assured me he would take care of. Then, with an aim to get to Valdosta that day, I headed back out to the bike. Lloyd and Kay came out and took a look at the Triumph while we said our good-byes. I lifted the kick stand, fired the Bonnie up, and continued on my way to Valdosta, taking US 84.

Along the way, I got my chance to get a few photos of the bike in front of a cotton field, a shot I had meant to get on previous rides through cotton country, but somehow had never accomplished. Arriving at Interstate 75 at Valdosta, it was just one exit north and a couple miles west and I would be at my friend's house.

I usually don't mind a stop in Valdosta. It gives me a chance to catch up with another old high school friend, Julie, who manages the gallery and teaches at Valdosta State University. Julie was part of that knot of friends back in high school that Brenda had been part of, and the only one I get to see on a regular basis. Living in Valdosta, she is pretty much at the gateway to most other parts of the country I might ride to coming north from central Florida. I often make it a point to crash at her place and catch up with her and her dad, Jack, who lives with her. Only 280 or so miles from home, it is a nice distance for a day's ride, and perfect when combined with a three day weekend, when I am in the mood for seeing my old school chum.

As usual, Julie welcomed me with open arms and even took me and some friends out for a steak dinner and beer, of course, plenty of beer. More beer and stories flowed back at her place the rest of the evening, and I went to bed fat and happy. Tomorrow would be an easy day—a nice way to end a long trip.

I woke to coffee brewing, and, not being in a rush, I took my time having coffee, talking, and loading the bike. I didn't want to leave too early, because I planned on stopping at a place Julie told me about to pick up a large bag of shelled pecans, and I didn't want to get there before they opened. Finally, I said good-bye to Jack and gave Julie a thankful hug and headed back out to a morning enveloped in a thick fog.

I rode through Valdosta and picked up the pecans, then headed south on US 41 and into Florida. Just inside my home state, I turned right on FL 143 at Jennings, and in a few miles I was on Interstate 75, racing south toward home.

I normally eschew Interstates, partly because most of my riding, until I got my Triumph, had been on top of my ancient CB350, which, although it would run at Interstate speeds, sounded pretty wound out at 6,500 rpm and just made me uneasy. But the main reason I avoided Interstate travel was because on them you just didn't get to see much countryside and local color, each mile looking roughly like the one before it and the one after. This time I was on the Bonnie, which seemed to thrive at 75 miles per hour, and I had extended the trip already by a day and wanted to make good time in order to arrive before school was out, so I could walk up to the school crossing, a half mile from our home, and walk my daughter home from school as a surprise.

After a final fuel stop at FL 44, I hopped back on 75 for only a minute before merging left onto the Florida Turnpike and heading towards US 27, which runs past Lake Wales. I made a final shift of my track at Davenport to FL 17 and continued south on the now local roads into my little town and into my drive. I had just enough time to hop off the bike and walk to the crossing where my daughter ran to me with shouts of joy and, of course, "What did you bring me?!"

So the balance had shifted. It was time for me to be the dad who stays at home and spends time with the family. I'd do my best to be that guy and do a good job of it. It would be months before I could plan my spring escape, when he scales would tip the other way.

Morning Deer

It had become my yearly ritual over the last few years to ride up to the Barber Vintage Festival, in Leeds, Alabama. Other than the first year, when I had ridden over from Maggie Valley, North Carolina, with the Motorcycle Kickstart Classic ride, the usual procedure was to ride up to Pinetta, Florida, just inside the Florida line, south of Valdosta, Georgia, and meet up friends, Debbie and Luis, who have a bike shop there and also have a swapmeet spot at the festival. I would ride the two hundred and fifty or so miles to Pinetta, stay the night, then in the morning my friends and other local riders would show up, and we would all ride the remaining three hundred and twenty-five miles to Barber. As a result, Deb and Luis had a night guard at their booth, and I had a tent camping spot, free of charge. My friends, although they had no obligation to do so, had also generously provided me with my pass into the festival. When we had all said our good-byes last year, the plan was on to do it all again in the fall of 2013. In the spring, there was another check-in from Debbie to see who was planning to go.

A couple weeks before the 2013 festival, I emailed Deb one

last time to find out what the plans were, only to discover that she and Luis and their friends were not going to make it this time. I had blocked out time for this. It is my usual break after a long summer of being daycare for my kids and before school gets going in earnest. I started scrambling to see what my options were. A check of the Barber Vintage Festival website revealed that all camp sites were sold out. My guess was that if they were sold out then any campground any practical distance from the festival would be, too. That left hotels. They were probably going to be full up for a wide distance around, too, and if I could find a room it would probably mean a long ride in each day to the Barber Motorsports Park. Added to this, I had to consider that my financial situation had been marginal for going to Barber this year. Now that the cost had increased by the expense of a hotel room for several nights and of a pass for all the days at the festival, not to mention the cost of eating out all the time I would be there, going was too much of a strain on my pocketbook. What to do?

Let me back up here a bit and tell you that for years, when my younger brother, Tim, had lived close by in Florida, we tried hunting deer together. After year after year of being skunked, with only one exceptional year, when Tim had gotten a small deer and I had shot a tiny dog-sized deer, we had pretty much given up on providing our families with a supply of venison. Eventually, Tim moved to South Carolina and bought a place in an ideal spot, set back on the edge of a clearing ringed by woods and bordered by a creek. Tim invited me up to hunt last year on the opening weekend, which happened to coincide with Barber Vintage Festival. I was riding to Barber and so had to miss hunting with Tim then, while he brought in his limit, only yards from his back door. By the time I made it up a month later, the magic was over, with no deer to be found. Now, all that had changed. I could ride up, shotgun strapped across the bike, and take advantage of the opening day and the feeders Tim had installed below the stands, something that was not allowed the year before. I'd only have to spend money for fuel for the Bonneville and a little food on the way up and back. It would cost nothing while at Tim's. I called Tim, and we hatched a plan.

The day came when I would have left for Barber, but instead it found my headlight pointing northeast on I-4, headed for the promised land of deer and plenty, and plenty of deer. I considered my options and wanted to make this excursion as short as possible. My wife had changed jobs and was now driving a substantial distance to an office, instead of working from home. She had lost much of her flexibility when it came to picking up and caring for the kids. I made arrangements with my parents to pick up and watch the kids on a Friday after school, until Andrea could get there to bring them home after work. All she would have to do as far as child care on Friday morning would be to get them up and off to school, and then she would be home with the kids for the weekend. I would leave Tim's Sunday evening and be back in Lake Wales before the kids went off to school on Monday morning.

That plan would work, so I considered my options to fine tune my departure. Of course, now was the season for deer to become mobile, not just in South Carolina, but across Georgia. I wanted to avoid any surprise meetings of my headlight and a deer on the way up. Hitting a deer with a car is a messy thing, and a deer for a hood ornament does not bode well for a car or its occupants, but on a bike the same often results in the rider's quick and final good-bye. I decided it would be best to avoid that danger as much as possible by staying on the Interstates during the dark of night. Considering that, as far as Andrea and her caring for the kids was concerned, it made no difference if I left in the daylight, which would seriously cut into hunting time, or whether I left the night before, which would get me a full weekend in the tree stands, I decided on a night departure.

I headed out on Thursday night at eleven, with a plan to ride northeast through Orlando on I-4—something I would do anything to avoid any other time of day. By the time I got to the city, though, it would be midnight, and most of the vehicles that make I-4 a nightmare at rush hour would be snoozing in driveways or garages across central Florida. It should be a breeze, and it was. I sped northeastward through the night toward my eventual connection with I-95, upon which I would hurtle north, escaping Florida, and the other city bottleneck, Jacksonville, before daylight. Florida is not known as a high incidence state for deer strikes, but it still pays to be vigilant, and the Interstates gave me the best chance for avoiding hazards of the antlered variety. Expecting to be at Brunswick, Georgia, by daylight, I hurried north into our neighboring state, the road all but to myself.

If you take Interstates all the way to Tim's, it entails taking I-4 northeast, to I-95 north-northeast, curving to northeast along the coast to I-26, just inland from Charleston, for the final run northwest to Inman, where the deer awaited. While you can maintain good speed on this route, Inman happens to be almost due north from Lake Wales, where I live, so the Interstate route means a huge detour out of the rhumb line course. At Brunswick, Georgia, the route wandered east by a insignificant amount, but after that, I-95 swerves more eastward with every mile. Brunswick looked to be the perfect jumping off point to head cross-country across east Georgia and South Carolina to Inman. This would cut off the dog leg, and I would rejoin I-26 just thirty miles short of my destination. With any luck, the sun would be coming up when I departed I-95 at Brunswick, and heading north on small roads in daylight would pose the least risk of encountering road-hogging deer. It turned out I made such good time on the Interstate that I arrived at Brunswick at about four thirty—the morning still dark as pitch. I had planned on stopping for a decent breakfast anyway, so I pulled into a Waffle House with the intent to kill some time while the sun made more progress toward the horizon.

I had been going non-stop, other than quick fuel ups. There was a chill in the air, and, in spite of my warm clothing, a bit of the cold had seeped in while my hunger had grown, so the restaurant was a welcome stop. The stop also happened to be pretty close to the halfway point of my northward trudge. I filled up on scrambled eggs, hash browns, and coffee, while the feeling started to return to my fingers. When I had cleaned my plate, paid, made my farewell bathroom pit stop, and stepped outside the world, at least that corner of it, was still in darkness. I started north on US 25, grateful for my foresight to have installed my two LED auxiliary lights, each of which threw out 1,500 lumens into the Georgia darkness. I bought these at advmonster.com from a fellow advrider forum inmate. They were Model 30 spots and one of the best motorcycling investments I had made, especially considering the anemic headlight on the Bonnie that shone on the ground ten feet ahead on "low," and on the upper leafy boughs of trees on "high." I took my time, kept my speed down, and watched the roadside, ahead and to either side, like a mouse watching for a low sweeping hawk.

It became even chillier as sunrise slowly came on, and, as it curiously always seems to do just after daylight, it got colder still. As I rode northward through the familiar east Georgia countryside, details appeared slowly while the sun made its way over the top of the passing trees. Off the highways now, I could smell the pleasant balsam scent I have grown to love in this part of the country. Soon, the scenery was bathed in full light and the cold withdrew. US 25 shot north-northwest, away from the coast, then north into Augusta, and across the Savannah River into South Carolina. I peeled off US 25 onto SC 121, and by mid-morning I was at Saluda and was shedding my windproof liner. From there I took SC 39 to Clinton, where SC 56 connected to I-26, just south of the I-385 and I-26 split.

I was on the home stretch and barreled north on 26, passing between Spartanburg, on my right, and Greenville, on my left.

Soon, I was at Exit 15 and US 176, fifteen miles short of the North Carolina line. It was then just a couple more turns, a right across a field on a dirt path, over the railroad tracks, and down the other side and into the woods, finally entering the wood-encompassed clearing and Tim's place, tucked neatly on the far side, in a tree-lined nook.

I arrived just about noon, greeting Tim thirteen hours after I left home. I grabbed my bags, installed them in my room, and pulled on my camo. Then, it was a quick lunch of venison on bread, bounty from Tim's hunt last year. Energy renewed, we exited the house. I assembled the two halves of my Winchester, loaded it with buckshot, and we walked into the woods, each taking different paths to our deer stands.

I wearily climbed the tree to my deer stand, nailed between three trunks of a hickory. By now I had been up since six thirty the previous morning, a tiring eighteen and a half hours earlier, but the excitement and anticipation of the hunt kept my eyes and ears open. I sat in the still of the woods, in view of the gurgling creek and the feeder, but by the time night had fallen no deer had taken our invitation. I climbed back up the hill, out of the woods, and to the house.

All was not lost. This was only our first attempt, we had hardly started, and today's hunt had been in the afternoon. We talked about hunting over more venison on the grill for dinner, and Tim made sure to point out that, in all the years he had hunted deer, here and in Florida and also Virginia, where he lived previously and had brilliant success, he didn't recall ever getting a deer in the afternoon. These were "morning deer" we kept telling ourselves, and, surely, a morning hunt would yield results. Tim and his wife, Pam, and I chatted on the deck until fatigue finally overtook me. I said my goodnights about eleven o'clock, after twenty-nine and a half hours of being awake. After the long ride and the day in the trees, I could not find the energy to shower. I undressed and fell in a heap on the waiting bed.

Five o'clock came early, much earlier than my body wanted to accept, but I clawed my way out of bed and into my camo, once again. In the kitchen, the critically necessary black coffee was already ready, and I poured myself cup after cup. Tim busied himself at the stove, fixing, what else, venison sausage and gravy over biscuits. Suitably reinforced, we headed outside and into the woods, being careful to break as few twigs as possible as we walked out to the stands in the dark. I chose the same stand I had been in the day before, ascended to the platform, and settled in, waiting for daylight and the "morning deer."

Morning grew to midday, but with no sign of deer. It became quite warm and was bordering on hot when we came in for a lunch break and more venison, of course. After lunch, Tim took me around the woods, and, as we quietly tread through the fallen leaves, he showed me where the third stand was and where he scored his deer last year.

We separated again, and this time I chose a stand farther from the house, to the southwest in the woods. This was near the edge of a swampy area, which abounded in deer tracks—buck tracks, no less—around the feeder. I had only barely recovered from the ride up, and, as the afternoon wore on, my eyes began to droop. From time to time I would close my eyes, leaving only my ears to detect movement in the surrounding brush. On a couple occasions, I nodded off completely, awakening with a start, followed by a quick assessment of what I might have missed in my brief moment of drowsing. Eventually, the sun sank again, and the woods were filled with darkness. I drug myself back along the path to the house in the darkness, shining my meager flashlight ahead of me in search of the reflective markers Tim had attached to various branches and stumps. Losing the path several times, I finally found the treeline and the house.

For a change, beef tenderloins were on the grill, which sufficiently woke me up for the remainder of the evening. We all caught up on old times and family news and gradually wandered off to bed, vowing tomorrow would be the day. After all, we had only been hunting *one* morning, and, as we well knew, these were "morning deer." One attempt was not enough; tomorrow our fortunes would surely change.

Another five o'clock awakening, more venison for breakfast, and gulps of hot coffee, and, once again, we were off into the woods for a meeting with our "morning deer." Finally recovered from the sleepless day on the way up, I managed to find the stand by the swamp in the blackness without cracking too many limbs and announcing to the forest dwellers Man's presence in their home. Dark grew to gray, and, while the colors returned to the leafy canopy and low lying brush, I kept my eyes and ears tuned for the shapes and sounds of forest creatures that had the potential to fill our freezers. Hours passed. I quietly sat and watched the squirrels playing in nearby boughs, and mice and chipmunks compete for the corn scattered at the foot of the feeder, while they watched nervously overhead for the presence of an owl or a hawk. They would dash out from hiding and grab a couple kernels, chewing them on the spot, until another of their kind would approach and demand their share, followed by a chattering and a scrambling of the losing party off into the underbrush, while the victor gnawed and watched for danger. First the chipmunks did this dance, then the squirrels, and occasionally a tiny, flitting bird. But the "morning deer" ignored the corn. As the morning dissolved into noon, not a single deer had showed the least interest in our breakfast offerings. I finally climbed down and, with a discouraged gait, walked out to meet up with Tim.

Perhaps we needed to change our strategy. Tim and I had a quick phone conversation and decided to walk, he from his side of the woods and me from the other. So off we traipsed, walking quietly through the woods, hoping that if the deer would not come to us we might come to the deer. We took a route to circle around the woods, that likewise circled the house and clearing, and which would meet up at the road that ran briefly along the railroad tracks before entering the woods on its way back to the house. I had one excited moment when, upon entering a thicket in a wet area, to my right, in the thickest of brush and tangles, I heard something big bound off toward the tracks. I walked though the center, following an animal trail the best I could. I made my way out of the thicket as quietly as possible, but no more sounds returned to my ears, and I was not rewarded with even the sight a tuft of a white tail bouncing off into the woods.

Tim and I met up at the tracks. Sure enough, fresh tracks led up and across the tracks that had to have been made only minutes earlier. Alas, those were the last "morning deer" of which we were to see fresh signs. We followed the railroad tracks toward the creek and then followed a power line cut-off to the right, and then another to the left, ending at the creek, where it was obvious many deer had crossed. We started along a game trail that meandered away from the creek, through a tangle of brambles, and through some shallow wet areas back into the woods. After thoroughly wetting our feet, we emerged at the game trail leading to the deer stand where I had been stationed during the last two hunts. Deer tracks were showing along the muddy trail, but none had made it to the feeder.

It was then back into the stands for another try, me staying on this one and Tim moving on to the ground stand he had been in earlier in the day. As light faded on this final day of hunting, I lost hope of seeing a deer and was just filling the remaining time in the stand, hoping on the off chance that one of the "morning deer," who perhaps had lost track of the time, might accidentally wander by. As I sat, I was thinking of my ride back. The strategy of staying out of deer territory in the dark and the fact that I would now be leaving in the middle of night to make it home according to my original plan, made me reconsider the wisdom of that plan. I would have to take I-26, and even that, in this area, would not be the relatively safe passage I had on the Interstate in Florida, where the chances of hitting deer are a distant third on the list behind alligators and wild boar. The Interstate in this area would only be marginally safer in that respect than country roads, and it would take me far out of the way, east of a straight north-south route. I have never been a fan of Interstates anyway, and the memory of that long hard ride north made me reconsider returning directly after the hunt.

After arriving back at the house, after our final and disappointing hunt, we discussed what had happened. One thing was sure and that was that someone had turned the thermostat way up in South Carolina, and the needed cold snap to set the deer into rut, making them just careless enough to fall for our feeders in the daylight, had never happened. When the cold snap would occur, I would be six hundred miles away.

At the house after dinner, I made a call to Andrea. If I left in the morning, I could head cross country in the daylight. All we would have to do is call in one more favor from my folks and have them pick up the kids, and then Andrea could get them after work, like before. I resisted furthering the burden on her and my parents, but the thought of the danger and resultant exhaustion from a ride through the dark countryside outweighed that. I resolved to leave early in the morning just before light, peeling off I-26 at Clinton to retrace my steps south. By the time I got to Clinton, not far from Tim's, the sun should be up. With luck, I would be home before six in the evening. After gaining Andrea's approval of the plan, I loaded the bike with all but the essential stuff I would need in the morning and went off to bed for one last night. In the morning I could just hop out of bed, throw on my clothes, and ride away.

Tim rode his Star Stratoliner to work that morning, so we rode together until he rolled onto the exit for I-85, as I continued south, giving him a wave and toot of my pathetic horn. The eastern sky was just beginning to lighten as I left the Interstate at Clinton, where I stopped for a bite and some black coffee. By the time I had finished my breakfast, the sky was light, and I headed off onto the South Carolina country roads, bound for Augusta. Not long after my stop in Clinton, I came around a wide, sweeping curve and, lo and behold, there, crossing the road directly in front of me, was a deer. I slowed, and, by the time I passed where it had crossed, it was gone. With morning growing around me, I had to admit they were, indeed, "morning deer."

By midday, I zipped through the fragrant Georgia countryside and made the Florida state line, where I stopped to eat and call home with my status report. Florida was hot, as usual, and I followed an old, and what I thought was a familiar, route in order to avoid Jacksonville, but I slipped up somewhere and ended up back on Interstate 95. At least I had Jacksonville behind me, so I settled into the Interstate rhythm and watched for signs of FL 40, at Ormond Beach, where I could leave the highway and head west to US 19, in the Ocala National Forest. That would get me south, avoiding Orlando, and bring me to one of my favorite roads in central Florida, CR 561. Winding and rolling on 561 through the Sugarloaf Mountain area put me, finally, on US 27, which goes all the way to Lake Wales. By six, I was in the drive at home. Soon after, I was in my own bed, sleeping the sleep that only comes after hours on the road.

I missed that chance of getting a deer, but we are taking the entire family up for Thanksgiving to share the holiday with Tim, Pam, and his daughter, son, and son-in-law. I've been watching the weather reports. The cold has made it to Inman. Once there, I'll get up early, and maybe that would be my chance to put some "morning deer" in our freezer.

REFLECTING

Expensive Distractions

Always, and necessarily, being a frugal man, the cost of all things "motorcycle" sometimes astounds me. After reading motorcycle magazines, someone of slight or even moderate means just getting into riding must reel and might reconsider their choice of transportation when confronted with the newest and best motorcycle gear and accessories. It reminds me of my sailing days when anything with "marine" stamped on it was claimed to be worth the equivalent value of five or six of the same item without that special label.

Every month I read of helmets unabashedly offered with price tags of four or even six hundred dollars. You need a good pair of boots for riding?—get ready to cough up $600. And, of course, you must ATGATT if you value your life at all—four hundred for leather pants and the same for leather jacket is a small price to pay for your safety. Now, also, almost everyone has to ride in different seasons, which logically requires different clothing for each and a wardrobe budget of thousands. After all, you'd be a fool to ride without heated clothing in the cold or in the summer in a full-face helmet. While buying all this, you have already spent so much that you might as well get that certain label; it hardly makes any difference, percentage-wise—it may as well be emblazoned with "Harley-Davidson," "Alpinestars," or "Aerostich."

And the bike, well, how are you going to go anywhere without hard bags that match the color of the bike. And when the cold fronts roll in you are going to be glad you have those heated grips. Can you imagine crossing the flat plains of the Midwest without a good stereo to listen to for passing the monotonous time? Your pipes are too quiet and you've heard that "Loud Pipes Save Lives"?—here are some aftermarket ones that are LOUD.

None of these things are bad in themselves, but it's wise to consider the cost-benefit ratio for each. If I was a wealthy man, sure, I'd buy a complete Aerostich suit, and boots custom made from exact measurements of my feet. Why not? Those products will probably perform great. Like many of us, however, I must balance the cost of those things against others, like my ability to go where and when I want on my motorcycle. If those extra four hundred dollars I paid for my boots means shortening my two week motorcycle trip to one, are they worth it? Will wearing a hundred and fifty dollar pair keep me from going the distance on that trip? In other words, especially with limited means, I must decide what is more important to me; I must prioritize. This seems pretty simple when you think about it, but often the logical gets blurred in the world of marketing we all live in. Yeah, I *want* those new saddlebags, but do I *need* them? Will I be able to do anything more or go anywhere farther with new ones that I cannot go with the old ones, in spite of what the magazine ads tell me?

For some, the choice is often made easier by simply not having the means to purchase "newer and better." While that can deny some kind of enjoyment, it also frees one from all the rigmarole of superfluous complications and expenses.

I bought a used set of leather saddlebags at a yard sale back when I got my CB350 going. They cost me the sum of eight dollars. They are not nice and shiny, they are not watertight, but they have held half of my kit for thousands of miles with little trouble (and not more than a few ziplock bags to contain the stuff within). Sure, someday I will spend $250 on bigger, waterproof, and more flexible bags, but I know I do not *have* *to* and can choose to whenever a windfall comes my way. Two hundred and fifty dollars is two nights, at least, in motels on the road—an automatic extension of any trip I take.

I bought an aftermarket windscreen for my CB350; one of those that attach to the handlebars of about any bike. It was relatively inexpensive, but, in spite of its small size, it made a huge difference in comfort at highway speeds. I am not sorry I spent the money on it, but that I could get by without even that was proven when I dropped the bike and broke the windshield on the way out of my drive on the way to Michigan during a cold April. It was not until I got to Michigan, a thousand miles later, that I was able to procure a replacement, but by then I knew that having one, while nice, was not a necessity.

Not giving oneself over to the advertising gods, gives a rider a chance to collect his or her thoughts about gear and accessories and decide on a rational and personal level of what is important to him or her. For me, a windscreen and a good saddle are important parts of a pleasant riding experience, and worth some expenditure. I have never felt the need, however, to spend many hundreds of dollars on motorcycle clothing. Early on I bought a mesh jacket with CE armor for less than a hundred dollars. It is usually all I need, and I can zip in its thermal jacket for all but the coldest times here in Florida. For those times, I can wear my old sailing fleece and nylon shell jacket underneath and stay toasty warm in the 40s. When in colder weather than that, I layer thermal underwear and a long sleeve shirt. Would I be more comfortable in a jacket made for the cold or one with a heater, without the need for all those bulky layers? Yes, of course, but not much warmer and, certainly, not richer.

My boots? Eighty-nine dollars, a lucky find when my local bike shop owner, Vince, decided he didn't like the way they fit his feet. Even at retail, I would have been out no more than a hundred and twenty-five dollars. My riding pants, well, I have to confess to often riding in plain jeans, but, for more serious non-local riding, I do have jeans with leather lining in the seat and knees and CE armor that cost me less than ninety dollars.

I'd like to reassure those riders who, like me, are shocked at the price of motorcycling gear, that it is not necessary to mortgage a house to ride a motorcycle. Heck, you can stay pretty damned warm just lining yourself under your jacket with newspaper—ask an old-schooler; they'll confirm it. You can navigate all over North America with nothing but an atlas and a few folding maps, no GPS necessary—really. You can get a tent for less than fifty dollars that will pack small behind you on your saddle or you can even form a lean-to "tent," as I once saw an intrepid rider do, by draping a tarp over your bike and tacking the other edge to the ground, crawling in to sleep between the tarp and motorcycle—no REI catalog necessary.

So, if you can afford the expensive stuff, then great. Just don't let the appurtenances of motorcycling overshadow the act of riding. They don't have to. Much of the freedom of riding a motorcycle is tied to independence, of being unattached to many of life's distractions that others are bound to. The rider should be in control of his direction and his machine. Where he goes should be decided by him, not a voice on a GPS telling him where to turn. To be a slave to all the superfluous stuff that can be attached to a motorcycle takes some of that independence away. I say, if you drop your bike in your driveway and break your windscreen, ride anyway.

Modern Life and Motorcycling

These days, in so-called civilized countries, we live in a largely artificial world. We watch television, which displays simulations of things that we are expected to accept as real. We live and work in containers shielded from the rain, the heat, the cold, the outside sounds. We drive in glass and steel cocoons away from the distractions of wind, sound, and smell, insulated from the inconvenient vagaries of the street surfaces we pass over.

Movies want us to believe that a car can be chased at high speeds through a city, crash innumerable times, still keep going, and never hurt anyone but the "bad guys"—but it can't. We see a psychologist and a distraught family talking in front of a live audience, and a remote audience of millions, and we are supposed to believe what we are seeing is psychotherapy—but it's not. Reality shows want us to believe they reveal how others actually go about their lives—but they don't.

During commercial breaks scientific diagrams flash before our eyes describing the next breakthrough in toothbrush design; we know it is real science because the characters are wearing lab coats—but it's not. Everything new is good and everything old is bad, so buy—but it's not true. We eat homemade meals in restaurants—but they're not.

Politicians say they know the truth and have solutions to our problems—but they don't. For them, truth is something fluid and moldable to whatever they need it to be. The solutions are whatever is convenient to their campaigns and that which pleases their lobbyists. Truth is sacrificed for political expediency.

Wall Street brokers and bankers want you to believe they're honest and have your interests at heart—but they aren't and they don't. Morality and honesty are replaced by legality. Doing right is doing what they can get by with without breaking the law.

These few examples, out of many other possible examples, illustrate how pervasive this artifice is. At its worst, we are presented with misinformation and, at its best, entertainment meant to persuade us to consume, or vote for someone, or spend. We are so bombarded with this alternate reality on a daily basis that it becomes easy to accept.

In this world that civilization weaves around us, we can easily become spectators of the unreal lives of scripted characters, created with an eye to audience response or political persuasion, but with no regard for reality. If we are not careful, we can end up following story lines, instead of living our own lives.

But not all entertainment and convenience is bad. If we keep in mind how superfluous these things really are, it can be fun to watch a story unfold on television, momentarily suspending disbelief, or relaxing to take advantage of some of our modern conveniences. But, for many, this is not a momentary escape. Instead, many want to believe and to wrap themselves up in the cocoon of the modern world and not deal with the good, bad, and the ugly of the physical world. They trade their lives for sameness, predictability, and safety. Hopefully, for most of us, modern life's distractions are seen for what they are. We realize there is a bigger world of which we are all a part, behind the smoke and mirrors. We realize we are connected with that real world, and want to participate in it in an intimate and physical way. For me, riding a motorcycle makes that connection.

When riding a motorcycle, one can't bend the rules of physics or trade the truth for comfortable beliefs. Riding demands we pay attention to reality. If we choose to ignore it, or if we think we can make it what we want by wishing it so, reality will let us know, in usually painful ways, that we can not. Take that curve at a hundred and ten miles per hour (an easy thing to do for any movie character), and reality will slap you—hard.

Riding a motorcycle removes the facade of wood, steel, plastic, and glass that usually isolates us from the world. We cannot ride and decline the invitation to smell the pleasant incense of spring in Georgia or the freshly fertilized fields of Indiana. We cannot ride and turn off the wind or the sound of the motor between our legs. We cannot ride in the rain and ignore it, or in the cold and not feel the icy fingers of the wind. We cannot multi-task by taking that important phone call while riding, without reality showing us just how stupid that is. We cannot put the motorcycle on cruise, ride half awake, and wake up at our destination. Constant vigilance is a requirement and a blessing.

While riding, one must embrace the world and be a part of it. You must be a participant, not an observer. Riding demands our attention and activity. It is not a passive function of existence; it is a hands-on and pay-attention action. You must hold on and react to the road, the traffic, and the natural world around you. Riding is both pleasant and demanding, painful and pleasurable.

Most of all, riding connects us with reality, from which everyday life often conspires to disconnect us. It is our escape from the fog of unreality and our awakening from a dream-state. When we ride, we live, instead of simply exist. Riding makes us acknowledge life, and invites us to take part in the world around us. Riding reconnects us with cause and effect and forces us to accept the truth of things. Riding rewards us with the state of being fully awake and living in the moment, a state so seldom attained by many in the modern world. Riding motorcycles reminds us of who we really are and where we really live.

Riding is the Zen slap that awakes our consciousness and reminds us that we are part of the world and not simply observers of it. Accepting the world and participating in it is such a richer way to live and much more rewarding than being insulated from it, only to realize at the end you had not really lived at all.

Solo Riding

I like to take long rides. No, not *like*, I *yearn* to be on the road heading somewhere, or nowhere, far away. I have thought about this often. What is different about those road trips? What is different about me that makes me want to ride those kind of rides?

I think, in essence, I am a loner. I always have been. I have never desired to join a group for some kind of self-identity. I have been a part of groups: woodworking forums, motorcycle forums, a vintage motorcycle club, and the American Motorcyclist Association. But I have always joined these groups for more or less selfish reasons—to gather needed information about this or that mechanical or other problem. I joined the Savage Motorcycle Forum because I had an old Savage that needed much work and repairs and these people knew the Savage. I joined Woodnet forum when I started more than dabbling in woodworking and had questions about technique and machinery.

Not that I did not enjoy the camaraderie these organizations provided. I made friends, I even hosted get-togethers of members, many of whom I still count as friends even after I moved on from the forum on which I met them. But in the end, I worked on woodworking projects alone, I worked on my motorcycles alone, I rode alone. While I do enjoy riding with one or maybe two other bikes, I am perfectly happy to be rolling along by myself.

I think this trait in me came from a place long ago, or maybe my DNA determined it before I took my first baby breaths. I recall growing up in the late '60s, a time of peace and love and people who claimed to be "doing their own thing." But doing their own thing often meant doing something that a lot of others were doing, it meant being "in." It had more to do with doing something different from The Establishment than about really living as an individual, apart and distinct from others. But I took that ideal of individualism to heart, regardless of all those around me declaring their independence, while really having none.

I was young when much of the '60s upheaval took place, but not so young as to be unaffected by it. As the decade waned and I grew into a teen-aged, high school student at the beginning of the '70s, drug use was everywhere. Many of my friends smoked grass, some did much more, but the crowd I was in was mainly late-blooming hippies who smoked pot.

I recall one night at my friend's cabin on Brandywine Creek, away from the prying eyes of parents in the house above on the hill, the usual crowd was sitting by the fire, playing music on the stereo, and toking. Two girls from the class more senior than mine, class of '74, asked if I wanted to smoke. I declined. I had not smoked weed before and was never urged to do so by any of my close friends, but these girls wanted me to try it, wanted me to do like they and everyone else was doing. They urged me to "Go ahead, try it," "What's wrong? Are you afraid?..." It was like a bad scene from some public school anti-drug movie.

I was not going to do anything that I did not choose to do just to be a part of the crowd. I did not have much of a moral objection to smoking marijuana, I still don't, but I sure as hell wasn't going to do it because two high school girls somehow felt obliged to introduce me to its pleasures so that I would be a validated part of their group. And if I was *expected* to do something, anything, then I was determined I would not. Groups were not for me, not then, not now.

Later on, I had dreams of sailing to far away, tropical places with exotic sounding names seemingly lifted from a pirate story—Spanish Wells, Abacos, Puerto Plata, and Providenciales. As I had always done, and still do when I get my mind set on pursuing something new, I read everything I could get my hands on about the subject. Of all those tales, the ones that most appealed to me were about little, uncomplicated but sturdy, boats like *Jester*, *Dove*, and *Chidiock Tichborne* and, unsurprisingly, those boats were often sailed single-handed; their voyages extended across the Atlantic or around the world.

When I left for sea, I sailed alone about half the time. I reveled in the quietness of no voices. I sat anchored contentedly for a week up the Shark River in the Everglades while a Norther passed. I threaded drifting sand shoals along the Exumas alone, sometimes walking up to my waist and tugging my little boat along in the quiet water, the white hulled little vessel my only, and best, companion.

And, of course, with more and more experience of being on my own came more self-reliance and competency. I could do more things because I did more things. I favored action over inaction. Something in me was restless and unsettled if not doing something or going somewhere. I often have this idea in the very back of my mind to just start walking and keep walking, like a modern-day Thoreau on his journey by foot from New England to the Midwest.

My parents deserve some of the credit for this ambulatory impulse. Every summer we would pack everyone into whatever we were driving that year and hit the road. From South Bend, Indiana, our routes stretched out in varying directions—once or twice toward Colorado and the mountains my dad loved, or east to the battlefields of the Civil War in Pennsylvania, or to Maryland or Missouri to see long-distance relatives and to search for ancestors' gravestones. We clambered through caves in Kentucky, took a wild ride down Sliding Rock in North Carolina, spent a week in a West Virginia coal camp, and were amazed at the sight of palm tress in Florida. Our little VW Beetle hauled all five of us out and back across the Kansas plains. We bounced about in the topper of an old pickup while climbing up and racing down the hills of the Blue Ridge Mountains.

Family traveling for us was not from hotel door to hotel door. We parked in the dark of mountain forests and pitched a tent. We occasionally pulled a homemade camper, affectionately called "The Thing" behind, that was made for two people but which we made do for all five of us. Our meals were cooked over a Coleman stove and our light was from the bright mantles of a lantern. The old canvas tent leaked, and our beds were the ground.

Those travels set the mood for my future motorcycle wandering and, combined with my sense of independence, prompted me to often be a lone rider.

Of course, life changes. I got older, got married, and we had children. But that impulse remained—to be doing something, going somewhere alone. Now it is a struggle to balance the responsibilities to those who depend on me and my own inward need to find new roads and blaze new trails. The challenge is to find a balance between being there for others and being alone for myself, not shirking my responsibilities to others or to myself. I must be a parent, a partner to my spouse, and true to myself, allowing myself to roam occasionally. The need for individuality doesn't dissolve into thin air once married, or once a child is born. I keep in mind the saying: moderation in everything, including moderation. I must take care of others, but also must take care of myself.

Managing Wanderlust

Wanderlust—that's a fitting word for that condition that afflicts me and many other riders. Wanderlust, like lust, is something that demands fulfillment, and if not fulfilled causes anxiety in the afflicted. Even when one is distracted by other mundane things, lust is lurking in the background, demanding attention. Lust is hard to ignore.

The question is, what to do about wanderlust once you have it? How do you go about breaking free from the rote world most of us live in and, instead, travel for weeks, months, or perhaps years? Before that question can be answered, however, perhaps a more important question needs to be asked: should you fulfill that desire?

If you're young and unattached to a spouse and children, and all that arrangement entails, you can save up, pay off, and ride away, fulfilling your desire with a reasonable expectation that you will have the time when you return to find rewarding employment and establish a family for yourself, if that is what you want. You can go for "as long as it's fun" or until you run out of funds. This is precisely what I did when I was young, fresh off a divorce and having no children. I worked and paid off all my debts, worked some more and saved, and finally one day I slipped away from the dock and headed south on my sailboat. That voyage lasted a year and a half. If you can do the same, then I say follow your dreams. I don't regret a minute of the time that I did it. Even if you are in a similar situation, remember, though, that those times usually do not last. Enjoy them while you can.

Most of us do not have that kind of freedom for long, or we have left it behind by accident or deliberately. Life is often— no, usually—messy. Decisions made years before wanderlust set in may determine, if you are a responsible person, how, when, and for how long you can ride. Responsibility must be weighed against desire.

I've heard people say that if you want something you simply need to pursue it and let nothing get in your way. You could do that, but if you have a family at home and you do, well, don't look to me for absolution. Life often throws other people and responsibilities across our paths. To simply "not let them get in the way" and just sweep them aside is irresponsible. It is all well and good to say, "Follow your dreams, at all costs," when no one else pays the costs for that action other than yourself, but when a family is left behind, a wife and perhaps children, because of our actions we need to pause and consider what we are about to do and how we are about to do it.

Not many are independently wealthy, young and in the prime of life, with no responsibilities to anyone but themselves. Many who are lucky enough to be in ideal situations denigrate those who are not in the same situation in life; a kind of "blame yourself" game that serves to hold that person on a higher plane than the one not so situated. It reminds me of something my sister-in-law once said in response to someone who was complaining about their work situation and lack of vacation time. She is a teacher and jokingly replied, "I guess you didn't check the right box when you went to college, did you?" In other words, "I made the right decision, you didn't, so quit complaining and live with it." This is akin to those who claim that anyone who is not wealthy or as successful as themselves has not made the right decisions in life and have no one to blame but themselves. Or, "Anyone who is poor simply has not worked hard and did not have enough ambition." This is a kind of convenient philosophy that legitimizes their own success while illegitimizing others who have failed to succeed.

The truth, however, is never so simple. Yes, there is a need to strive for what you desire, to work hard and do all you can to achieve it, but sometimes when you have done all that, you still fall short; you still fail. Blaming the poor for their poverty does nothing to help them rise above that poverty. Likewise, so many of us who are infected by wanderlust just do not have the options that others may have, and determining who's at fault does nothing to help.

People's needs and desires change over time. They had that family, but now long to spread their wings. Should they be a slave to yesterday's decisions? Did they "check the wrong box" and now should pay the price by giving up their dreams? Is it an all or nothing game? Consider whether you'd want your children to deny themselves happiness because of a decision or mistake made early in their lives? Should they be responsible for the part they played in their own lives that put them in today's situation? Yes. Should that situation be chains that hold them from any future joy or happiness? I think not. Follow your dreams, yes. Take charge of your responsibilities, yes. But should doing one preclude the other? I don't think so. Is it better to be an example to your children by showing them they must give up their dreams, or should you rather show them that they can be both responsible and follow their dreams? To deny ourselves our dreams in the one short life we have is to leave the worst message we could to our children: "Let life pin you down and forget about your own happiness." How would you prefer to see them live their life: defeated by their situation or overcoming it?

Life is not one thing or the other, responsibility or freedom, one canceling the other. There must be room in one's life for both—a way to balance these forces; a way to be fair to others while being fair to oneself. Life's passions always put on hold is a waste of our very limited time on earth; once it's gone, we're gone. I plan to stuff as much living into the rest of my time as possible before going "into that good night" and I hope my children do, too.

So, how to go about following the dream of motorcycling adventure while being loyal to those who depend on you? For most of us this means having a plan, and every person's plan will be different. One may have to put off that ride while preparing and taking measures in anticipation of what their absence will mean for others. It may mean making several shorter rides, instead of one extended one. It may mean delaying the dream while other matters take precedence.

I am an "inmate" of an Internet forum dedicated to adventure touring, and many of the members there don't dream of a couple weeks away riding the Rocky Mountains or doing the Tale of the Dragon and Appalachian parkways. Instead, they might ship their bike overseas and ride them from the western edge of Europe to the eastern edge of Asia, or from the Arctic Ocean to the Southern Ocean off Patagonia. They ride "The Road of Bones" and "Dalton Highway" and their thoughts are how to get their bikes across the Darien Gap from Panama to Colombia where no road connects the two. Those kind of rides involve planning for possibly years of being gone with perhaps no income or requires finding a way to make an income while on the road.

While this long distance trekking is certainly adventurous, luckily, adventure isn't solely measured by miles ridden or countries ticked off a map. You don't have to be a world traveler to be an adventurer. There are riding adventures all around us, and they can be on Interstates or single track National Forest roads, country back roads or city streets. What makes the ride an adventure is what is inside us, not where we go. Adventure is different for each person. Finding a way to get out for a few weeks twice a year can be as satisfying for some as a round the world trip can be for another. Either way, planning is essential and can be a pleasant obsession while waiting for that departure date.

For many of us, planning means working out vacation times that coincide with the times of the year suitable weather-wise to riding in the specific locations we may want to visit. Of course, these times must often also coincide with times at work when things are slow. Another thing to be mindful of is choosing times that minimize the impact of your absence on family and loved ones.

What will work for one may not work for another. While it will be different for each rider, for me it's still an imperfect art and how I've gone about it seems to be working for us. Although I have to admit to a twinge of guilt leaving my wife to be a single parent for a couple weeks twice a year, it has given me the opportunity to chase my riding dreams and still do what I expect and demand of myself as a father and a husband.

My office is in our home, so for economics' sake I am also the daycare attendant after school hours and through the summer months. This complicates arranging time for long rides. Summer is out, other than perhaps three or four day weekends, unless extraordinary measures are taken. Luckily, my wife can work from home if she chooses and so a couple days at home over a few months is not an issue for her, especially if those days are during school and only requires her to leave the office mid-afternoon, rather than taking entire days off.

For these reasons I limit my long tours to the between the time school starts in mid-August and the beginning of June when it ends. For these reasons, also, I avoid times around holidays when the children may have breaks. Given these constraints, that allows me to ride north to cooler climes without freezing and gives me a much-needed break from children after a long summer home alone with them and a nice break before it all starts again.

I have been careful to arrange my business, a book publishing company, to be as automated as possible, and anything I must attend to can usually be taken care of on the road via a cell phone or laptop. This works for me.

Once you have decided that you owe it to yourself to live your dream, whatever your situation, there is almost always a way to work in an adventure or two each year, even if your definition of adventure has to be modified a bit. The most important thing is to not let responsibilities force you to miss out on living your life. There are ways to be responsible and still fulfill the need for wanderlust, striking a balance between being good to others and being good to yourself. Life keeps going whether we get going or not; don't be left behind. Plan and provide and go out and grab that joy that touring on a motorcycle provides so well.

Riding What You Have

At some point for each rider it's good to know; is it the ride or the bike? Neither answer is incorrect, but it's better to know the answer for oneself and not be deluded into believing it's the opposite.

Some love bikes themselves; that's the thing for them. A couple years ago, I heard of a local fellow who had a couple CB350s, so I rode the five miles or so south to see him and what he was working on. As we talked about the venerable CB350 and together extricated a motor from one, I asked him about riding. "Riding? I don't *ride* them." Here was a guy not confused by who he thought he should be; he honestly loved futzing with old bikes. That was it for him, and he knew it.

As much as I have worked on old bikes, even with some enjoyment at times, my goal was always to provide me with the means of hitting the road, and never was the work or the bike ends in themselves.

My seemingly always limited funds forces it upon me maybe, or perhaps it is an inherited trait of making-do that forms this bent in my psyche, but I'll ride what I have, rather than put off adventure until I am "properly outfitted." A Honda Rebel 250 can take you everywhere a Ultraglide Classic can and if I'm dealt a Rebel, then that's what I'll ride. The biggest, newest, or right brand is not a prerequisite for a great tour.

Of course, there is always that bike that is so unreliable and handles so poorly that the fun of riding it disappears like air from a deflating balloon, so I want a bike that is mechanically sound and not constantly threatening the menace of breakdowns and high maintenance. But I'm also not waiting for that dream bike to be mine, or that new accessory to arrive, before I kick the starter or push the start button and I'm off. If the dream is to ride, and if not having exactly what I want will keep me from leaving, I must reevaluate if it truly is the ride that's important to me.

There is so much chatter about which is the better bike that the chatter can come to seem more important than a bike's purpose and overshadow the fact that they are all made so we can ride. The bikes become ends in themselves. It's easy to be distracted, even if you are enamored with the ride, and become lost in all the glitter and glitz of big new bikes and all their accessories. You can get tangled up in arguments about which is better, V-twin or parallel fours, or perhaps transverse Vs, or thumpers. Is it superior to have a 360 degree or 180 degree firing motor or should the cylinders be arranged at thirty-eight, forty-five, or ninety degrees? Should a twin's pistons rise together or alternately? Can you really tour without hard bags and heated grips?

If chrome and pistons get your blood pumping, or seeing the smooth lines of a custom melts your heart, or if the sound of a Harley revving with aftermarket pipes curls your toes, own it. Don't be that guy who buys the big cruiser and thinks that by owning the right bike, and doing biker things, it makes him a rider. For him, the bike is the thing but he doesn't admit it, perhaps even to himself. There's nothing wrong with being a lover of bikes and not a rider.

For me, motorcycling is about adventure, and adventure is about the rider and the road, not the bike. Good riders are just as good on small bikes as they are on a big ones, are still as good riders on old bikes as they are on a new ones. The Cherohala Skyway is just as beautiful from the back of an old Triumph as it is from the back of a new Gold Wing.

It is the rider and the road that define those great moments in motorcycling, the ones we remember fondly years after the act, not the bike. So, if your core drive is riding, too, don't get caught up in the bigger and better and newer. Just ride. Ride what you have and enjoy the ride.

Post Ride Funk

I've got to admit it; I'm bummed. This last trip I didn't even ride my bike, but ever since I got back from North Carolina I've been in this funk, and I can't seem to shake it. If I had come home from a ride the funk would have been much greater.

An inevitable part of any tour is coming home. Usually that homecoming is to a life much more drab and monotonous than just about any moment on the road.

After care-free days of swimming in mountain streams whenever the mood struck me, I came back to long days of sitting here at the computer and perusing emails, flagging junk mail, replying to legitimate ones, and dealing with whatever business crisis had arisen while I was gone. "Damage control" being another of my duties (aka household and business accounting), means a return to constant vigilance and juggling of various accounts to make sure the power bill gets paid and the kids get fed.

Add to that having two young kids at home, where my office happens to be, for the entire summer vacation and all the trouble and turmoil that goes with two constantly competing children and...well...you get the picture.

So, I get out the bike and do a couple rides to blow out the cobwebs and clear my head, but, instead, I am reminded how great the riding was in the mountains. Not to say the riding around here is not fun, but you have to look hard for those good riding roads in central Florida, and, once you've ridden the same ones within a day-circle of the house numerous times, well, they don't hold the thrills and chills they once did. (I wonder if anyone ever tires of the "monotony" of NC 215.)

Now that I've mentioned "chills," I am also reminded how un-"chilled" it is here in the summer. I fondly remember how I considered zipping my thermal liner in my jacket up on the Blue Ridge Parkway not that long ago, while here before I have finished putting on jacket, gloves, and helmet and rolled the bike out of the garage, I am soaked in sweat and my eyes are swimming. Ah, mid-summer in humid central Florida.

Maybe its just me. Maybe other riders come home to a life of continued excitement and familial bliss. Maybe they come home to a business thriving in their absence, maybe they come home in time to send the kids off to summer camp, maybe they come home to a canyon carving paradise. But not me.

For me the question is: What do I do about the post-trip blues?

I might have found the secret, and it may already be working to de-funkify me. I pull out the atlas or, now days, I more often visit Google Maps. I survey all those squiggly lines in areas away from cities, a sure sign of good riding. I look around Birmingham, to the north and east. Looks good. Friends from north Florida have once again invited me to ride with them to Barber Vintage Festival in October. I'm in; let the planning begin. There might even be time before then to get in a ride to Key West on the thumper. A fellow rider I know from Fuzzy's wants to go, too. I'll have to check out places to stay in the Conch Republic.

I'm feeling better already.

Three Keys to Riding Safely

I've been reading frequent discussions on a motorcycle forum lately on riding safely. I have a few miles of riding under my belt and thought I would share my thoughts.

Riding is a complex activity, where many minor and major technical skills are used. It is good to know and develop every skill you can, but this chapter is not focused on the minutiae of riding technique. In my experience, safe riding can be broken down into three major elements, or *keys*.

Living in the Future

As you ride, keep your eye out for anything and everything that is taking place, or will take place, when you are fourteen seconds or so farther down the road. I have found this little bit of wisdom to be a major cornerstone to riding safely.

Looking ahead, both in time and distance, gives you time to assess your environment and make a plan for anything that could happen or is developing. Anticipating problems is the key to avoiding them. As much as it is wise to practice your technical skills in avoidance and stopping, it's always best if you never have to put those skills to the test in an emergency situation. Living in the future could also be described as "avoiding the use of emergency procedures."

Don't focus on the rear of the vehicle directly in front of you, but also watch for telltale signs ahead of possible dangerous situations developing. Pay attention to the brake lights or turn signals of the car ahead of the car you're behind, and the car in front of them. Constantly scanning and using your peripheral vision, watch for side streets and stopped cars waiting to cross or join traffic. Look for white backup lights in driveways ahead, which tell you to be ready for them to back into the roadway. Notice that railroad crossing ahead and decide before you get there if you need to change lane position to enable you to cross the tracks at a better angle. Watch for dogs or other animals near the side of the road ahead and be ready for them to act unpredictably.

It is important to periodically glance in your mirrors for anything developing there, but most of the time the real danger is ahead of you, so keep your mind on watching that area ahead of you where you will be in about fourteen seconds.

Living in the future has been my mantra and has kept me from having to use my emergency skills for many miles. A couple years ago my brother and I rode from central Florida to Michigan, a round trip of about 2,800 miles in both rural and city traffic. During the entire journey neither of us had to utilize our emergency skills. It wasn't that we didn't observe all sorts of crazy behaviors from other drivers, but when we saw these dangers ahead of us developing we were ready for them. The only incident that could have ended badly was a pickup truck backing out of its drive into our path, but we were watching that truck. Before it became an emergency, although we braked quickly, we were stopped well away from the hazard.

Riding a motorcycle has its dangers, but living in the future goes a long ways toward improving the odds of avoiding them.

Don't Panic

I think we've all done this: You're coming into a tight curve and in the middle of it you realize you're in too hot. I've done it; I ran wide in a local corner that for some reason often catches me off guard when it doesn't straighten out as early as it looks like it should. The time I did that, I purposely ran off into the grass. I stood the bike up, braked, released the brakes before leaving the pavement, and my Honda became a dirt bike on a gentle ride across the grass on the right shoulder. I should have judged that corner better, but I didn't panic, I chose what to do and I did it, straightening the bike up and readying myself for a ride off-road. Was that the best option? Nope. I could have misjudged the shoulder and gone down. However, having ridden on the grass and off-pavement gave me an idea of what I could expect, as did knowing and seeing the condition of the shoulder. Braking upright reduced my speed enough that riding through the grass was not much different than riding on my front lawn, something I do every time I leave home. But most of the time, running off the road is not a good option. On a right-hand curve, there are often other vehicles in your path. And going off-road in the Blue Ridge Mountains is usually the last thing you want to do.

Now I take that same curve occasionally on purpose, so I can hone my cornering skills to the point it doesn't surprise me anymore. Now, I don't run off, I lean more. Often, a rider when faced with this situation will panic and throw on the brakes, or at least chop the throttle. At first thought it seems like slowing down would be a good idea, but hard-braking when leaned is a course of action that can have devastating effects. When you roll off the throttle, the bike will want to stand up. When the bike is no longer leaning it will not turn, so the rider accomplishes just what he or she wanted to avoid.

Your tires only have so much available traction. When you brake, either with the levers, or by engine braking by chopping the throttle while in gear, you are asking for more traction for stopping at a critical time when you need all the traction you can get for turning. Often, the loss of traction for turning is enough to cause the tires to slide and you end up in a low side slide or the rear instantly regains its grip and you end up over the bars in a high side. Both of these things are something to avoid and can have less than desirable effects on your bike and your body.

What the panicking rider is doing is not having faith in his or her bike's ability to lean, and, by leaning, its ability to turn. If anyone has watched motorcycles racing, one thing that is striking is how much they can lean and still retain traction. While we don't all ride racing bikes, the bikes we do ride on the street are usually far more capable of leaning than we realize. Instead of panicking and bailing in a turn, have faith in the bike and lean. Unless you are dragging the hard parts of your motorcycle you haven't leaned as far as you can, and you haven't turned in the direction you want to go as far as you can. Even when dragging a peg, you can shift your weight to the inside and get a tighter turn with the same amount of lean.

How do you lean? You countersteer; you turn the bars opposite the direction you want to go, often described as "push right [the right end of the handlebar] to go right." It might be counter-intuitive to actually turn the bars opposite the direction you want to go, but it works, and the task for the rider is to practice this until it becomes intuitive and a natural response. Part of learning that is thinking about it each and every time you take a curve. Panicking is not thinking; it is reacting without thinking. Keep a clear head and don't panic; do what you know you need to do. If you practice turns while consciously thinking countersteering, when the time comes and you're in too hot, you will naturally repeat the practice of "thinking through the turn."

On straightaways it also pays not to panic. When that car pulls out in front of you, squeeze the brakes progressively; don't just snatch the lever and pull for all you're worth. A skidding tire is a tire that has lost traction, and a tire without traction takes much longer to stop than one with grip. Moderate your braking to ensure your wheels keep turning until you are at zero miles per hour. When you panic and lock your tires, you have relinquished control and have resigned yourself to luck. Once your panic has caused you to lock up, unless you can release and reapply properly in time, the accident controls you.

I recall reading about race car drivers and how they "drive through the crash," in other words, they never relinquish control of their vehicle but do everything they can, even when a crash is imminent. That last second controlling your braking before hitting an object, might mean the difference between minor and major injuries, or death.

Target fixation is another form of panic. You see an obstacle, be it sand, a car, or a guardrail, and instead of watching where you want to go you stare right at the thing that is scaring you. It's almost magical. When you stare at something, that is where you go. You want to exit the turn; look at your exit. You want to hit the guardrail; look at the guardrail. Again, this is a matter of ignoring your natural instinct of staring at the threat and trusting your mind, instead.

Controlling panic will help in many situations. Our natural instinct when things go wrong is to stop, and stop quickly, but thinking may tell you something completely different. When that tire blows, throwing on the brakes will do little to help the situation, but using your head will tell you to slow gradually and apply braking to the good wheel. When the back locks up, your natural instinct will be to let go of the brakes, while your head will tell you to determine if you are straight or sliding sideways before taking any action. If something runs out in front of you in a curve your natural instinct will tell you to slam on the brakes, but your head will tell you to straighten up, *then* use the brakes. Your head will tell you these things instantly if you have practiced, practiced, practiced. Once learned, these skills will replace your natural instincts with what might be called "informed instinct," the difference being that what you have thought through and practiced now is what you do automatically. Practice is the best antidote to panic.

Ride Your Own Ride

Another easy way to avoid accidents is to "ride your own ride," as I quote every time I sign off on a new blog entry. Riding your own ride means to control your own riding and not let others' behaviors control yours.

If you are riding in a group, and the rest of the riders blow through a late yellow for which you would normally stop, then stop. When the pack is turning right after stopping at a red light, roaring onto the pavement to get ahead of oncoming traffic that is getting closer the further back you are in the pack, if you would stop when riding alone, then stop when riding in a group. Don't let being part of the pack put you in harm's way. Don't relinquish control of your fate to others. If the pack doesn't like it, find a new group with which to ride.

Other vehicles can also cause one to ride unwisely. Don't let that tailgater who won't pass you force you to ride at an unsafe speed. Be willing to first signal clearly, then pull off the road if necessary to get them past you. Choose the road you feel comfortable riding on, don't just choose an Interstate, for instance, because everyone tells you, "But it's the fastest route!" When someone doesn't yield the right of way to you, don't let having the right of way make you do something unsafe.

Riding in a place like the Tail of the Dragon, or any number of other popular twisty roads, is differently challenging for each motorcyclist. Street riding shouldn't be a competition. Don't try keeping up with riders much more experienced than you, or perhaps more foolhardy than you. Ride your own ride, within your own comfort level and envelope of ability. Don't be sucked into trying to ride like everyone else. If competition is your bag, then schedule a track day. Don't turn the road into a track and don't let ego control your actions, possibly causing you and others harm. There is no shame at riding twisties slower than other riders. Not a single GP racer had mad skills in the beginning. Let your mad skill be using your brain and making the right decisions. Really talented riders will admire that more than your cornering speed.

With all the myriad skills you can employ riding a motorcycle, keeping these three keys in mind while riding will help you avoid or minimize many dangers. Best of all, they may save you from having to use any emergency techniques in the first place.

.

The Why of Riding

While I wait for the new throttle cable for Old Faithful, my venerable little CB350, I thought I might turn my thoughts to the *why* of riding. Without getting too philosophical, a simple experience last night reminded me of why I like to ride.

On Thursday nights I usually hop on one or the other of my bikes and head out in quest of dinner, followed by a stop at our local biker watering hole, Fuzzy's.

Last night, as I have done many nights before, I got on the Savage, fired it up, and headed for home, a couple miles away.

It was dark now, about 9:30, and I was enjoying the relative cool of the evening air passing through my mesh jacket. The Savage's engine was pleasantly thrumming under me with that typical sound only a big single can make, running as well as it ever has, and I sped through the large double sweeper curves north of Mountain Lake with a smile on my face. I made my turn at the last light, and, rolling slowly down the hill, I turned the final corner, negotiated the short and gentle double curve just before the house, and then something clicked in me.

I looked to my left, and rising there an inviting full moon, a third of its way to the zenith, above the hills

283

surrounding Lake Wailes. I idled past the house and onto Lakeshore Boulevard picking back up to normal riding speed with the moon leading me westward along the north shore of the lake.

I ran west from the lake and then south, out of Lake Wales and into the country surrounding it. I sped on through the night, the motor thrumming and the breeze cooling me. I turned left onto Scenic Highway, through Babson Park, and back through another couple large sweepers to the top of the ridge just beyond. Now descending, I rolled past a large lake on my left, the moon illuminating the chop of its waters while lightning could be seen off to the south and west, along with the sound of distant delayed cracks of muffled thunder breaking the night air.

I continued to Frostproof, where I turned west, catching US 27 for the ride back north to Lake Wales.

I guess the question is: Would I have ever have driven thirty-some miles out of my way if I had been in a car? The answer: Nope.

There is something completely different about being on a bike, and those rare and special moments, like last evening's ride, drive home the differences in a lucid way. Unlike driving, there is no frame through which you are looking. There is nothing containing you in a micro-environment, isolating you from the world you see zipping by. You may be tired, hot, and dirty, riding through some isolated part of east Georgia, but you will smell the wonderful scent of pine in the air. You may be riding in the Rockies, sore and weary, but you will feel the pleasant temperature change as your road runs along a mountain stream.

Instead, on a motorcycle you are in the environment and a part of it. Instead of moving past the world, you are moving in it. You are an integral part of the world, and when the outdoors is like it was last night, it offers an invitation which is hard to ignore.

Every time you ride, it may not be as special as last night

was for me, but it is always different than a ride in a "cage." You are always a participant, not a spectator. There are, of course, many other things that draw people to motorcycling, it may be the thrill of racing, the challenge of riding dirt, the coolness of rolling on that low black cruiser, or the camaraderie of being part of a biker family. But for me, this participation in life that is riding appeals to me the most.

A Cold Ride and Why We Do What We Do

My high school friend, Julie Bowland, is the only one of a group of us in school that grew up with the dream of being artists who stuck with it and now makes her living painting and teaching painting to others. The rest of us either ended up with jobs that had no connection with the arts or jobs that used that creative side of us as a small part of a bigger whole. One close friend is now a graphic designer, and I started in the publishing world on the graphic design side creating book covers. But Julie is the real deal—a painter through and through.

I often make Julie's place an overnight stop on my way to distance places outside of Florida. It is conveniently about 250 to 260 miles from home, depending on whether I take back roads or the Interstate, and it is virtually at the gateway to all places northwest, north, and northeast I may be heading to or returning from on my way into or out of central Florida. Stopping there gives me a good night's rest and an easy ride home on the final day of a road trip so I arrive refreshed instead of exhausted. Julie and I have been able to reconnect on those short stopovers over the years, but I always hope she doesn't get the impression that I am just using her for a convenient hotel, but that I truly enjoy the opportunities these visits present to spend time with her.

I happened to see on Facebook that there was to be a reception for Julie at a gallery at North Florida Community College, where some of her *plein aire* painting [painting done outdoors, at the scene] was being shown. I thought it would be fun to ride up and surprise her at the reception. It is only about 230 miles from Lake Wales; I could be up there by noon for the reception, have lunch with Julie, then speed home and arrive around dusk. Julie would be surprised, and it would be a sign to her that I truly enjoy her company, bed or no bed.

The only problem with the plan was it was January twenty-third, and, even in Florida, January can be cold. This twenty-third was going to turn out to be one of the coldest days of the year. As the time approached, I watched the forecast and the cold only became more likely and deeper, although as a consolation I could expect sunny skies and no rain. I pulled my cold weather gear out of the drawers and got prepared to do some cold weather riding.

I laid all my gear out the night before, so getting rolling would be a matter of popping out of bed, jumping into the gear, and going. The reception was at noon, so I decided to leave early, in case I had to stop to warm up on the ride north, causing me take more time to get there than the minimum.

Over my regular underwear I wore a pair of thermal pants and my Kevlar lined riding pants over those. Knowing I could always remove a layer if I got too warm I put a pair of leather chaps over all this. A lot of riders like to laugh and make fun of chaps, but if they ever have to ride in really cold temperatures I wonder how many would refuse to wear a pair if they had the option. If the temps are really down, chaps are very handy for keeping the wind off your legs and are easily removable if they prove unnecessary. When I am riding in sub-freezing conditions, they can laugh all they want while my legs stay nice and warm. Harsh weather riding is no time to be a motorcycling fashionista—I use what works.

On top, I wore a regular T-shirt and over it a L. L. Bean "River Driver" shirt. This shirt is a little secret of mine for cold weather wear. I used to wear one at sea sailing small boats and it works equally as well on a motorcycle ride. This long sleeve shirt is made up of two layers, the inner cotton and the outer wool. It is not bulky and keeps the core warm, and even I, cheapskate that I am, do not regret the thirty dollars I spent on it when I'm out in the cold. I find it to be the perfect layer under a riding jacket. The wool keeps it warm and the cotton makes it comfortable against the skin. Next came the coat. This one happened to be a Sliders Kevlar-lined mesh all-season jacket. It works well for very hot summer days with no inner layers in, but also works well in the cold or rain with the additional layers zipped in. On this ride, I put in both the thermal liner as the bottom layer, then the rain and wind liner above that, with the mesh jacket on top of it all.

In anticipation of days like this, I finally bought a balaclava to shield my neck and face from those icy blasts I would receive tearing down the highways. I put it on under the helmet and tucked it down into the collar of my jacket. In my boots I wore Smart Wool socks which stay warm wet or dry and are not too hot, even in the summer. The boots were my every day First Gear waterproofs, and my hands were inside a no name brand of fleece lined leather gauntlet gloves, which turned out to be a big mistake later on.

I rolled out from under the covers and was on the road by five am—more than enough time to cover the 231 miles Google Maps had spit out.

I had ridden in cold weather before but nothing could prepare me for the icy needles finding every crack and crevice in my armor as I rolled up US 27 in the dark, en route to my crossover via the Florida Turnpike to Interstate 75. When I left Michigan years ago on a cold April morning, there was a sheet of ice covering my saddle, but that day warmed quickly as the Midwest spring sun rose; but this day was cold before light, cold at dawn, and cold as the day grew. Any increase in temperature was compensated by the extended duration of my exposure and my route that lead me into ever higher latitudes. I found out later that it had been below freezing when I left, as evidenced by the frost on the sides of the roads even after the sun rose. At the speeds I was moving, the wind chill brought that number down to single digits.

My fingers suffered the worse, feeling like skinny, brittle icicles, frozen in their position wrapped around the grips. I cursed myself for not getting better gloves and made a note to remedy that. Each gas stop was a routine of filling the tank and drinking hot coffee. I was taking advantage of stop lights on US 27 to warm my right hand on the cylinder, while as I was moving, I would continually hunch down and move my free left hand onto the cylinder on that side. If I left my hands on for two or three minutes I would get five or so minutes of relief before my fingers would return to their semi-frostbit and rigid state.

By Ocala, I had as much as I could take, and I shivered my way off of the bike and into a Cracker Barrel restaurant for some hot breakfast. For at least a half hour I ignored my food and kept ordering more coffee, only releasing my grip on the hot ceramic mug when the waitress took it to refill. When I finally had most of the feeling back in my fingers, I dug into pecan pancakes and ordered more coffee. Warm once again, I headed out on I-75 and accelerated back up to that bone chilling seventy miles per hour. No matter how many layers you have on at those temps, the cold finally finds you; all the layers do is slow down how long that search takes. In the dawn's special brand of cold I was finally feeling the freeze in my legs and my chest.

Coffee at every gas stop, along with the delay of thawing out at Cracker Barrel, stretched a five hour ride to almost seven, but I arrived enough early enough to find a diner in

Madison and have a couple more coffees before trying to find the campus. I entered the gallery before Julie arrived and took a look at her work while munching on treats put out by the gallery staff for the group of attendees.

After a while, Jack, Julie's dad, walked in with Julie, and he was the first to recognize me. Julie didn't have a clue until the gallery director filled her in on my presence. Mission accomplished—she was completely surprised.

After Julie was introduced to the crowd and had done her talk on her work and answered questions from visitors and art students, Jack, Julie, and I met up at a Mexican restaurant, where we chatted about art, friends, and old times and made future plans to get together. I had a hardy lunch of chips with extra hot green salsa, refried beans, and flautas then said my good-byes and remounted the Bonnie for the ride home.

The temperature had relented a little by the time I left for home, getting somewhere into the upper forties, I would guess. I rolled south fairly comfortably, even as evening approached, with my hands the only part suffering, but not getting as frozen as they had been on the way north. The continued progress south also helped compensate for the lowering temperatures as the sun got low on the horizon and finally left me in darkness again. It was not long after sunset, though, that I arrived back home, tired and chilled, but with a feeling of satisfaction at getting though the challenging ride.

If you've ridden for hours you know one thing you have is time to think (or time to try to stop singing that song that's sticking in your head—"...Just give me a reason, just a little bit's enough, just a second we're not broken just bent..."), and as I was doing this ride I was wondering what made me do stuff like this, stuff I know will be hard and painful, stuff that will make me uncomfortable for hours, stuff that will leave me sore and tired for days after. I could have stayed home; Julie would not have been disappointed; she didn't even know I was going to show up anyway. I knew the forecast; I could have gone to see her some other time, some time warmer.

The more I thought about it the more I realized I was not alone, not unique. There are thousands of riders who do that. They know the trips they do will test and even scare them, and maybe even break them, but they go anyway. There are hundreds of them on advrider.com telling the stories of their trials and triumphs. I'm not unique or rare, or even very adventurous compared to many other riders. But I do share some of their motorcycling genetics. I ride whether it will be warm or cold, dry or wet, because riding in the long run is a bigger reward than all those risks and pains are a punishment.

Why? My guess is that a ride, a sailing trip, a hike, any kind of an adventure is really not an adventure if nothing goes wrong, if it's cakewalk. We don't sit around campfires telling stories of that ride that went so well, where the temperature was seventy-eight degrees and the clouds were out just enough to take the glare off the sunlight. Instead, we tell about the time the rain came down in torrents and the wind was howling as we crossed Beartooth Pass with the cold front and snow approaching fast, and we just made camp in time...or the time we didn't clean the camp area up well enough before hitting the sack and we woke to a bear sitting outside our tent...or the time it was 109 and we were crossing Death Valley and our reserve light came on...

Not only are the memories from tough trips vivid and enduring, but the feeling of accomplishment is long lasting. Sometimes the very idea that a trip will probably take a hard turn and become a challenge is the very reason we go out riding in the first place. Riders don't go around the world because it is easy; they go because it is hard. Those are the opportunities to test ourselves and see what we are made of, and more times than not we find out we are made of much tougher stuff than we thought. When we push ourselves and persevere, each subsequent time we find we can push further still.

We don't all have to circle the globe, ride to Ushuaia, cross Mongolia, or dip the front wheel in the Arctic Ocean. Each person's challenge is different. To some it may be to simply ride overnight somewhere and return home the next day; to another it might be to see the West Coast, and for another it may be to just learn to ride a motorcycle on their own. The common thread, though, is that each time a limit is challenged and surpassed, we have confidence that we'll clear the next hurdle, too.

The next time you feel a goal is just out of reach, reach anyway. You might surprise yourself and begin a journey that may open a new world of things to you that you once thought were not possible.